I0009694

Fan-Gang Tseng and Tuhin Subhra Santra (Eds.)

# Micro/Nanofluidic Devices for Single Cell Analysis

This book is a reprint of the special issue that appeared in the online open access journal *Micromachines* (ISSN 2072-666X) in 2013 (available at: http://www.mdpi.com/journal/micromachines/special_issues/single_cells_analysis).

*Guest Editors*
Fan-Gang Tseng and Tuhin Subhra Santra
Department of Engineering and System Science
National Tsing Hua University
#101, Sec. 2, Kuang-Fu Road
30013 Hsinchu
Taiwan

*Editorial Office*
MDPI AG
Klybeckstrasse 64
Basel, Switzerland

*Publisher*
Shu-Kun Lin

*Editorial Manager*
Alistair Freeland

**1. Edition 2015**

MDPI • Basel • Beijing • Wuhan

ISBN 978-3-03842-090-3 (PDF)
ISBN 978-3-03842-146-7 (Hbk)

# Table of Contents

# List of Contributors

**Caroline B. Adiels:** Department of Physics, University of Gothenburg, Gothenburg, SE-412 96, Sweden

**Doryaneh Ahmadpour:** Department of Physics, University of Gothenburg, Gothenburg, SE-412 96, Sweden

**Visham Appadoo:** Department of Chemistry, Stanford University, Stanford, CA 94305, USA

**Fumihito Arai:** Department of Micro-Nano Systems Engineering, Graduate School of Engineering, Nagoya University, 1 Furo-cho, Chikusa

**Amin Abbaszadeh Banaeiyan:** Department of Physics, University of Gothenburg, Gothenburg, SE-412 96, Sweden

**Charlotte Hamngren Blomqvist:** Department of Physics, University of Gothenburg, Göteborg S-412 96, Sweden; Department of Applied Physics, Chalmers University of Technology, Göteborg S-412 96, Sweden

**Athanasia E. Christakou:** Department of Applied Physics, KTH—Royal Institute of Technology, SE-106 91 Stockholm, Sweden

**Peter Dinér:** Department of Chemistry, KTH-Royal Institute of Technology, Teknikringen 30, SE-10044 Stockholm, Sweden;; Department of Chemistry and Molecular Biology, University of Gothenburg, Göteborg S-413 90, Sweden

**Lin Feng:** Department of Micro-Nano Systems Engineering, Graduate School of Engineering, Nagoya University, 1 Furo-cho, Chikusa-ku, Nagoya 464-8603, Japan

**Thomas Frisk:** Department of Applied Physics, KTH—Royal Institute of Technology, SE-106 91 Stockholm, Sweden

**Mattias Goksör:** Department of Physics, University of Gothenburg, Gothenburg, SE-412 96, Sweden

**Morten Grøtli:** Department of Chemistry and Molecular Biology, University of Gothenburg, Göteborg S-413 90, Sweden

**Alexander Grünberger:** Institute of Bio- and Geosciences, IBG-1: Biotechnology, Forschungszentrum Jülich GmbH, D-52428 Jülich, Germany

**Masaya Hagiwara:** Department of Aerospace and Mechanical Engineering, University of California, Los Angeles, CA 90095, USA

**Eric W. Hall:** Department of Chemistry, Stanford University, Stanford, CA 94305, USA

**Akihiko Ichikawa:** Department of Micro-Nano Systems Engineering, Graduate School of Engineering, Nagoya University, 1 Furo-cho, Chikusa-ku, Nagoya 464-8603, Japan

**Ida Iranmanesh:** Department of Applied Physics, KTH—Royal Institute of Technology, SE-106 91 Stockholm, Sweden

**Samuel Kim:** Department of Chemistry, Stanford University, Stanford, CA 94305, USA; Department of New Biology, DGIST, Daegu 711-873, Korea

**Dietrich Kohlheyer:** Institute of Bio- and Geosciences, IBG-1: Biotechnology, Forschungszentrum Jülich GmbH, D-52428 Jülich, Germany

**Kin Fong Lei:** Graduate Institute of Medical Mechatronics, Department of Mechanical Engineering, Chang Gung University, 259 Wen-Hwa 1st Road, Kwei-Shan, Tao-Yuan 333, Taiwan

**Bashir I. Morshed:** The Department of Electrical and Computer Engineering, The University of Memphis, Memphis, TN 38152, USA

**Tofy Mussivand:** Medical Devices Innovation Institute, The University of Ottawa, Ottawa, ON K1Y 4W7, Canada

**Mathias Ohlin:** Department of Applied Physics, KTH—Royal Institute of Technology, SE-106 91 Stockholm, Sweden

**Björn Önfelt:** Department of Applied Physics, KTH—Royal Institute of Technology, SE-106 91 Stockholm, Sweden; Department of Microbiology, Tumor and Cell Biology, Karolinska Institute, SE-171 21 Stockholm, Sweden

**Christopher Probst:** Institute of Bio- and Geosciences, IBG-1: Biotechnology, Forschungszentrum Jülich GmbH, D-52428 Jülich, Germany

**Tuhin Subhra Santra:** Institute of Nano Engineering and Microsystems, National Tsing Hua University, Kuang Fu Road, No. 101, Section 2, Hsinchu 30013, Taiwan

**Maitham Shams:** Department of Electronics, Carleton University, Ottawa, ON K1S 5B6, Canada

**Fan-Gang Tseng:** Institute of Nano Engineering and Microsystems, National Tsing Hua University, Kuang Fu Road, No. 101, Section 2, Hsinchu 30013, Taiwan; Department of Engineering and System Science, National Tsing Hua University, Kuang Fu Road, No. 101, Section 2, Hsinchu 30013, Taiwan; Division of Mechanics, Research Center for Applied Sciences, Academia Sinica, Nankang, 115 Taipei, Taiwan

**Bruno Vanherberghen:** Department of Applied Physics, KTH—Royal Institute of Technology, SE-106 91 Stockholm, Sweden

**Wolfgang Wiechert:** Institute of Bio- and Geosciences, IBG-1: Biotechnology, Forschungszentrum Jülich GmbH, D-52428 Jülich, Germany

**Martin Wiklund:** Department of Applied Physics, KTH—Royal Institute of Technology, SE-106 91 Stockholm, Sweden

**Richard N. Zare:** Department of Chemistry, Stanford University, Stanford, CA 94305, USA

# About the Guest Editors

 **Fan-Gang (Kevin) Tseng** received his PhD in Microelectro Mechanical System (MEMS) from the University of California, Los Angeles, USA (UCLA), under the supervision of Professor C-M. Ho and C.J. Kim. Dr. Tseng joined as an Assistant Professor in the Department of Engineering and System Science, National Tsing Hua University, Taiwan in August 1999. Currently he is a Distinguished Professor in the Department of Engineering and System Science (ESS). He has also been a Deputy Director of the Biomedical Technology Research Center, National Tsing-Hua University since 2009. Further, he is also an affiliated Professor at the Institute of Nanoengineering and Microsystems (NEMS), National Tsing Hua University and a Research Fellow in Academia Sinica, Taiwan. Dr. Tseng focuses his research in the following areas: MEMS, bio-MEMS, nano-biotechnology, nanomedicine, fuel cell, MEMS packaging, and integration. Dr. Tseng has been on the Editorial Board of Applied Sciences from 2010, the Journal of Circuits and Systems from 2010, the Open Micromachine Journal from 2009, the Open Nanomedicine Journal from 2008, the MEMS special issue, Electronic Magazine from 2009, the Chinese Micro Electromechanical System magazine in 2002 and 2004. He was the editor of a book entitled "Micro Electromechanical System Technology and Applications", published by the Precision Instrument Development Center of National Science Council, in 2003. Dr. Tseng was elected an ASME fellow in 2014, and received several awards, including Outstanding in Research Awards (2010 and 2014) and Mr. Wu, Da-Yo Memorial Award (2005) from MOST, Taiwan, National Innovation Award in 2014, nine Best Paper/Poster awards (1991, 2003, 2004, 2005, 2008, 2010, 2012, 2013, 2014), among others. He has received 40 patents, written eight books/book chapters, published more than 200 SCI Journal papers and 350 conference technical papers in biosensors, bio-N/MEMS, micro fuel cells, and micro/nano fluidics related fields, and co-organized or co-chaired many conferences including IEEE MEMS, IEEE NEMS, IEEE Transducers, Micro TAS, ISMM, IEEE Nano, and IEEE Nanomed.

**Tuhin Subhra Santra** received his PhD degree in Bio-Nano Electro Mechanical Systems (Bio-NEMS), especially for single cell analysis from the Institute of Nanoengineering and Microsystems (NEMS), National Tsing Hua University (NTHU), Taiwan in 2013, under the supervision of Professor Fan-Gang Tseng. Currently he is a Post-Doctoral researcher at the California Nano System Institute (CNSI), University of California, Los Angeles (UCLA), USA. His main research areas are bio-NEMS, MEMS, single cell analysis, bio-micro/nano fabrication, biomedical microdevices, nanomedicine. Dr. Santra serves as a Guest Editor for the Journal of Micromachines, International Journal of Molecular Science, Sensors and Transducers Journal, American Journal of Nanoresearch and Application, among others. Dr. Santra has received many awards such as the NTHU outstanding student award in 2011 and 2013, IEEE-NEMS best conference paper award in 2014, best poster award at 15th Nano/Microsystem Conference in 2012, Junior Research Fellowship at IIT-Kharagpur in 2008, outstanding student awards at NTHU and Jadavpur University in 2005, 2006, 2010 and 2012, silver medal from Vidyasagar University in 2004. Dr. Santra has published more than 15 international journal papers, has one US and Taiwan pending patents, five proceedings, six book chapters, 25 International Conference papers in his research field and is currently editing a book entitled "Essentials of Single Cell Analysis" with Springer-Verlag, Germany.

# Preface

On December 29, 1959, Nobel Laureate, Richard Feynman's lecture at the American Physical Society (APS) meeting in Caltech, USA, entitled "There's plenty of room at the bottom" is often held to provide inspiration for the field of micro/nanotechnology. Later his vision was captured and published on February 1960 in the Caltech "Engineering and Science" journal. Feynman described the need in micro/nanotechnologies for scaling down of lathes and drilling machines, drilling holes, molding, stamping, *etc*. After this visionary publication, a lot of micromachining research and developments were initiated in the following few decades and was later related with Micro-Electro-Mechanical-Systems (MEMS) which was defined as miniaturized mechanical and electro-mechanical elements (*i.e.*, devices and structures) that are made using microfabrication techniques. With the turn of another century, the development of MEMS started with integration of chemical engineering, chemistry, and life science with micro/nanofluidic devices to become Bio-MEMS, Lab on a Chip, or micro total analysis systems (µTAS), which can enable more complex manipulations of chemicals and biological agents in fluidic environments in addition to the handling of electrical, optical, or mechanical signals/actuations.

Micro/nanofluidic devices with the power to manipulate and detect bio-samples, reagents, or biomolecules at micro/nano scale can well fulfill the requirements for single cells analyses. In the conventional method, the ensemble measurement of millions of cells together cannot provide accurate information, such as stem cell proliferation and differentiation, neural network coordination, and cardiomyocytes synchronization. To understand the behaviors of cell to cell or cell to the environment with their organelles and their intracellular physical/biochemical/biological phenomena, single cells analyses (SCA) can be conducted by employing miniaturized devices, whose dimension is similar or smaller to that of the single cell. Micro/nanofluidic devices are not only useful for cell manipulation, cell lysis, and cell separation, but also can easily control biochemical, electrical, mechanical parameters for SCA analyses. This special issue book emphasizes the integration of micro or nano systems dealing with the manipulation, separation, or lysis of single cells and the study of single cell dynamics with the use of micro/nanofluidic devices, combined with various detection schemes. The role of single cell analysis is recognized as one of the most important pathways for system biology, proteomics, genomics, metabolomics and fluxomics, and has the potential to lead to a paradigm shift. The applications and future challenges with their advantages and limitations for single cell analyses are also discussed.

This special issue book entitled "Micro/nanofluidic devices for Single Cell Analysis" is also uniquely comprehensive insofar as it not only deals with problems that are directly related to fluidics with cells such as a cell lysis, intracellular delivery, electrokinetic phenomenon, transport mechanism, flow resistance, molecular diffusion into cells, but also it deals with the advance concept of micro/nano fabrication and their challenges, from which readers can gain knowledge regarding cellular analyses using different devices.

Fang-Gang Tseng and Tuhin Subhra Santra
*Guest Editors*

# Micro/Nanofluidic Devices for Single Cell Analysis

Tuhin Subhra Santra and Fan-Gang Tseng

Adapted from *Micromachines*. Cite as: Santra, T.S.; Tseng, F.G. Micro/Nanofluidic Devices for Single Cell Analysis. *Micromachines* **2014**, *5*, 154-157.

The Special Issue of *Micromachines* entitled "Micro/Nanofluidic Devices for Single Cell Analysis" covers recent advancements regarding the analysis of single cells by different microfluidic approaches. To understand cell to cell behavior with their organelles and their intracellular biochemical effect, single cell analysis (SCA) can provide much more detailed information from small groups of cells or even single cells, compared to conventional approaches, which only provide ensemble-average information of millions of cells together. Earlier reviews provided single cell analysis using different approaches [1–3]. The author demonstrates invasive and noninvasive with time and non-time resolved SCA [1]; whereas some other literature provided destructive (with dyes, DNA, RNA, proteins and amino acids) and nondestructive (electroporation, impedance measurement and fluorescence based methods) cellular content analysis using microfluidic devices [3]. Further literature also suggest that single cell analysis is possible with capillary electrophoresis (CE) combined with a detection method such as electrochemical detection (ED), laser induced fluorescence (LIF) detection and mass spectrometry (MS) [4,5].

This special issue mainly focuses on the recent development of SCA with different microfluidic devices based technologies. Feng *et al.* [6] proposed on-chip enucleation of bovine oocytes by using magnetically driven microrobot flow control. The microrobot can control the flow speed with fluid resistance adjustment in a microfluidic device and was specifically designed for enucleation. Their device can: (a) promote fluid flow control; (b) the volume of the oocyte can be adjusted resulting in less damage of the oocyte; (c) and to control microrobot and hydrodynamic forces, the nucleus can be removed. To use this device, they achieved minimally invasive enucleation with 2.5 s average enucleation time and 20% average removal volume ratio.

Hall *et al.* [7] described single cyanobacterium lysis for whole genome amplification. They present a lysis protocol, which can extract genomic information from single cyanobacterium of Synechocystis sp. PCC 6803, which have multilayer cell wall structures usually preventing the use of a conventional lysis mechanism. The high-fidelity genome sequencing of single cells of Synechocystis can be achieved by performing microfluidic MDA (Multiple Displacement Amplification) reactions with selected genes (15 loci nearly equally spaced throughout the main chromosome).

Santra *et al.* [8] reviewed recent progress of micro/nanaofluidic single cell electroporation for intracellular and extracellular delivery. The electroporation technique is not only useful for cell lysis, cell to cell fusion or separation, insertion of drugs, DNA and antibodies inside single cell, but also it can control biochemical, electrical and mechanical parameters. The single cell electroporation technique can provide high transfection efficiency, higher cell viability, lower sample contamination, lower joule heating effect, and low toxicity during experiments compared to bulk measurement. As a result, single cells with their organelles can be measured more precisely by using micro/nanaofluidic devices. The authors describe in detail recent single cell and localized single cell electroporation techniques and their impact on single cell analysis.

Maorshed and coworkers [9], provided theoretical and experimental information on single cell electrical lysis in a microfluidic device and effects in a microchannel. They suggested that the generation of an electric field in a microchannel can provide sufficient energy with low current requirements. Single cell lysis in a microfluidic device was found to apply an external applied voltage approximately 700 V to 900 V within seven seconds and used less than 300 mW power consumption. For this single cell lysis, they used an 8 mm long microchannel with dimensions of 100 μm × 20 μm. Another author, Kin Fong Lei, in this special issue, reviewed the impedance detection of cellular response in a micro/nano environment [10]. The author reviewed the impact of a microfluidic system combined with the impedance measurement technique, which can provide non-invasive and label-free monitoring of cellular responses in 2D and 3D culture systems.

Probst et al. [11] suggested PDMS based submicron traps for single cell analysis of bacteria. The authors presented a hundred submicron size-based trapped barrier structure in a microfluidic device for immobilization and cultivation of individual bacteria. However, the study of prokaryotic cells, such as E. coli, encountered some challenges because of their small size and fast growth rates. They cultivated E. Coli for several hours within their microfluidic trapped structure, and it showed constant division times with rod-shaped morphology, indicating excellent cell growth with high cell viability.

Banaeiyan et al. [12] presents a specific microfluidic device as a cell comb, which is capable of high throughput single cell experiments. The microfluidic device can trap at least six cells in each V shape structure by using hydrodynamic forces giving a cellular response, such as protein migration followed by bright field and fluorescence imaging. They monitored arsenite (As (III)) uptaken in Saccharomyces cerevisiae cells with different flow rates (low = 25 nL min-1, moderate = 50 nL min-1, and high = 100 nL min-1). The device might be applicable for cell signaling pathways and to their modes of function and regulation.

Wiklund et al. [13] reviewed the cell to cell interaction in multi-well microplates combined with live cell fluorescence microcopy by using an ultrasound method. They describe the interaction between natural killer (NK) cells and cancer cells at an individual level. This review not only elucidates on the heterogeneity in cytotoxicity of NK cells and their ability to form one or several immune synapses simultaneously, but also on the impact of ultrasound exposure for cell viability, proliferation rate and their function.

Blomqvist et al. [14] studied single yeast cells with highly effective Hog1 inhibitor and the use of osmotic stress. They have used four channel microfluidic systems to enable multiple signal inputs (Hog 1 and sorbitol) to a yeast signal transduction pathway for studying single cell response. To activate the Hog 1 signaling pathways for the presence or absence of the cellular response, was monitored by the imaging of the nuclear translocation of the cytosolic MAPK, Hog1 on a single-cell level.

In conclusion, this special issue of *Micromachines*, "Micro/Nanofluidic Devices for Single Cell Analysis" not only emphasizes the new microfluidic devices for SCA, but also reviews recent advancements of SCA with different techniques such as electroporation, ultrasound, and impedance measurement. In the last couple of years, SCA has not only been at the forefront of biological cell studies and therapeutic research, but also it has been in close collaboration with human health. Recently microfabricated devices called "Laboratory on a chip" (LOC) perform a tremendous role in single cell analysis. Micro/nanofluidic devices are not only useful for cell manipulation, cell lysis, and cell separation, but also can easily control biochemical, electrical, mechanical parameters for single cell analysis. By miniaturizing the device such as in micro total analysis ($\mu$TAS) systems, analysis of single cell organelles with precise biochemical control can be achieved inside the single cell. SCA for system biology, genomics, transcriptomics, proteomics, metabolomics and fluxomics is not only a broad research area, but also a challenging task for application in biology, medicine, pathology and clinical trials, *etc.* With the continuous progress of single cell analysis, development of biomedical technologies which are essential to our daily life could be extended to offer many possibilities in the future.

## Author Contributions

Tuhin Subhra Santra wrote this editorial and Fan-Gang Tseng provided the concept to write an editorial and finally corrected it.

## Conflicts of Interest

The authors declare no conflict of interest.

## References

1. Fritzsch, F.S.O.; Dusny, C.; Frick, O.; Schmid, A. Single-cell analysis in biotechnology, systems biology, and biocatalysis. Annu. Rev. Chem. Biomol. Eng. 2012, 3, 129–155.
2. Andersson, H.; van den Berg, A. Microtechnologies and nanotechnologies for single cell analysis. Curr. Opin. Biotechnol. 2004, 15, 44–49.
3. Chiao, T-C.; Ros, A. Microfluidic single-cell analysis of intracellular compounds. J. R. Soc. Interface 2008, 5, S139–S150.
4. Lu, X.; Huang, W-H.; Wang, Z-L, Cheng, J-K. Recent developments in single cell analysis. *Anal. Chim. Acta* **2004**, *510*, 127–138.
5. Wu, R-G.; Yang, C-S.; Cheing, C-C.; Tseng, F-G. Nanocapillary electrophoretic electrochemical chip: towards analysis of biochemicals released by single cell. *J. R. Soc. Interface Focus* **2011**, *1*, 744–753.
6. Feng, L.; Hagiwara, M.; Ichikawa, A.; Arai, F. On-chip enucleation of bovine oocytes using microrobot-assisted flow-speed control. *Micromachines* **2013**, *4*, 227–285.
7. Hall, E.W.; Kim, S.; Appadoo, V.; Zare, R.N. Lysis of a single cyanobacterium for whole genome amplification. *Micromachines* **2013**, *4*, 321–332.
8. Santra, T.S.; Tseng, F-G. Recent trends on micro/nanofluidic single cell electroporation. *Micromachines* **2013**, *4*, 333–356.

9.  Morshed, B.I.; Shams, M.; Mussivand, T. Analysis of electric fields inside microchannels and single cell electrical lysis with a microfluidic device. *Micromachines* **2013**, *4*, 243–256.

10. Lei, K.F. Review on impedance detection of cellular responses in micro/nano environment. *Micromachines* **2014**, *5*, 1–12.

11. Probst, C.; Grunberger, A.; Weichert, W.; Kohlheyer, D. Polydimethylsiloxane (PDMS) sub-micron traps for single-cell analysis of bacteria. *Micromachines* **2013**, *4*, 357–369.

12. Banaeiyan, A.B.; Ahmadpour, D.; Adiels, C.B.; Goksor, M. Hydrodynamic cell trapping for high throughput single-cell applications. *Micromachines* **2013**, *4*, 414–430.

13. Wiklund, M.; Christakou, A.E.; Ohlin, M.; Iranmanesh, I.; Frist, T.; Vanherberghen, B.; Onfelt, B. Ultrasound-induced cell–cell interaction studies in a multi-well microplate. *Micromachines* **2014**, *5*, 27–49.

14. Blomqvist, C.H.; Diner, P.; Grotli, M.; Goksor, M.; Adiels, C.B. A single-cell study of a highly effective Hog1 inhibitor for *in situ* yeast cell manipulation. *Micromachines* **2014**, *5*, 81–96.

# On-Chip Enucleation of Bovine Oocytes using Microrobot-Assisted Flow-Speed Control

Lin Feng, Masaya Hagiwara, Akihiko Ichikawa and Fumihito Arai

**Abstract:** In this study, we developed a microfluidic chip with a magnetically driven microrobot for oocyte enucleation. A microfluidic system was specially designed for enucleation, and the microrobot actively controls the local flow-speed distribution in the microfluidic chip. The microrobot can adjust fluid resistances in a channel and can open or close the channel to control the flow distribution. Analytical modeling was conducted to control the fluid speed distribution using the microrobot, and the model was experimentally validated. The novelties of the developed microfluidic system are as follows: (1) the cutting speed improved significantly owing to the local fluid flow control; (2) the cutting volume of the oocyte can be adjusted so that the oocyte undergoes less damage; and (3) the nucleus can be removed properly using the combination of a microrobot and hydrodynamic forces. Using this device, we achieved a minimally invasive enucleation process. The average enucleation time was 2.5 s and the average removal volume ratio was 20%. The proposed new system has the advantages of better operation speed, greater cutting precision, and potential for repeatable enucleation.

Reprinted from *Micromachines*. Cite as: Feng, L.; Hagiwara, M.; Ichikawa, A.; Arai, F. Micro/Nanofluidic Devices for Single Cell Analysis. *Micromachines* **2013**, *4*, 272-285.

## 1. Introduction

"Dolly" is famous for being the first mammal to be successfully cloned from an adult cell [1]. Despite low success rates, several mammalian species have been successfully cloned since then [2–4]. Embryo manipulation is a potential technique for the genetic improvement of domestic animals and the preservation of genes of rare animals. Oocyte enucleation is a primary technique for the cloning process. The cloning of Dolly the sheep had a low success rate; 277 eggs were used to create 29 embryos, of which only three resulted in lambs, and eventually only one lived. Peura *et al.* conducted a viability test of the oocyte volume during nuclear transfer and determined that the nucleocytoplasmic ratio is an important parameter for embryo development [5]. Therefore, the low success rate of cloning techniques is a bottleneck for developing this field. Conventional techniques for the enucleation process mainly include the following: manual manipulator operation, microfluidic cutting methods in a microchip, and chemical treatment methods [6–8]. However, these methods tend to have a long operation time, low success rate, contamination, and low repeatability. Additionally, such types of complicated cell manipulation processes can only be undertaken by skilled people. During the chemical treatment processes, a person unaware of toxicities may poison the cells.

Recently, researchers invented many techniques that do not require manual operation for the treatment of cells by fabricating a microrobot on a microchip. Magnetically actuated microrobots appear to be the most promising because of this method is minimally invasive to a cell, features a

6

noncontact drive, and has a low production cost [9–13]. Nelson *et al.* controlled the untethered microrobots using electromagnetic fields [14]. Sitti *et al.* designed a biologically inspired miniature robot [15]. These methods reduced the technical skills of operation and increased the throughput and repeatability. These robots can be operated precisely, but they do not have enough power to separate an oocyte. Previously, we have developed magnetically driven microtools (MMTs) in order to apply the microrobot to a wide range of cell manipulations. A permanent magnet possesses a magnetic field that drives an MMT 10–100 times more forcefully than an electromagnetic coil of the same size, effortlessly causing the output of mN-order forces. In order to reduce significantly the effective friction of the MMT, we arranged permanent magnets parallel to the driving plane [16] and piezoelectric ceramics were employed on the drive plane to induce ultrasonic vibrations so that the effective friction reduced significantly [17]. As a result, we achieved μm-order positioning accuracy while maintaining a mN output force.

Enucleation by a dual arm MMT was conducted previously [18]; however, it was difficult to remove the nucleus because the oocyte is a viscoelastic material. The cutting process is a complicated model because the oocyte is soft and sticky. Once the tip of the MMT blade touched the surface of the oocyte, a resistance force generated by the oocyte decreased the position accuracy. In addition, achieving the enucleation process was difficult because the oocyte flow was not well-controlled.

The contribution of this paper is the development of an enucleation system using cooperation of an MMT with fluid control. Our new enucleation system contains three remarkable improvements: the oocyte enucleation process can be conducted one by one; the removal ratio in the volume is controllable, minimizing damage to the oocyte; and the nucleus can be removed with a hydrodynamic force controlled by the MMT. The methods of how to achieve these merits will be introduced sequentially in this manuscript.

Figure 1a shows the concept of the enucleation chip that we used to conduct oocyte enucleation experiments. Two large chambers with a height of 300 μm and a diameter of 5 mm were designed. The MMT with a height of 200 μm was placed in one chamber with its blade inserted in the microchannel branch. To conduct the enucleation process, the other inlet of the Y-shaped microchannel was used to inject continually the oocytes. On the other side of the inlet is a shallow withdrawal microchannel with a height of 50 μm that was used to confine the oocyte to a position to cut accurately the oocyte by a given volume.

The first stage involves oocytes in a cell culture medium being injected from the inlet of the microchip. By connecting a digital pump to the outlet, the medium containing the oocytes from the inlet flowed through the microchamber towards the outlet. The tip of the MMT cutting blade was placed at the interface of the chamber and the withdrawal microchannel. The oocyte was delivered by the flow to the withdrawal microchannel, as shown in Figure 1b. Then, the tip of the MMT controls the oocyte orientation so that the nucleus comes to suction port. The delivered oocyte is obstructed at the interface because of the height limitation (50 μm) of the microchannel, as shown in Figure 1f. Then, the hydraulic pressure deformed the oocyte, allowing the lower part of the oocyte to be suctioned into the withdrawal microchannel, as shown in Figure 1c. After the nucleus was in the withdrawal microchannel, the tip of the MMT was actuated to the left in order to close the interface, as shown in Figure 1d. Next, under the protection of the MMT, the initial portion of the oocyte was reserved and only the separated nucleus was flushed away with the flow (Figure 1e). After the nucleus separated from the oocyte, the remaining part was also sucked out and collected from the outlet. Figure 1f shows the cross-sectional view of the microchannel; there is a height difference between the main chamber and the withdrawal microchannel. The oocyte can be stopped at the intersectional junction where the oocyte enucleation was conducted because of the height difference.

Figure 1. (a) Overview of the enucleation microchip. (b–e) Concept of the oocyte enucleation process by the use of magnetically driven microtools (MMTs) in a microfluidic chip. Blue arrows show the flow direction. (f) Height differences in the microchannel design. The white arrow shows the movement of the MMT.

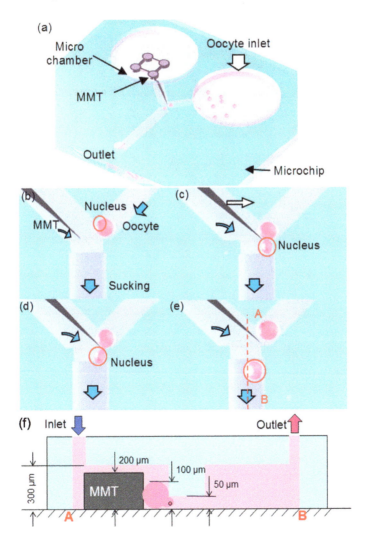

## 2. Material and Methods

### 2.1. Fluid Control by MMT

In this enucleation procedure, the nucleus is removed from the oocyte by hydraulic force. The force on a moving object due to a fluid is:

$$F_D = \frac{1}{2} \rho v^2 C_d A \qquad (1)$$

where $F_D$ is the drag force, $\rho$ is the density of the fluid, $v$ is the speed of the object relative to the fluid, $C_d$ is the drag coefficient, and $A$ is the reference area. As evidenced in the equation, the drag force is relative to the velocity of the fluid. Therefore, in order to utilize the flow effectively for the oocyte enucleation process, the local velocity of the fluid must be precisely controlled by MMT; this method is proposed below.

In representing the flow of a fluid as the flow of electricity, some insight into the process is gained; the fluid in a hydraulic circuit behaves similar to electrons in an electrical circuit. An electric circuit analogy is used in Figure 2 to specify the parameters of the microchannel [19]. The total volumetric flow rate $Q$ (m$^3$/s) in a rectangular microchannel is described by Hagen–Poiseuille's law [20] as

$$Q = \frac{\Delta p}{R_H} \qquad (2)$$

$$\Delta p = Q R_H \qquad (3)$$

where $\Delta p$ is the pressure difference (Pa) through a finite channel length $L$. The hydraulic resistance $R_H$ (Pa s$^3$/m) is defined as

$$R_H = \frac{8\eta L}{\pi R^4} \approx \frac{8\eta L}{\pi r_H} \qquad (4)$$

where $\eta$ is the viscosity (Pa s). The hydraulic radius of the channel $r_H$ (m) is a geometric constant and is defined as $r_H = 2A/P$, where $A$ is the cross-sectional area of the channel (m$^2$) and $P$ is the wetted perimeter (m).

Based on the equations mentioned above, we determined that the structure of the microchannel strongly influences the volumetric flow rate. The area-averaged velocity of the fluid $U$ (m s$^{-1}$) is [21]:

$$U = \frac{Q}{wh} = \frac{\Delta p}{whR_H} = \frac{\Delta p \pi w^3 h^3}{8\eta L (w+h)^4} \qquad (5)$$

where $w$ and $h$ are the width and the height of the microchannel, respectively. By changing the position of the MMT, the microchannel structures on both sides are slightly modified. Therefore, the fluid distribution is actively controlled by the MMT. By employing the MMT-controlled fluid, the oocytes can be individually delivered to the suction port. Considering oocytes are typically 100 μm in diameter, the oocyte inlet microchannel is 150 μm in width, and length is 300 μm. Because the height of the MMT is 200 μm, the chamber height and width are both 300 μm, and to confine the oocyte at the suction port. In order to have allowed the MMT enough space to conduct all the processes, the MMT works similar to a rheostatic controller, which is governed by the distribution of flow, $Q_2$ and $Q_3$. The flow allows the oocyte to load to the location of operation, *i.e.*, separating the nucleus from the oocyte, by increasing the hydraulic pressure.

We conducted the experiments by loading fluorescent microbeads ($\Phi$: 2 µm) into the microfluidic chip to demonstrate the effectiveness of the MMT movements on the velocity of the fluid. Figure 3 shows the fluid velocity with respect to the position changes of the MMT. In Figure 3a, when the MMT is near the right-side corner of the withdrawal microchannel, the velocity of fluid on the left side is higher than on the right side of the MMT. In Figure 3b, when the MMT is near the left side, the velocity of fluid in the microchannel on the right side is higher than on the left side. Three representative points were selected to assess the velocity distribution in the microchannel. The pressure distribution on the oocyte was derived from the velocity distribution. Points A and B show the distribution of velocity on both sides of the MMT at the suction port, while point C was used to the observe velocity changes in the suction channel. The width of the microchannel is 200 µm and we measured the distance $L$ at points along the range of 0–200 µm. Figure 3c shows the experimental results as well as the theoretical results for the fluid velocity changes with respect to the MMT position at each point. When the position of the MMT was at the right edge of the channel ($L = 0$ µm), the flow from the right side of the channel ceased, whereas when the position of the MMT was at the left edge of the channel ($L = 200$ µm), the flow from the left side ceased. The experimental values reasonably corresponded to the theoretical values, proving that the flow distribution in the channel was well-controlled by the MMT position, similar to an adjustable valve. As a result, the surface traction forces (FD) affecting the oocyte can be adjusted to conduct the oocyte enucleation process by allowing the oocyte to split via the hydraulic force and to be flushed away by the flow.

**Figure 2.** Electric circuit analogy of the enucleation chip.

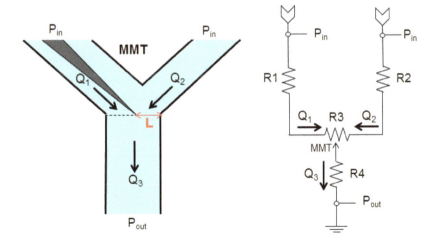

**Figure 3.** Theoretical and experimental values of the fluid velocity changes at three points in the channel. The velocity of the outflow is set to 3.5 mm/s. (**a**) In case that the MMT is near the right-side corner, (**b**) In case that the MMT is the left-side corner.

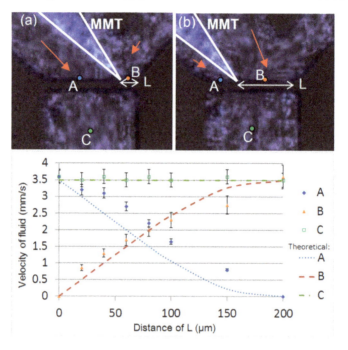

## 2.2. Cutting Volume Estimation

In order to achieve precise separation of the nucleus from the oocyte with minimal damage, the effect of the oocyte removal volume is significant. It is crucial to remove the nucleus in the smallest volume possible to increase the potential for the development of the nuclear transfer embryos [22]. The MMT controls the volume of the suctioned oocyte by closing the channel after a certain amount of time. To determine the correlation between the suction time and the oocyte volume suctioned into the channel, experiments were conducted.

In the experiment, the outlet velocity (point C in Figure 3) was fixed to avoid interference from the pump. The outlet of the polydimethylsiloxane (PDMS) chip was connected to a syringe pump using a Teflon tube. The relationship between the oocyte volume sucked into the outlet microchannel and the suction time was obtained. The distance between the MMT tip and the right edge of the withdrawal microchannel, $L$ in Figure 4, can vary, which would result in a change in the velocity of the sucked volume. In our experiment, the MMT position was fixed at a distance of 40 μm from the right edge of the channel, and the oocyte with a nucleus had enough space to be suctioned into the withdrawal microchannel. The suctioned volume of the oocyte was measured by the oocyte area in the channel and the height of the channel (Figure 4a). Figure 4b shows the experimental results of the volume ratio of the sucked volume into the channel to the original oocyte volume with respect to time. The graph shows that the error bars at each data point are small. Especially, the volume suctioned in the channel in less than 3 s was consistent and the variation was less than 5%. This indicates that the volume control over time using an MMT and fluid forces is highly accurate, enabling a precise enucleation process.

**Figure 4.** Correlations of the volume sucked into the outlet microchannel with respect to the time under the fixed position of the MMT. The velocity of the outflow is set to 3.5 mm/s. (**a**) The definition of volume ratio, (**b**) the experimental result.

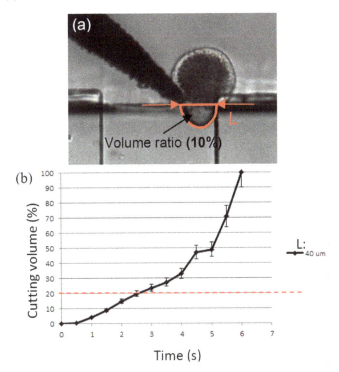

### 2.3. Separation of Oocyte by Hydraulic Force

Separating an oocyte using two MMTs is difficult because the perfect alignment of two cutting edges is difficult [17]. Therefore, we propose a new cutting method employing only one MMT. We squeeze an oocyte using an MMT towards the wall of the microchannel, allowing the nucleus portion to be separated by fluidic forces. A 3D structure was modeled using COMSOL Multiphysics 4.1 to analyze the distribution of the surface traction on the oocyte; this model also allowed the flow conditions in the microchannel to be observed. The MMT angle and the exit velocity are set to 150° and 3.5 mm/s, respectively. Figure 5 shows the COMSOL simulation results; from this figure, the surface traction on the oocyte is completely different with respect to the velocities in separate areas. The lower part of an oocyte that enters the withdrawal microchannel suffers a high traction force with a maximum value of 72.2 Pa from the hydraulic pressure in the Y-direction. Meanwhile, the part that is not being suctioned into the microchannel experiences almost 0 Pa because it is protected by the MMT from the impact of the medium.

**Figure 5.** FEM results of the velocity distribution and the surface traction of oocytes in the Y-direction. Object surface: y component of surface traction (force/area) (Pa). Arrow: Velocity field, Slice: y component of velocity field (m/s).

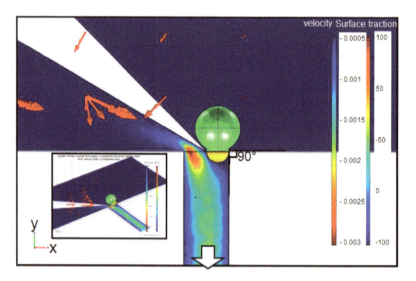

*2.4. Fabrication of Hybrid MMT and Microfluidic Chip*

A microfluidic chip consists of a PDMS microchannel and is bonded to a glass substrate. A PDMS microchannel was produced via replica molding with a photolithography-fabricated master mold. Ultraviolet light was exposed through a photomask to produce a microchannel pattern using a mask aligner (LA410, Nanometrich Technology Inc., Tokyo, Japan). The substrate was then developed and rinsed. We employed SU-8 film (DuPont Co., Wilmington, DE, USA) and a two-step exposure process to produce the height difference in the microchannel of the microfluidic chip. The two-step exposure was performed to fabricate a precise and uneven channel for cell confinement. The main channel and the withdrawal microchannel had heights of 300 μm and 50 μm, respectively.

Ni is ferromagnetic and can be magnetically attracted by a permanent magnet, but it is easy to bend during handling because of its ductility and thinness. As a result, smooth Ni is difficult to maintain, which is essential for flow control in the channel. Therefore, we employed a hybrid MMT composed of Ni and Si, which is both rigid and bio-compatible. The Ni-Si MMT fabrication process is shown in Figure 6. At first, Au and then Cr were sputtered onto the Si wafer (thickness = 200 μm). Then, the wafer was coated with a thick negative photoresist (SU-8, Tokyo Ohka Kogyo Co., Kanagawa, Japan) and then exposed on the Si substrate so it could be utilized as a support layer. The other side of the Si wafer was coated with the photoresist OFPR (Tokyo Ohka Kogyo Co., Kanagawa, Japan). After the exposure on the OFPR side, the OFPR pattern was developed. Next, deep reactive-ion etching (DRIE) was conducted on the OFPR side, and the Si was etched to a depth of 200 μm, until the Cr/Au layer stopped the etching process. After the wet etching of the Cr, the Au surface was exposed. Then, Ni was grown on the Au surface by the electroplating method to a thickness of 200 μm. After the Ni accumulated in the holes on the Si substrate, we again conducted the OFPR coating, exposure, and DRIE processes to form the MMT shape. At last, by removing the photoresist and the Au layer, a hybrid MMT was fabricated.

In order to prevent contamination after 2–3 h experiments, one disposable microfluidic chip that costs only 0.2 dollars was available. However, the MMT could be repeatedly cleaned and reused.

**Figure 6.** Fabrication process of the MMT and a fabricated chip with a magnified figure of the MMT.

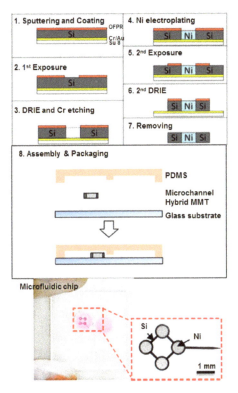

## 3. Oocyte Enucleation Experiments

### 3.1. Experimental Setup

Figure 7a shows the system components of the platform, including a linear stage for the magnet actuation, a microscope with a CCD camera, a joystick, a high-response pump, and a microfluidic chip. The microscope with the CCD camera sends the captured image data to the PC and the stage movement is controlled by the joystick. A high-response syringe pump connected to the microchip is used to control the velocity in the microchannel.

Figure 7b shows the overview of the microchip setup, including the driving concept of the MMT using horizontal polar drive (HPD) with ultrasonic vibration [17]. The MMT is actuated by HPD and the four neodymium ($Nd_2Fe_{14}B$) (diameter: 1.0 mm, grade: N40) permanent magnets, which are arranged on a swivel base set on a 2 degrees-of-freedom (DOF) linear stage [16]. The commercially available piezoelectric ceramic (W-40, MKT Taisei Co., Tokyo, Japan) has the following parameters: the size is $\varphi = 42.0 \times 3.5$ mm; the resonance frequency is 55 kHz; and the electrostatic capacitance is 4600 pF. This was attached to the microfluidic chip and an AC of 150 $V_{p-p}$ was applied at 52.5 kHz to vibrate the sliding surface of the MMTs [17]. By controlling the 2-DOF linear stage, the MMT could be actuated in the X- and Y-directions. The swivel base rotated the MMT in the X-Y plane. In summary, an MMT with 3-DOF on the X-Y plane is sufficient for performing the enucleation process.

**Figure 7.** Components of experimental system: (**a**) experimental setup for the enucleation of oocytes including the linear stage for magnet actuation, a microfluidic chip, and a piezoceramic for generating vibrations on the microfluidic chip and (**b**) system architecture.

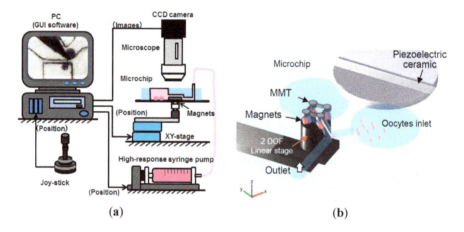

(**a**)            (**b**)

*3.2. Experimental Process and Result*

Prior to the oocyte enucleation process, the bovine oocyte must be prepared in advance with hyaluronidase (0.1% of medium) for 10 min in order to remove the cumulus cells surrounding the oocytes and pronase (0.5% of Phosphate buffered saline) for 10 min to remove the zona pellucida. Next, Hoechst 34580 is applied to stain the nucleus of the oocyte; the nucleus portion was florescent when exposed to a mercury lamp.

Figure 8 shows the experimental results of the bovine oocyte enucleation process (Supplemental video file available online). The oocyte inserted from the inlet flowed to the narrow channel. The MMT pushed the oocyte towards the wall of the microchannel so the oocyte orientation could be adjusted by letting the nucleus face towards the suctioning microchannel. The oocyte was too large to pass into the microchannel with a height of 50 μm (Figure 8a). After the nucleus position was confirmed, the downside of the oocyte was drawn towards the withdrawal microchannel by the outward flow until the nucleus, visualized by the bright spot, was sucked in the channel (Figure 8b). Then, the tip of the MMT held the oocyte by pressing it towards the corner of the channel (Figure 8c). Next, the lower part of the oocyte with the nucleus was torn by hydraulic forces and was washed away with the outward flow (Figure 8d). After the separation experiments, the remainder of the oocytes were suctioned from the outlet and immediately sent to an extraction chamber to evaluate the status of the cell membranes. Although deformation of the oocyte could happen during the separation process, Figure 8e shows that the cell membrane of the enucleated oocyte, which is spherical, remained intact. The removed nucleus can also be observed in this figure. The nucleus was successfully removed and the oocyte shape remained circular, even after the separation. The procedure time, *i.e.*, the duration from the oocyte reaching the narrow channel until the nucleus was removed from the oocyte, was less than 5 s and the volume removed from the oocyte is approximately 17.8% of the original volume.

**Figure 8. (a–d)** Experimental results of the oocyte enucleation process with an MMT. **(e)** Nucleus after being removed from the oocyte. The incision of the enucleated oocyte is smooth and the remaining oocyte is remains smooth; the enucleated nucleus is also shown in this figure with a removal volume of 17.8% from the original volume. (Supplemental Video file available online).

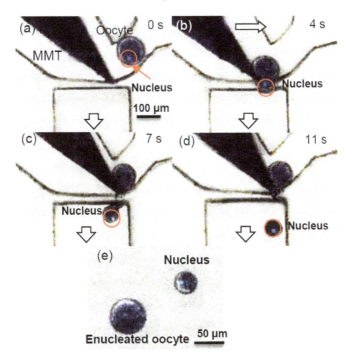

*3.3. Separation Time and Removal Proportion Evaluation*

The dot graphs of Figure 9 show the evaluations of both the enucleation time and the removal proportion of oocytes based on 15 samples. Figure 9a shows that the enucleation time was an average of 2.5 s for a single oocyte enucleation. The slowest processing time was less than 5 s. In mammalian cells, the average diameter of the nucleus is approximately 6 μm, which occupies about 10% of the total cell volume [23]. Using our approach, the removal volume of the oocyte was 20%

16

on average; the 20% removal of the cytoplasm ratio is significant for early cloned bovine embryos [22]. Depending on the nucleus position, the removal volume can be slightly increased, but the highest volume removed was 36%. The precise control of oocyte orientation in a few seconds assists in improving the separation accuracy, which will be further covered in our future work.

**Figure 9.** (**a**) Enucleation processing time for 15 samples; the average enucleation time is 2.5 s for one oocyte. (**b**) Removal proportion of the nucleus from the original oocyte for 15 samples; the average removal proportion is 20%.

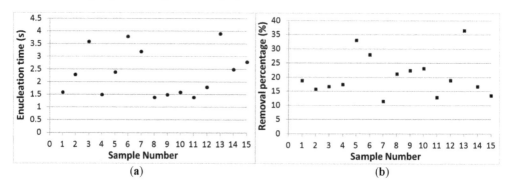

(a)  (b)

## 4. Conclusions

A new scheme that involves use of hydraulic forces controlled by a microrobot to perform an oocyte enucleation process in a microfluidic chip has been demonstrated. Using this novel design for oocyte enucleation, the nucleus was removed from the oocyte successfully. This system is advantageous for the following three reasons: (1) that oocyte enucleation can be conducted at a higher speed as compared to conventional enucleation methods; (2) that it minimizes the damage to the oocyte, and that the removal volume of the nucleus portion is small, which is important because the cytoplasmic volume affects the development of nuclear transfer embryos; and (3) that the incision of the enucleated oocyte is smooth, which may also reduce the influence of the viability on the oocyte. Viability examinations of enucleated oocyte by proposed method are our ongoing work. However, the advantage of separating an oocyte by fluid force is confirmed by Ichikawa *et al.* [7].

The precise and faster orientation control of the oocyte needs to be studied more because it takes several seconds to minutes to properly orient the oocyte positions. Then, the next step is a fusion process using the enucleated oocyte. After this, our study will include a repeatable enucleation process via more automatic control. For instance, automatically detecting oocytes and adding a dispensing module, which could dispense the enucleated portion to the culture automatically, will achieve high-speed, high-precision, and repeatable results. This work will conclude with the automation of the oocyte enucleation process, similar to a manufacturing production line.

## Acknowledgments

This work is partially supported by SENTAN, JST; the Nagoya University Global COE program for Education and Research of Micro-Nano Mechatronics; and Scientific Research from the Ministry of Education, Culture, Sports, Science and Technology (25630090).

## Conflict of Interest

The authors declare no conflict of interest.

## References

1. Lassen, J.; Gjerris, M.; Sandøe, P. After Dolly—Ethical limits to the use of biotechnology on farm animals. *Theriogenology* **2005**, *65*, 992–1004.
2. Edwards, J.L.; Schrick, F.N.; McCracken, M.D.; van Amstel, S.R.; Hopkins, F.M.; Welborn, M.G.; Davies, C.J. Cloning adult farm animals: A review of the possibilities and problems associated with somatic cell nuclear transfer. *Am. J. Reprod. Immunol.* **2003**, *50*, 113–123.
3. Vanderwall, D.K.; Woods, G.L.; Aston, K.I.; Bunch, T.D.; Li, G.P.; Meerdo, L.N.; White, K.L. 76 cloned horse pregnancies produced using adult cumulus cells. *Reprod. Fertil. Dev.* **2003**, *16*, 160–160.
4. Schramm, R.D.; Paprocki, A.M. Strategies for the production of genetically identical monkeys by embryo splitting. *Reprod. Biol. Endocrinol.* **2004**, *2*, 38, doi:10.1186/1477-7827-2-38.
5. Peura, T.T.; Lewis, I.M.; Trounson, A.O. The effect of recipient oocyte volume on nuclear transfer in cattle. *Mol. Reprod. Dev.* **1998**, *50*, 185–191.
6. Wang, H.L.; Chang, Z.L.; Li, K.L.; Lian, H.Y.; Han, D.; Cui, W.; Tan, J.H. Caffeine can be used for oocyte enucleation. *Cell. Reprogramming* **2011**, *13*, 225–232.
7. Ichikawa, A.; Tanikawa, T.; Akagi, S.; Ohba, K. Automatic cell cutting by high-precision microfluidic control. *J. Rob. Mechatron.* **2011**, *23*, 13–18.
8. Costa-Borges, N.; Paramio, M.T.; Calderón, G.; Santaló, J.; Ibáñez, E. Antimitotic treatments for chemically assisted oocyte enucleation in nuclear transfer procedures. *Cloning Stem Cells* **2009**, *11*, 153–166.
9. Barbic, M.; Mock, J.J.; Gray, A.P.; Schultz, S. Electromagnetic micromotor for microfluidics applications. *Appl. Phys. Lett.* **2001**, *79*, 1399–1401.
10. Mensing, G.A.; Pearce, T.M.; Graham, M.D.; Beebe, D.J. An externally driven magnetic microstirrer. *Phil. Trans. R. Soc. Lond. A* **2004**, *362*, 1059–1068.
11. Atencia, J.; Beebe, D.J. Magnetically driven biomimetic micro pumping using vortices. *Lab Chip* **2004**, *4*, 598–602.
12. Roper, M.; Dreyfus, R.; Baudry, J.; Fermigier, M.; Bibette, J.; Stone, H.A. On the dynamics of magnetically driven elastic filaments. *J. Fluid Mech.* **2006**, *554*, 167–190.
13. Gao, L.; Gottron, N.J., III; Virgin, L.N.; Yellen, B.B. The synchronization of superparamagnetic beads driven by a micro-magnetic ratchet. *Lab Chip* **2010**, *10*, 2108–2114.

14. Zhang, L.; Abbott, J.J.; Dong, L.; Kratochvil, B.E.; Bell, D.; Nelson, B.J. Artificial bacterial flagella: Fabrication and magnetic control. *Appl. Phys. Lett.* **2009**, *94*, 064107, doi:10.1063/1.3079655.

15. Park, H.S.; Floyd, S.; Sitti, M. Roll and pitch motion analysis of a biologically inspired water runner robot. *Int. J. Rob. Res.* **2010**, *29*, 1281–1297.

16. Hagiwara, M.; Kawahara, T.; Yamanishi, Y.; Arai, F. Driving method of microtool by horizontally arranged permanent magnets for single cell manipulation. *Appl. Phys. Lett.* **2010**, *97*, 013701, doi:10.1063/1.3459040.

17. Hagiwara, M.; Kawahara, T.; Yamanishi, Y.; Masuda, T.; Feng, L.; Arai, F. On-chip magnetically actuated robot with ultrasonic vibration for single cell manipulations. *Lab Chip* **2011**, *11*, 2049–2054.

18. Hagiwara, M.; Kawahara, T.; Yamanishi, Y.; Arai, F. Precise control of magnetically driven microtools for enucleation of oocytes in a microfluidic chip. *Adv. Rob.* **2011**, *25*, 991–1005.

19. Oh, K.W.; Lee, K.; Ahn, B.; Furlani, E.P. Design of pressure-driven microfluidic networks using electric circuit analogy. *Lab Chip* **2012**, *12*, 515–545.

20. Pfitzner, J. Poiseuille and his law. *Anaesthesia* **1976**, *31*, 273–275.

21. Cornish, R.J. Flow in a pipe of rectangular cross-section. *Proc. R. Soc. Lond. A* **1928**, *120*, 691–700.

22. Hua, S.; Zhang, H.; Su, J.M.; Zhang, T.; Quan, F.S.; Liu, L.; Wang, Y.S.; Zhang, Y. Effects of the removal of cytoplasm on the development of early cloned bovine embryos. *Anim. Reprod. Sci.* **2011**, *126*, 37–44.

23. Alberts, B.; Johnson, A.; Lewis, J.; Raff, M.; Roberts, K.; Walter, P. DNA and Chromosomes. In *Molecular Biology of the Cell*, 4th ed.; Garland Science: New York, NY, USA, 2002; pp. 191–234.

# Lysis of a Single Cyanobacterium for Whole Genome Amplification

Eric W. Hall, Samuel Kim, Visham Appadoo and Richard N. Zare

**Abstract:** Bacterial species from natural environments, exhibiting a great degree of genetic diversity that has yet to be characterized, pose a specific challenge to whole genome amplification (WGA) from single cells. A major challenge is establishing an effective, compatible, and controlled lysis protocol. We present a novel lysis protocol that can be used to extract genomic information from a single cyanobacterium of *Synechocystis* sp. PCC 6803 known to have multilayer cell wall structures that resist conventional lysis methods. Simple but effective strategies for releasing genomic DNA from captured cells while retaining cellular identities for single-cell analysis are presented. Successful sequencing of genetic elements from single-cell amplicons prepared by multiple displacement amplification (MDA) is demonstrated for selected genes (15 loci nearly equally spaced throughout the main chromosome).

Reprinted from *Micromachines*. Cite as: Hall, E.W.; Kim, S.; Appadoo, V.; Zare, R.N. Micro/Nanofluidic Devices for Single Cell Analysis. *Micromachines* **2013**, *4*, 321-332.

## 1. Introduction

Single-cell genomics is an emerging field that holds great promise for understanding the nature and function of genetic diversity in biological systems [1–3]. Obviously, this fast-growing area of study relies on DNA amplification techniques that can be applied to an extremely small amount of starting material, that is, genomic DNA from one cell. Multiple displacement amplification (MDA) [4], based on φ29 DNA polymerase and random primers, has been the method of choice for single-cell whole genome amplification (WGA) [5–8]. It generates a sufficient amount of replicated DNA of high fidelity from template DNA of unknown sequence and exhibits lower error rates and longer fragment sizes than genome-wide amplification based on polymerase chain reaction (PCR). Although a new WGA method with lower amplification bias has recently been reported [9], MDA is still the prevailing approach because of commercially available reagents and relatively simple procedures.

Microfluidic platforms have been developed for achieving single-cell isolation and a miniaturised MDA reaction for the purpose of WGA and successfully applied to a few cell types: lab-cultured bacteria [10], uncultured bacteria and archaea [11,12], and human sperm cells [13]. However, analysis of bacterial species from environmental samples is particularly challenging because of the thick, multiple-layer cell wall structures often found in these microorganisms, which may obstruct cell lysis. Development of an effective bacterial lysis protocol is important for expanding the applicability of single-cell genomics in view of the relevance of this culture-independent approach to the hugely diverse realm of uncultured or hard-to-culture environmental prokaryotes. We chose as a model system *Synechocystis* sp. PCC 6803, a unicellular cyanobacterium with a fully sequenced genome [14]. Significant difficulty is encountered in breaking cells of this species via chemical treatment compatible with microchip MDA. It should be noted that conventional mechanical lysis methods such as French press or bead beating are not suitable for single-cell WGA.

The lysis protocol proposed in this study is based on the combined use of enzymes and detergents for disrupting the *Synechocystis* cell wall structures composed of four chemically distinct layers: the external surface layers (proteins and polysaccharides), the outer lipid membrane, the crosslinked peptidoglycan layer, and the inner cytosolic membrane [15,16]. The order of chemical treatments, which include denaturants and proteases, was carefully designed to avoid interference with the downstream amplification activity of φ29 DNA polymerase. As a requisite for preserved single-cell identities, additional washing steps to remove extraneous genetic materials were implemented on the basis of quantitation of extracellular DNA. The efficacy of the lysis protocol for single-cell WGA was demonstrated by sequencing 15 selected genes that are nearly equally spaced across the entire chromosome using the MDA products obtained from single *Synechocystis* cells.

## 2. Materials and Methods

Figure 1 summarizes the lysis protocol. Briefly, *Synechocystis* cells from 400 μL of liquid culture were pelleted by centrifuging at 3 krpm (RCF = 735 g) for 10 min (5145C, Eppendorf, Hamburg, Germany) and resuspended in 0.1% (w/v) Sarkosyl (Sigma, St. Louis, MO, USA) in TES Buffer (10 mM Tris (pH 8), 50 mM EDTA, and 50 mM NaCl). The cell suspension was incubated at room temperature for 10 min with gentle mixing, followed by centrifugation. Then, the pellet was resuspended in 10 μg/mL Proteinase K (RNA grade, Life Technologies, Carlsbad, CA, USA) and 0.1% (w/v) SDS in TES Buffer and the sample was incubated at 57 °C for 2 h. After centrifugation and supernatant removal, 200 U/μL lysozyme (Ready-Lyse, Epicentre, Madison, WI, USA) in SoluLyse (Genlantis, San Diego, CA, USA) was added and the suspension was incubated at 37 °C for 2 h. Finally, an equivalent volume of alkaline DLB reagent from Repli-g Midi kit (Qiagen, Venlo, The Netherlands) was added to complete cell lysis. In the case of microfluidic single-cell analysis, multiple washing steps with TES Buffer were performed immediately after the Proteinase K + SDS incubation step to remove contaminant DNA, and the cell suspension was transferred to the MDA microchip for subsequent microfluidic procedures.

The amount of DNA, either released by lysis or amplified via MDA, was quantified using a dsDNA-specific fluorescent dye (PicoGreen Kit, Life Technologies, Grand Island, NY, USA) for labeling and a 96-well plate reader (SpectraMAX Gemini EM, Molecular Devices, Sunnyvale, CA, USA) for fluorescence measurements, following the manufacturers' protocols. The level of contaminant DNA, which was below the detection limit of the PicoGreen assay, was quantified by employing digital MDA (dMDA) as described elsewhere [17]. The dMDA assay is based on small-scale MDA reactions performed on a commercially available microfluidic chip (765 9-nL wells as MDA microreactors; BioMark 12.765 Digital Array, Fluidigm, South San Francisco, USA) and subsequent detection of fluorescent wells using the companion BioMark imaging system. The number of DNA template molecules in the original sample was calculated by counting the number of "lit" fluorescent wells and applying a Poisson correction.

**Figure 1.** Schematic of the lysis protocol. Cellular layers and chemical reagents used to remove them are shown. The letter D stands for DNA molecules; D in black represents genomic materials originated from captured single cyanobacteria cells whereas D in grey indicates DNA from other cells, either cyanobacteria of interest or different species; this type of DNA is termed "contaminant DNA" in the text for describing single-cell genome amplification experiments.

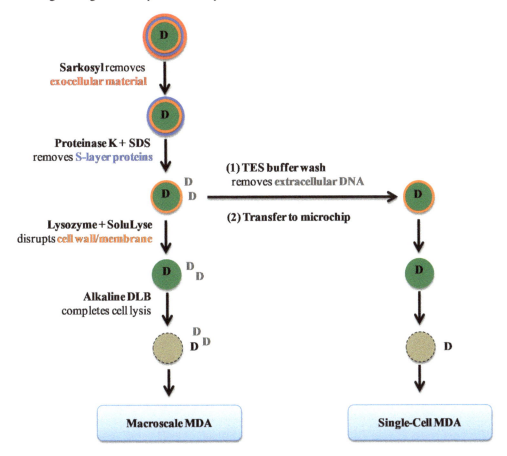

Macroscale MDA (50-µL reaction) was performed using the released DNA from cell lysis as template and the Repli-g Midi kit reagents (Qiagen) as per the manufacturer's protocol. Single-cell MDA (scMDA; 60-nL reaction) was performed on an integrated microfluidic device, which closely resembles that developed by Quake and coworkers [10,11]. Microchip fabrication and operation procedures were similar to those reported previously [18] with details in Supplementary Methods (Figure S1). To obtain sufficient amounts of DNA for downstream PCR and sequencing, 1 µL of each amplification product extracted from the microchip was used as a template in a second-round 50-µL MDA reaction (33 °C incubation for 16 h) and the final amplicon was stored at 4 °C until further analysis. DNA yields from both rounds of amplification were quantified via the PicoGreen assay.

To estimate the genome coverage of the amplification product from scMDA, 15 PCR primer sets were designed for genes evenly dispersed over the main 3.57 Mbp chromosome of *Synechocystis* sp. PCC 6803 (See Supplementary Table S1). Sequence specificities of the expected PCR products were checked using NCBI Primer-BLAST software [19] (See Supplementary Table S2). Primers were synthesized at the PAN Facility of Stanford University. PCR (20 µL reactions using 25 ng of template DNA) was performed using LightCycler 480 System (Roche) with the following conditions: 95 °C for 3 min; 39 cycles of 95 °C for 30 s, 59 °C for 30 s (annealing) and 72 °C for 1 min; 72 °C for 15 min. The PCR products, the presence of which at 1-kb region was confirmed by gel electrophoresis (1% agarose, 100 V, 15 min), were submitted for Sanger sequencing at the PAN Facility.

Initial experiments on *Synechocystis* sp. PCC 6803 were carried out on a cell line provided by Devaki Bhaya from the Carnegie Institution for Science, but all work reported here is based on a new culture (ATCC# 27184), which was purchased from American Type Culture Collection. The culture was maintained at 30°C in BG-11 media (C3061, Sigma, St. Louis, MO, USA). All chemicals were purchased at highest purity and care was taken to avoid introducing extraneous DNA; all of the buffers were filtered with 0.2-µm filters and exposed to UV irradiation for one hour before use, which is reported to eliminate amplification of contaminant DNA [20].

## 3. Results and Discussion

The initial attempts to lyse *Synechocystis* cells were made using the protocol reported by Wu *et al.* [21], which employs stepwise treatments with detergents and enzymes. Lysis effectiveness was qualitatively assessed by visual inspection of the cell pellet after each chemical treatment. The original protocol produced intact, dark green pellets, indicating that it is unsatisfactory for this type of cyanobacteria. However, improvement of cell breakage was observed when (*a*) proteinase K treatment was performed in the presence of 0.1% SDS and (*b*) lysozyme step was combined with SoluLyse, a proprietary detergent for bacterial lysis (See Supplementary Table S3). The amounts of DNA released into the supernatants by these modified protocols, as measured by PicoGreen assay, were comparable to the DNA level obtained from sonication-induced lysis, indicating that near-complete lysis was achieved [22].

The lysis protocol was further optimized for microfluidic scMDA, our target application, by testing its compatibility with φ29 DNA polymerase activity and on-chip single-cell isolation procedure. First, we investigated the effect of the lysis reagents on the polymerase activity by performing standard macroscale MDA reactions supplemented with a series of lysis reagents and determined the resulting amplification factors (Figure 2). The detergents were the most inhibitive against the MDA reactions, with 0.1% sarkosyl reducing the amplification by a factor of ~$10^4$ and 0.1% SDS suppressing the polymerase activity completely. The deleterious effects of proteinase K and lysozyme were relatively small at the tested concentrations, retaining amplification factors greater than $10^5$. SoluLyse, with or without lysozyme additive, resulted in amplification factors between $10^3$ and $10^4$. Based on these results, we decided to carry out the first two lysis steps utilizing sarkosyl and proteinase K in SDS "off-chip" followed by supernatant removal and on-chip isolation of single cells, and finally addition of lysozyme in SoluLyse to each cell "on-chip".

**Figure 2.** Inhibition of 50-μL Multiple displacement amplification (MDA) reactions by lysis reagents. Amplification factor was calculated by dividing the amount of amplified DNA, as quantified via PicoGreen assay, with that of the starting template (50 pg). The MDA reaction with 0.1% SDS yielded an amount of product (<10 pg/μL) that could not be detected within the limits of the PicoGreen assay, meaning that its amplification factor was below 10. Sark and ProK refer to sarkosyl and proteinase K, respectively. Error bars are not shown on this figure but are approximately 10% of each value.

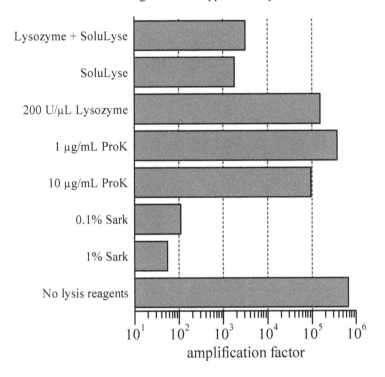

In order to retain cellular identities for each MDA reaction, it is crucial to prevent extraneous DNA from entering a microchamber together with the desired cell during the single-cell isolation process. Even a minuscule amount of DNA, either from the same organism or foreign species, can interfere with the analysis by competing with the targeted intracellular DNA during the amplification reaction. A facile strategy involving multiple washings of the cell pellet immediately prior to introduction of the cell suspension to the microfluidic device was developed in order to eliminate contaminant DNA from the environmental samples. To determine the number of washing steps necessary to eliminate extraneous DNA, we quantified the level of DNA present in the supernatant after each washing step (Figure 3). Although the reduction of DNA amounts within the supernatant by consecutive washings was obvious, the PicoGreen assay was not sensitive enough to detect DNA present below single-cell quantities. When the dMDA assay was employed to quantify DNA present in the supernatants, the level of extracellular DNA in the cell suspension after the fourth TES wash and subsequent 200-fold dilution with Injection Buffer (PBS pH 7.4 with 0.1%

Tween-20) was comparable to that of the no-template-DNA control sample (Figure 4). Therefore, for scMDA experiments, five TES washing steps were inserted between the off-chip and on-chip lysis procedures to preclude DNA contamination.

**Figure 3.** Removal of extracellular DNA via multiple washings of cell pellets before injecting into the microfluidic device. dsDNA concentration of the supernatant solutions were determined via PicoGreen fluorescence assay. ProK refers to proteinase K.

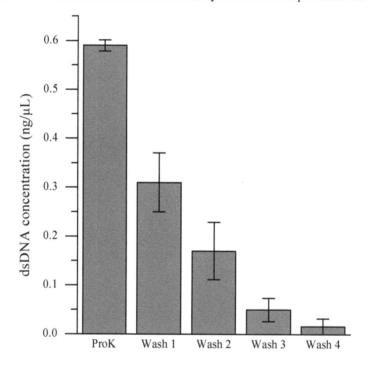

With the established lysis protocol, microfluidic scMDA of *Synechocystis* was performed. Three independent experimental sets (Sets A–C) were prepared, each of which consisted of six single-cell-containing 60-nL microchambers and two negative control chambers (that is, containing no cell). The amplification factors for the first-round on-chip MDA reactions were estimated to be ~$10^5$, which are significantly greater than those of macroscale reactions under the same conditions (See Supplementary Figure S2). This increase is consistent with the previous reports [10] that a confined reaction volume increases the yield of MDA. It is also notable that the inhibitory effects of added lysis reagents do not seem to be similarly enhanced.

**Figure 4.** dMDA confirmation of extracellular DNA removal via multiple washings of cell pellets before injection into the microfluidic device. The amounts of DNA fragments in the supernatants from the third and fourth successive TES Buffer washes were quantified with dMDA (as explained in Materials & Methods). Fluorescence images of the dMDA chips containing (**a**) the supernatant from the third wash and (**b**) its 200-fold dilution with Injection Buffer; (**c**) and (**d**) show the same set from the fourth wash, and (**e**) is the no-template-DNA control result.

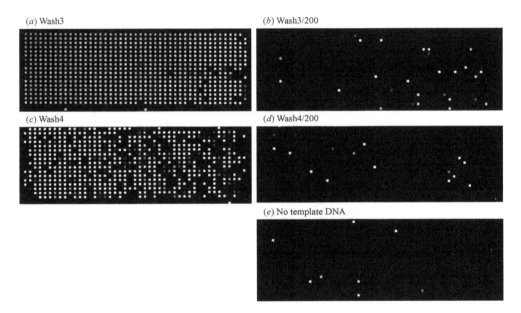

(*a*) Wash3  (*b*) Wash3/200

(*c*) Wash4  (*d*) Wash4/200

(*e*) No template DNA

   The MDA amplicons from the "on-chip" experiment were amplified via macroscale 50-μL MDA reactions and then PCR-amplified for sequencing using 15 *Synechocystis*-specific primer pairs targeting genes across the entire chromosome (See Supplementary Table S1). When PCR products of expected fragment sizes, assessed from gel electrophoresis results, were Sanger-sequenced and their sequences were compared against the reference genome, 13 out of 17 single-cell amplicons (one sample lost) and 3 out of 6 negative controls were found to contain at least one *Synechocystis*-specific target sequence. Sequences matching organisms other than *Synechocystis* were not found via BLAST searches against known genome sequences. Figure 5 is a graphical representation of the results from all samples, broken down by sample sets and primer sets. The average occurrence of the specific target sequence from the three sets was 10 (out of 17 single-cell amplicons) with a standard deviation of 4. In an effort to gain preliminary insights into possible sources of variable genome coverage, the "on-chip" amplicons of Set C were divided and subjected to two parallel, off-chip 50-μL reactions (Set C1 and C2). Among the 67 *Synechocystis*-specific sequences produced by the two sets, 32 (48%) were present in both, 22 (33%) were produced only by Set C1, and 13 (19%) only by Set C2. These results indicate that the observed variation of genome coverage may be attributed partly to the stochastic property of the MDA reaction itself, and not those factors that might be the result of microchip complications such as incomplete lysis, obstruction of the template by cell debris, and a small starting amount of template [10].

**Figure 5.** Loci coverage across scMDA samples. The bar chart presents the occurrence of *Synechocystis*-specific sequences across scMDA samples, broken down by sample and primer sets.

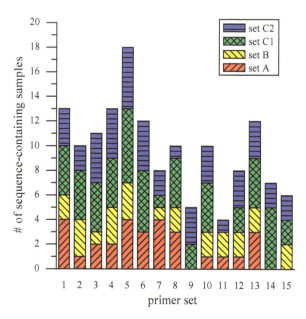

As mentioned above, half of all negative controls across the three sets produced *Synechocystis*-specfic target amplicons. To characterize the amount of extracellular DNA in the injected sample sets, the supernatants from the final TES washes of each sample were analyzed via dMDA (Figure 6). It should be noted that Set B's free DNA content is indistinguishable from the no-template control, which is consistent with the observation that no negative controls from Set B produced *Synechocystis*-specific amplicons. The no-template control is prepared according to all steps of the lysis protocol presented here, but no cells were added. We found that the no-template control gave negligible response after MDA amplification, demonstrating that our lysis reagents and sample handling do not introduce contaminating DNA. Therefore, the data from Set B represent a best-controlled single-cell experiment while other sets appear to still contain extracellular DNA, which must come from weakened cells leaking DNA into the solution,. In spite of these complications, we believe our data present a successful demonstration of the efficacy of our lysis protocol for *Synechocystis* and its compatibility with microfluidic scMDA. It should be recognized that prevention of leakage of genetic material into the isolation volume will be crucial to extend our lysis protocol toward the analysis of heterogeneous samples, such as those found in environmental bacterial communities.

**Figure 6.** Nucleic acid fragment content of final sample set washes. The supernatant of the final wash for each sample set was saved and diluted by a factor of 200. Nucleic acid fragments of the supernatants were quantified to obtain an idea of the level of sample exogenous contamination present in each set injection. Panels are lettered by sample ID (**a**) through (**c**) while the fourth (**d**) is a no-template control. Target counts are quantified per microliter of wash analyte (**e**), with error bars representing upper and lower 95% confidence interval estimates.

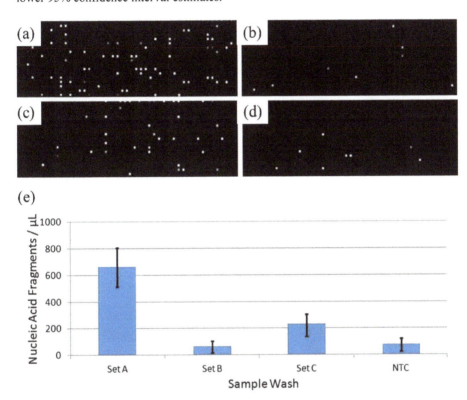

## 4. Conclusions

Whole genome analysis from single cells remains a topic of great interest. Significant progress has been made by combining microfluidic platforms with different kinds of gene amplification procedures [2,11,12]. For cells that easily lyse, such as mammalian cells, much progress has been achieved [13], but for cells having multiple cell wall layers, very few reports exist of their successful genomic analysis. This article has addressed this last issue by developing a lysis protocol that consists of off-chip partial removal and weakening of cell wall layers followed by on-chip lysis using reagents that do not interfere with the multiple displacement amplification reaction. This technique has been applied to *Synechocystis* sp. PCC 6803, a fully-genome-sequenced strain of photosynthetic cyanobacteria that commonly occurs in freshwater [14]. The challenge of single-cell genomic amplification is severe because of two types of interference, unwanted extraneous DNA arising from foreign sources and those arising from leaky cells [17,20]. These can dominate the amplification products because the lysing of a single cell releases so little genomic DNA. Consequently, much care has been taken to eliminate as best as we can these types of interference.

We have developed an effective lysis protocol for the model system *Synechocystis* and demonstrated its compatibility with microfluidic scMDA, thus extending this whole genome amplification technique to a strain of cyanobacteria. The protocol is both straightforward and flexible; it remains to be demonstrated that it is applicable with minor modifications to other prokaryotic species that are resistant to traditional lysis strategies. This chemical method, which is equally effective at a macro scale, also constitutes an alternative to conventional methods for preparing genomic DNA, which rely on mechanical cell breakage and extraction with organic solvents. We have shown that high-fidelity genome sequencing of single cells of *Synechocystis* can be achieved by performing microfluidic MDA reactions using this protocol, at least, as judged by performing sequencing on 15 loci that are widely separated. Whole genome sequencing was not performed in this study, but shotgun and next-generation sequencing and assembly might be done to assess how well this technique can cover the whole genome.

## Acknowledgments

The authors thank Paul Blainey (Department of Biological Engineering, Massachusetts Institute of Technology) and Anne-Kristin Kaster (Department of Civil and Environmental Engineering, Stanford University) for helpful discussions and advice provided, as well as samples of pure φ29 polymerase for purity comparisons. We also thank Devaki Bhaya (Department of Plant Biology, Carnegie Institution for Science) for a gift of the *Synechocystis* cells and for help in culturing them. Samuel Kim thanks Hong Gil Nam (Department of New Biology, DGIST, Daegu, Korea) and Visham Appadoo thanks HHMI for support. This work was supported by the US National Science Foundation (Grant Number MCB-0749638), the Research Center Program of IBS (Institute for Basic Science, No. CA1208) and the National Honor Scientist Support Program (National Research Foundation of Korea, No. 20100020417) funded by the Korean government (MEST).

## Conflict of Interest

The authors declare no conflict of interest.

## References

1.  Walker, A.; Parkhill, J. Single-cell genomics. *Nat. Rev. Microbiol.* **2008**, *6*, 176–177.
2.  Kalisky, T.; Blainey, P.; Quake, S.R. Genomic analysis at the single-cell level. *Annu. Rev. Genet.* **2011**, *45*, 431–445.
3.  Stepanauskas, R. Single cell genomics: An individual look at microbes. *Curr. Opin. Microbiol.* **2012**, *15*, 613–620.
4.  Dean, F.B.; Nelson, J.R.; Giesler, T.L.; Lasken, R.S. Rapid amplification of plasmid and phage DNA using Phi29 DNA polymerase and multiply-primed rolling circle amplification. *Genome Res.* **2001**, *11*, 1095–1099.

5. Zhang, K.; Martiny, A.C.; Reppas, N.B.; Barry, K.W.; Malek, J.; Chisholm, S.W.; Church, G.M. Sequencing genomes from single cells by polymerase cloning. *Nat. Biotechnol.* **2006**, *24*, 680–686.

6. Woyke, T.; Xie, G.; Copeland, A.; González, J.M.; Han, C.; Kiss, H.; Saw, J.H.; Senin, P.; Yang, C.; Chatterji, S.; *et al.* Assembling the marine metagenome, one cell at a time. *PLoS One* **2009**, *4*, e5299, doi:10.1371/journal.pone.0005299.

7. Woyke, T.; Tighe, D.; Mavromatis, K.; Clum, A.; Copeland, A.; Schackwitz, W.; Lapidus, A.; Wu, D.; McCutcheon, J.P.; McDonald, B.R.; *et al.* One bacterial cell, one complete genome. *PLoS One* **2010**, *5*, e10314, doi:10.1371/journal.pone.0010314.

8. Arakaki, A.; Shibusawa, M.; Hosokawa, M.; Matsunaga, T. Preparation of genomic DNA from a single species of uncultured magnetotactic bacterium by multiple-displacement amplification. *Appl. Environ. Microbiol.* **2010**, *76*, 1480–1485.

9. Zong, C.; Lu, S.; Chapman, A.R.; Xie, X.S. Genome-wide detection of single-nucleotide and copy-number variations of a single human cell. *Science* **2012**, *338*, 1622–1626.

10. Marcy, Y.; Ishoey, T.; Lasken, R.S.; Stockwell, T.B.; Walenz, B.P.; Halpern, A.L.; Beeson, K.Y.; Goldberg, S.M.D.; Quake, S.R. Nanoliter reactors improve multiple displacement amplification of genomes from single cells. *Plos Genet.* **2007**, *3*, e155, doi:10.1371/journal.pgen.0030155.

11. Marcy, Y.; Ouverney, C.; Bik, E.M.; Lösekann, T.; Ivanova, N.; Martin, H.G.; Szeto, E.; Platt, D.; Hugenholtz, P.; Relman, D.A.; *et al.* Dissecting biological "dark matter" with single-cell genetic analysis of rare and uncultivated TM7 microbes from the human mouth. *Proc. Natl. Acad. Sci. USA* **2007**, *104*, 11889–11894.

12. Blainey, P.C.; Mosier, A.C.; Potanina, A.; Francis, C.A.; Quake, S.R. Genome of a low-salinity ammonia-oxidizing archaeon determined by single-cell and metagenomic analysis. *PLoS One* **2011**, *6*, e16626, doi:10.1371/journal.pone.0016626.

13. Wang, J.; Fan, H.C.; Behr, B.; Quake, S.R. Genome-wide single-cell analysis of recombination activity and de novo mutation rates in human sperm. *Cell* **2012**, *150*, 402–412.

14. Kaneko, T.; Sato, S.; Kotani, H.; Tanaka, A.; Asamizu, E.; Nakamura, Y.; Miyajima, N.; Hirosawa, M.; Sugiura, M.; Sasamoto, S.; *et al.* Sequence analysis of the genome of the unicellular cyanobacterium *Synechocystis* sp. strain PCC6803. II. Sequence determination of the entire genome and assignment of potential protein-coding regions. *DNA Res.* **1996**, *3*, 109–136.

15. Hoiczyk, E.; Hansel, A. Cyanobacterial cell walls: News from an unusual prokaryotic envelope. *J. Bacteriol.* **2000**, *182*, 1191–1199.

16. Liu, X.; Curtiss, R. Nickel-inducible lysis system in *Synechocystis* sp. PCC 6803. *Proc. Natl. Acad. Sci. USA* **2009**, *106*, 21550–21554.

17. Blainey, P.C.; Quake, S.R. Digital MDA for enumeration of total nucleic acid contamination. *Nucleic Acids Res.* **2011**, *39*, e19, doi:10.1093/nar/gkq1074.

18. Chueh, B.; Li, C.-W.; Wu, H.; Davison, M.; Wei, H.; Bhaya, D.; Zare, R.N. Whole gene amplification and protein separation from a few cells. *Anal. Biochem.* **2011**, *411*, 64–70.

19. Ye, J.; Coulouris, G.; Zaretskaya, I.; Cutcutache, I.; Rozen, S.; Madden, T.L. Primer-BLAST: A tool to design target-specific primers for polymerase chain reaction. *BMC Bioinforma.* **2012**, *13*, 134, doi:10.1186/1471-2105-13-134.

20. Woyke, T.; Sczyrba, A.; Lee, J.; Rinke, C.; Tighe, D.; Clingenpeel, S.; Malmstrom, R.; Stepanauskas, R.; Cheng, J.-F. Decontamination of MDA reagents for single cell whole genome amplification. *PLoS One* **2011**, *6*, e26161, doi:10.1371/journal.pone.0026161.

21. Wu, X.; Zarka, A.; Boussiba, S. A simplified protocol for preparing DNA from filamentous cyanobacteria. *Plant Mol. Biol. Report.* **2000**, *18*, 385–392.

22. Hall, E.W. Microfluidic platforms for single-cell analyses. Ph.D. Thesis, Stanford University, Stanford, CA, USA, October 2012.

# Recent Trends on Micro/Nanofluidic Single Cell Electroporation

**Tuhin Subhra Santra and Fang-Gang Tseng**

**Abstract:** The behaviors of cell to cell or cell to environment with their organelles and their intracellular physical or biochemical effects are still not fully understood. Analyzing millions of cells together cannot provide detailed information, such as cell proliferation, differentiation or different responses to external stimuli and intracellular reaction. Thus, single cell level research is becoming a pioneering research area that unveils the interaction details in high temporal and spatial resolution among cells. To analyze the cellular function, single cell electroporation can be conducted by employing a miniaturized device, whose dimension should be similar to that of a single cell. Micro/nanofluidic devices can fulfill this requirement for single cell electroporation. This device is not only useful for cell lysis, cell to cell fusion or separation, insertion of drug, DNA and antibodies inside single cell, but also it can control biochemical, electrical and mechanical parameters using electroporation technique. This device provides better performance such as high transfection efficiency, high cell viability, lower Joule heating effect, less sample contamination, lower toxicity during electroporation experiment when compared to bulk electroporation process. In addition, single organelles within a cell can be analyzed selectively by reducing the electrode size and gap at nanoscale level. This advanced technique can deliver (in/out) biomolecules precisely through a small membrane area (micro to nanoscale area) of the single cell, known as localized single cell membrane electroporation (LSCMEP). These articles emphasize the recent progress in micro/nanofluidic single cell electroporation, which is potentially beneficial for high-efficient therapeutic and delivery applications or understanding cell to cell interaction.

Reprinted from *Micromachines*. Cite as: Santra, T.S.; Tseng, F.G. Micro/Nanofluidic Devices for Single Cell Analysis. *Micromachines* **2013**, *4*, 333-356.

## 1. Introduction

Electroporation or electropermeabilization is a powerful technique for biological cell studies. To apply high external electric field, cell membranes can increase their electrical conductivity and permeability due to structural change of the membrane to create transient hydrophilic pores from initially formatted hydrophobic pores. This process is usually known as electroporation or electropermeabilization [1–5]. The transient hydrophilic pores enable the delivery of biomolecules such as drugs, antibodies, DNA, RNA, dyes, ions, oligonucleotides from outside to inside of the cell [6–9] or intracellular cytosolic compounds from inside to outside of the cell [10,11]. The formation of hydrophilic stable or unstable pores mainly depends upon electrical field strength, the number of pulses, time between two pulses, *etc.* After application of external electric field surrounding cell medium, ions can move and accumulate as charges on cell membrane surface. This accumulation of charges can create an electric field inside cell membrane. As a result, electrical field strength generated inside the cell membrane is completely different from outside of the cell membrane [12]. This potential difference is called as transmembrane potential (TMP), which linearly proportional to the external electric field and the diameter of the cell. For a spherical cell, the TMP can be expressed by Schwan's equation as:

$$TMP = \varphi_i - \varphi_e = 1.5rE_0 \cos\theta \tag{1}$$

where $\varphi_i - \varphi_e$ is the potential difference between intracellular and extracellular membrane, $r$ is the radius of the cell, $E_0$ is the applied electric field strength and $\theta$ is the angle between direction of electric field and the selected point of the cell surface [13,14]. To apply high external electric field with longer pulses (ms), TMP can increase and hydrophobic pores became hydrophilic one at threshold TMP values (0.2–1 V) [6,15–19]. After withdraw the pulse, the membrane can reseal again without mechanical rupture and the phenomenon is known as reversible electroporation [19,20]. However, to apply very high external electric field, the cell membrane can deform permanently, whereas the membrane cannot reseal again resulting cell lysis, and the process known as irreversible electroporation [21,22].

Micro/nanofluidic devices are potentially beneficial for single cell electroporation. The main advantage of these devices are easy operation, low cost, portability, lower power consumption, very short reaction time, less toxic issue, small volume of reagent consumption when compared to bulk electroporation process (BEP) [23–26]. These devices can isolate single cell from population of millions of cells together and an inhomogeneous electric field can be focused only on single cell where remaining cells are unaffected. As a result, single cell manipulation can be performed from population of cells together. These devices can analyze cell to cell behavior with their organelle, their orientation, changes of cell size and shape with different polarities of electric fields [14,23,24,26,27]. On the other hand, bulk electroporation needs two large electrodes surrounding millions of cells together and a homogeneous electric field is applied to electroporates millions of cells at once. As a result, cell to cell behavior is difficult to analyze clearly. Due to a large gap between two electrodes, an additional voltage is required (several hundred volts) for the electroporation process. Higher voltage can provide higher electrical field strength, by which some of the cells can rupture and some of them are unaffected from millions of cells, resulting in lower transfection rate and cell viability when compared with single cell electroporation [24]. Larger size electrode can provide a larger surface area to react with a large volume of cell medium; however, toxic issues during the electroporation process will arise and might reduce the cell viability. This toxic issue mainly depends upon electrode materials [28]. For micro/nanofluidic devices, where the dimension of the devices are in micro to nanoscale label, which is similar to single cell dimension (microchannel). As a result, single cell can trap/sort easily for electroporation experiment. Moreover for specific design of microchannel, the device can supply nutrients to the cells and experiment can be performed many times without resuspended the cells and removal of cells without cell adhesive reagent, which is not possible in bulk electroporation process.

Recently, single cell electroporation (SCEP) research approaches in more advance stages, where the dimension of the micro/nanofluidic devices reaches from micro to nanoscale level. To use this dimensional advantage, an electric field can easily intense in the local region of the single cell membrane, by which high transfection rate and high cell viability were achieved [27,29]. However localized electroporation can also be performed by nanochannel ion transportation using the electrophoresis method [30]. To apply electrical field in local region of the single cell membrane, the process is known as localized single cell membrane electroporation (LSCMEP), by which precise and controllable drug delivery is possible [27,29,30]. The LSCMEP process can provide very high transfection rate, high cell viability, low power consumption, lower toxicity, low thermal effect in comparison with SCEP or BEP process.

## 2. Bulk, Single and Localized Single Cell Membrane Electroporation

### 2.1. Bulk Electroporation (BEP)

In Bulk electroporation (BEP) process, a homogeneous electric field is applied with suspension of millions of cells together, where two large electrodes are separated with larger distance. To transfect cells with BEP process, a very high external electric field (KV cm$^{-1}$) is needed to induce transmembrane potential, which must be exceed the cell membrane threshold values [31]. As result, transient electropermeabilized pores can form on the cell membrane to deliver exogenous biomolecules from the outside to the inside of the cell. Figure 1a shows the cuvette with suspensions of millions of cells in between two metal electrodes (the distance between two metal electrodes varied inside the cuvette, as result induced electric field is different from top to bottom of the cuvette). Whereas in Figure 1b, cells are suspension into the cuvette and metal electrodes can introduce from outside to inside of the cuvette. The gap between two metal electrodes are almost same in each position of the cuvette and electric field can act uniformly onto the cell membrane inside the cuvette. Both of this cuvette, cells are suspension in between two metal electrodes, as result a homogeneous electric field can act on to the cell membrane to deliver substances inside the cells with high electric field.

### 2.2. Single Cell Electroporation (SCEP)

In single cell electroporation (SCEP), an inhomogeneous electric field is applied surrounded the single cell, where distance between two electrodes is in micro scale level (single cell dimension). Micro/nanofluidic devices dimension almost reaches to this level to position each single cell with micro-channel flow control and it can perform successful single cell transfection or single cell lysis. Figure 2 shows how an electric field influences single cells to form membrane nano-pores during the electroporation process. From this figure, the maximum electric field is at the poles of the cell (light color across the cell membrane position) and minimum is at the equators (deep color on top and bottom of the cell membrane). As a result, the transmembrane potential is different in each point of the cell membrane. High transmembrane potential induces at the poles of the cell and low transmembrane potential at the equators (according to Equation (1)), resulting formation of higher density of pores at the poles and lower density of pores at the equators. To reduce the gap between two electrodes by using micro/nanofluidic devices, the requirement of voltage should be lower compared to the bulk electroporation process. In this device, single cell manipulation with their cytosolic compound can be analyzed easily. Figure 3 shows single cell electroporation, where external electric field is applied outside of the single cell. Figure 3a shows the formation of different density of pores at different position of the single cell membrane due to variation of electric field strength. Maximum pores form at the poles due to higher electric field (see Equation (1)) and minimum density of pores form at the equators due to less electric filed affect. Figure 3b shows that, after withdrawing the electric field, cell membranes reseal again, as a result biomolecules enter successfully inside the single cell.

**Figure 1.** The bulk electroporation apparatus *in vitro* experiment with cross sectional view of two metal electrodes. The distance between two large electrodes varies from millimeter to centimeter range. To manufacture of this device is simple but the voltage requirement is very high to permeabilize of millions of cells together due to large distance between two electrodes (a) cells are in suspension within the cuvette, where two metal electrodes are fixed inside the cuvette for electroporation experiment (b) cells are suspension and metal electrodes can introduce from outside to inside of this cuvette. Figure has been redrawn from reference [31].

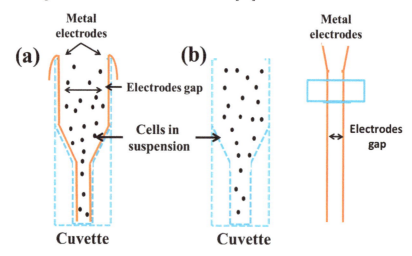

**Figure 2.** Electric field distribution for single cell electroporation where induced transmembrane potential is maximum at the cell pole and minimum at the equator.

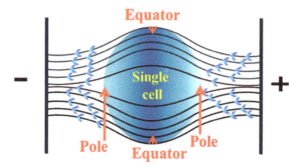

**Figure 3.** Single cell electroporation (SCEP), where an external electric field applied outside of the single cell (**a**) formation of pores due to electric field application (maximum pores open at poles and minimum pores open at the equators due to different field strength at different positions of the membrane); (**b**) after withdrawing the pulse, cell membranes reseal again and biomolecules enter successfully inside the single cell.

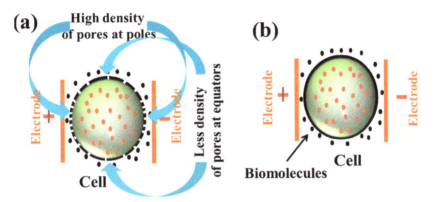

*2.3. Localized Single Cell Membrane Electroporation (LSCMEP)*

In the last couple of years, device fabrication approaches towards the nanoscale level, where the gap between two electrodes is reduced to nanometer scale. As the gap between the electrodes reduces significantly, the electric field can intensify only a nanometer region in-between two electrodes. To use micro/nanofluidic devices, single cells can be positioned on top of the nanoelectrode and cell membranes can deform only on nano-scale region (reaming cell membrane area will be unaffected) to deliver drugs from outside to inside of the cell. The process as known as localized single cell membrane electroporation (LSCMEP) [29]. Figure 4 shows the LSCMEP process, where Figure 4a shows how the cell membrane deforms and opens up the pores due to application of electric field. As a result, biomolecules enter from outside to inside of the single cell. Figure 4b shows the cell membrane resealing after withdrawing the pulses, where biomolecules enter successfully inside the single cell.

This new approach leads to lower voltage requirements, high transfection efficiency, high cell viability, low toxicity, low sample volume, very low Joule heating effect in compare with SCEP or BEP process. Until now, the fabrication of such devices is in the development stage. In the near future researchers need to pay more attention to developing micro/nanofluidic LSCMEP devices for better understanding of single cell analysis with their intracellular biochemical effect.

**Figure 4.** Localized single cell membrane electroporation (LSCMEP) where electric field is applied in a specific region (nano-scale region) of the cell membrane. (**a**) During electroporation, membrane pores open and biomolecules deliver from outside to inside of the single cell; (**b**) After electroporation cell membranes reseal again and biomolecules entered successfully inside the single cell. Permission to reprint obtained from Springer [27].

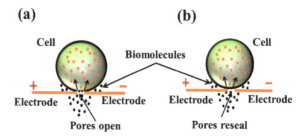

## 3. Micro/Nanofluidic Devices for Single Cell Electroporation

For single cell electroporation, micro/nanofluidic devices are essential to analyze intracellular reaction in response to external stimuli. The transfection rate depends upon electric field strength, number of pulses and duration of pulses. Generally, smaller size biomolecules can enter inside a single cell by the diffusion process whereas the larger size such as DNA can enter inside the single cell by the electrophoretically driven process. It was reported that short and strong electric field pulses can provide reversible electroporation [32,33]. However, ultrashort nanosecond pulses with higher electric field can provide irreversible electroporation [10]. The permeabilization area can be controlled with the pulse amplitude and the degree of permeabilization can be controlled with the duration of pulses, numbers of pulses, where longer pulses provide a larger perturbation area in the cell membrane [34,35]. In earlier studies of micro/nanofluidic based single cell electroporation, authors analyze cellular content and cellular properties [36–39], transfection of cells [17,40–42] and inactivating cells [43–45] with the use of micro-channel based electroporation [46–49], micro-capillary based electroporation [50–52], electroporation with solid microelectrode [36,53–55], membrane sandwich based microfluidic electroporation [56,57], microarray single cell electroporation [58], optofluidic based microfluidic devices [59–65], *etc.* Table 1 describes in detail micro/nanofluidic based single cell transfection, cell lysis, cell type with species, potential difference, pulse duration, *etc.*

In this article, we emphasize the details about single cell transfection and lysis by using micro/nanofluidic devices with cell trapping and droplet microfluidics technique, single cell transfection and lysis with localized single cell membrane electroporation (LSCMEP) technique. Also, we compared the advantage and future prospect of LSCMEP process with SCEP and BEP process. Finally, we have drawn some conclusions between BEP, SCEP and LSCMEP process.

**Table 1.** Performance of Micro/nanofludic single cell electroporation.

| Year and References | Potential difference | Pulse time | Cell type | Spices | Purpose |
|---|---|---|---|---|---|
| 1999 [66] | 0–60 V | 2 µs–100 ms | ND-1 ATCC#CRL-1439 | Human Rat | Transfection and lysis |
| 2001 [41] | 10 V | 5 ms | Huh-7 | Human | Transfection |
| 2003 [67] | 1125 V | Continuous DC | Jurkat | Human | Lysis |
| 2003 [38] | 20 V | ±20 s AC | S. cerevisiae | Yeast | Lysis |
| 2004 [68] | 1400 | 1 s | Erythrocytes | Human | Lysis |
| 2005 [69] | 0.1–1 V | 10 KHz AC | HeLa | Human | Transfection |
| 2006 [70] | 400 V/cm, 600–1200 V/cm | 10 µs–20 ms, 30 ms | CHO | Hamster | Transfection and lysis |
| 2006 [71] | 2000 V/cm | Continuous DC | E. coli | Bacterial | Lysis |
| 2007 [72] | 10 V$_{PP}$ | 1 MHz | Zucchini protoplast cells | Plant | Lysis |
| 2008 [73] | 1–3 V | 6 ms | C2C12 | Mouse | Transfection |
| 2008 [29] | 1 V$_{PP}$ | 0.5 Hz | Fibroblast cell | Rat | Transfection |
| 2008 [46] | <20 V | 100 KHz–1 MHz | A431 squamous cell | Human | Lysis |
| 2009 [74] | 5 V$_{rms}$ | 40 Hz | FITC-BSA-laden vesicle | - | Lysis |
| 2010 [75] | <3 V | Continuous DC | - | Yeast | Transfection |
| 2012 [27] | 10 µs, 20 ms | 8 VPP | HeLa | Human | Tranfection |
| 2012 [30] | 1–60 ms | 60–260 V/2 mm | K 562, Jurkat | Human | Transfection |
| 2012 [76] | 1.3 V | Continuous DC | Algal cell | Plant | Transfection |
| 2013 [77] | 600–90 m V$_{pp}$ | 2 ms | HT-29 | Human | Lysis |

*3.1. Single Cell Transfection*

3.1.1. Trapping Based Single Cell Transfection

The first microfluidic device with cell trapping was proposed by Huang *et al.* in 1999 [66]. This device was fabricated with two chambers (top and bottom), which were separated by silicon nitride layer (1 µm). Figure 5 shows the schematic of the device for single cell electroporation. The top and bottom layer were fabricated with n+ polysilicon layer, which was a conducting and transparent layer. As a result, the device was transparent and light from the microscope could pass throughout the device. One hole (2 µm to 10 µm) was formed in middle layer by reactive ion etching technique. Two chambers were filled with saline had different pressures: the top chamber was higher pressure than the bottom chamber, meaning cells had the tendency to flow from the top to bottom chamber. As the lowered pressure in the bottom chamber, the cell was trapped in a hole, which was formed in the middle layer. Then continuous DC power supply was supplied between two chambers with amplitude 0–120 V and 2 µs to 100 ms pulse duration. The distances between two electrodes were 900 µm. After application of electric field, it was constricted through the hole, which increased the transmembrane potential of the cell membrane, and finally the membrane was electrically permeabilized to enter exogenous molecules from outside to inside of the single cell.

Later, the same author has proposed different types of microfluidic devices for single cell transfection in 2001 and 2003 [78,79]. Figure 6 shows flow through based microfluidic chip for single cell transfection. In Figure 6a, cells flowed one by one through the micro-channel. The width of the micro-channel was higher than the cell dimension. When the cell was near the vicinity of the hole, due to back pressure (lower pressure) on the bottom channel, the single cell was trapped easily on the hole. As the application of electric field with proper pulse (10 V with 10 ms), the cell membrane was permeabilized, to enter foreign biomolecule inside the single cell. After electroporation, back pressure was withdrawn. As a result, a single cell was released from the hole and the next cell was ready to trap for another electroporation. With this microfluidic design, different cells can electroporate with different duration of pulses and different types of exogenous biomolecules can enter inside the single cell according to electroporation experiment requirement. Figure 6b shows the optical microscope image of micro-channel with hole and electrodes. The success rate for single cell trapping and electroporation effectiveness can be achieve 100% for this micro-electroporation method. This device transfected EGFP into SK-OV-3 cells with the application of 0.4 KV/cm electric field.

**Figure 5.** Microfluidic SCEP with cell trapping. Figure has been redrawn with reference [26,66].

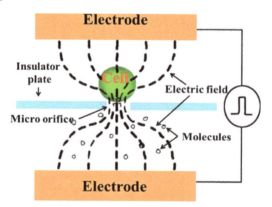

Another cell trapping with microfluidic device for single cell electroporation was proposed by Khine *et al.* in 2004 [80]. The device was fabricated with polydimethylsiloxane (PDMS), where silicon substrate was used as a mold for PDMS. In this device, two wider channels were used for cell inlet and outlet. The middle circular section, where cells can be released from the main channel and it was connected with many micro-channels for single cell trapping. The diameter of each micro-channel was 3.1 μm, which was one third of the cell diameter. As a result, localized electroporation was performed with this micro-channel based device. Later, the detailed manufacturing process of such trapping device was proposed by Suzuki *et al.* [81]. In this device, Ag/Agcl electrode was connected with each micro-channel and main inlet channel. After cell loading through the main inlet channel to the circular area, negative pressure was applied to the micro-channel. Then, the single cell was trapped with the micro-channel. The electroporation was measured to use the circuit model of this device. Cell membrane permeabilization was measured by characteristic "jumps" in the current that correspond to drops in cell resistance. The reversible electroporation was performed with this device by applying $0.76 \pm 0.095$ V with 6.5 ms pulse. This device can deliver drugs, DNA and protein inside the single cell. The feasibility of introducing foreign material with permeabilized single cell was tested with trypan blue for suspension of cells.

**Figure 6.** (a) Concept of flow through micro-electroporation chip; (b) Optical image of micro-channel, micro-hole and electrodes. Permission to reprint obtained from Elsevier [78].

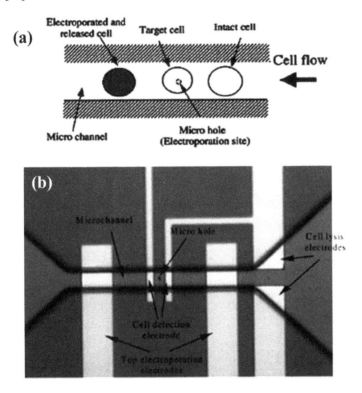

In 2008, Ionescu-Zantti *et al.* [82] proposed electrophoresis driven microfluidic based electroporation device for single cell trapping and transfection. Figure 7 shows the schematic steps for an electrophoresis based electroporation device. This device was fabricated with PDMS, where 3 μm × 3 μm capillaries microchannel was formed for single cell trapping and focusing the electric field. Initially, a cell was trapped through the capillary channel by using negative pressure and then 0–300 mV external field was applied (this field was below the cell membrane threshold values (0.5–2 V)) for electrophoretically preconcentrate the dyes near the cell membrane (see Figure 7a). After that, larger pulses were applied (5–30 ms) for the electroporation process (see Figure 7b) and dye was loaded during resealing of the cell membrane by applied lower electric field (Figure 7c). This method reduced the dye loading time into the single cell by its unique design.

**Figure 7.** The schematic steps for electrophoresis driven cell loading protocol **(a)** preconcentrate; **(b)** membrane electroporation; **(c)** apply electrophoretic driving force. Figure has been redrawn with reference [82].

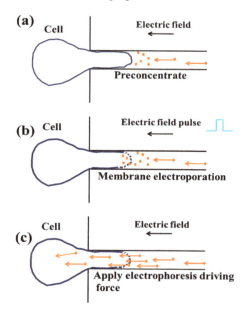

Another group, Valero *et al.* [73] in 2008, proposed microfluidic device which delivered PI dye to use single mouse myoblast $C_2C_{12}$ cells with high transfection efficiency (>75%). In 2012, Gac *et al.* [83] suggested a new microfluidic device by which they trapped individual cell in micrometer-size structure within a microchip and exposed an intense electric field with plasmid/dye. This device includes an array of independent electroporation sites, which electroporates nine cells together.

### 3.1.2. Droplet Microfluidics for Single Cell Transfection

Droplet microfluidic based single cell electroporation has raised a lot of interest in recent years for biological and therapeutic studies. This technique leads to high throughput screening application for single cell analysis. Droplets can encapsulate cells, DNA, dye, particles or molecules that are in the inner aqueous phase [84]. Recently, droplet microfluidic have wide applications in biotechnology such as animal cell growth in encapsulated droplet in picoliter range, with high cell viability [85]. The first droplet microfluidic based electroporation was proposed by Luo *et al.* [86] in 2006. They used the electrochemical detection method for aqueous droplet analysis in oil phase of microfluidic device. Electrochemical signal difference was held between oil and aqueous. This method provides the size information and ion concentration, which leads from 0.02 mmol/L to 1 mol/L of tens of picoliter to nanoliter aqueous droplet. In 2009 Zhan *et al.* proposed droplet microfluidic based single cell electroporation [87]. The device was fabricated with polydimethylsiloxane (PDMS) by using standard soft lithographic process. A 150 nm thickness based microelectrode was fabricated with e-beam evaporation and lithographic process. Figure 8 shows the droplet microfluidic based single cell electroporation process. This device has two inlets, one outlet and one pair of electrodes. Electroporation can be performed with droplet containing single cell. The buffer with cells and DNA was loaded in one inlet channel, where the cell was introduced by syringe pump with magnetic stair. In magnetic stair, the magnetic field can rotate to cause stair bar, which is immersed in medium with cells, making cells spin to avoid cells settling down. Another inlet channel was used for oil pumping. Droplets with cell of different sizes were produced by adjusting the flow rates between oil and buffer solution. The size of each droplet with a cell was 60–386 μm in length and this droplet containing a cell was electroporated with droplet velocity 1.38–8.86 m/min to apply 5–9 V constant DC voltage in-between 20 μm electrodes gap. Due to application of DC voltage, an electric field can act on a droplet containing conducting buffer solution and it electroporates a single cell within the droplet. This device achieved 68% cell viability with 4.7 volt applied voltage after electroporation; however, viability reduced down to 14% for 7.1 volt applied voltage. Also it transfected plasmid vector coding EGFP into Chinese Hamster Ovary (CHO) cell. The cell transfection rate was 11% due to 5.8 V, 1.8 ms pulse application. Thus droplet size, droplet velocity, electric field strength and distance between two electrodes are important to achieve high transfection and high cell viability. Droplet microfluidics is potentially applicable for high throughput functional screening of genes, which is not possible in the bulk electroporation process.

**Figure 8.** Layout and performance of a droplet based microfluidic device (**a**) two microelectrodes, where cells can be positioned for electroporation; (**b**) after electroporation, a droplet with a cell at the end of the device. Permission to reprint obtained from American Chemical Society (ACS) [87].

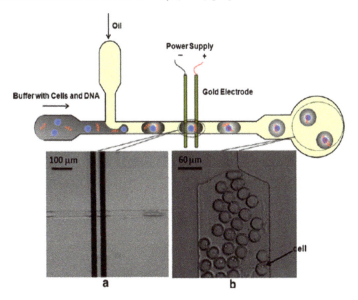

Recently, Qu *et al.* [76] proposed droplet electroporation with the use of microfluidic device. This device was fabricated with polydimethylsiloxane (PDMS) by using soft lithography process. Figure 9 shows the droplet microfluidic electroporation technique. Figure 9a,b shows a schematic of the droplet based microfluidic device and electroporation for algal cell. This device included two inlets and one outlet channel. One inlet channel contained DNA with algal cells whereas another inlet channel contained Fc oil. This cell content droplet flowed through the oil phase into the channel, where five pairs of micro-electrodes with constant DC voltage was present. A constant DC voltage with 1.3 V was applied to produce 393 V cm$^{-1}$ electric field for electroporation experiment. The electric current act, when the conducting droplet buffer with the cell passed through the microelectrodes. Oil passing through the microelectrodes leads to zero current due to nonconductive oil solution.

The gap between two electrodes were 33 μm. The electroporation time can be controlled by controlling the droplet size, flow rate of droplet size with droplet content cells and DNA, flow rate of oil, *etc.* When the flow rate of the droplet containing cell and the flow rate of the oil were 0.3 μL min$^{-1}$ and 0.5 μL min$^{-1}$, the electroporation time was 7 ms. The ratio of the cell counting droplet was 70% when the concentrations of the cells were $1.58 \times 10^7$ cells/mL. This device was achieved the transformation efficiency $8.14 \times 10^4$ and cell viability 81% by using serpentine channel with five pairs of parallel electrodes on the chip with DNA/algal cell ratio of 1000. This chip provided very high transfection efficiency (1600 times higher than that ($5.05 \times 10^{-7}$) compared to the bulk electroporation process.

**Figure 9.** Droplet microfluidic electroporation technique (**a**) schematic diagram; (**b**) electroporation process of algal cell. Figure has been redrawn from reference [76].

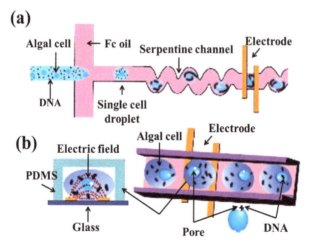

*3.2. Single Cell Lysis*

Microfluidic devices can provide single cell transfection as well as cell lysis by their unique design. Cell transfection can provide exogenous biomolecules delivery inside single cell with complete cell membrane resealing, which also known as reversible electroporation. This process can analyze intracellular biochemical effect and electrochemical cell membrane behavior. For irreversible electroporation, cell membrane cannot reseal due to high electric field affect and the membrane can rapture permanently resulting cell lysis. Both the processes have wide biological and therapeutic applications. Reversible electroporation or cell transfection can be applied to electrochemotherapy whereas irreversible electroporation or cell lysis can be applied to chemotherapeutic process. Figure 10 shows a microfluidic based single cell lysis device [88]. This device is designed with a continuous flow. The electric field strength was in periodic variation due to saw teeth geometry in each electrode. The overall channel was 1100 µm wide with 180 saw-teeth electrodes.

The distance between two electrodes tip was three times of the cell diameter to avoid cell clogging. Figure 10 shows the saw-teeth design of microelectrodes and electrical lysis zone in-between two electrodes. For this unique design of saw-teeth electrodes, the voltage requirement was very low and generation of heat was lower compared to bulk electroporation process. The results of this device shows that 81% cells were partially lysed where as 28% cells were completely lysed for 6 V, AC with 5 KHz frequency. Also, 74% cells became completely lysed and 71% cells were partially lysed for 8.5 V AC with 10 KHz frequency.

**Figure 10.** Schematic representation of microfluidic cell lysis device where saw-teeth microelectrodes acting as a dielectrophoresis effect on the device for focusing intracellular material after electroporation. Figure has been redrawn from reference [88].

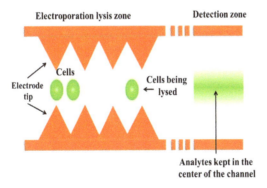

Another cell lysis device was proposed by Wang *et al.* in 2006 [71,89]. This microfluidic device was fabricated with PDMS by using the soft lithographic process. Figure 11 shows the microfluidic cell lysis device using electroporation technique. Initially, both reservoirs (sample reservoir and receiving reservoir) were filled with phosphate buffered saline. Then, cells were loaded in sample reservoir with $10^6$ cells/mL concentration. Both reservoirs contained 30 µL solutions during experiment. Platinum electrodes were connected with two reservoirs where positive electrode was in the receiving reservoir and the negative electrode was in the sample reservoir. Due to high electric field application, cells were moved from sample reservoir to the receiving reservoir through lysis section. The dimension of cell lysis section was 25 µm to avoid cell clogging and ensure stable performance. This section has higher electric field strength (because of narrow section) compared to two reservoirs. The cell lysis rate can be varied due to changes of length and width of the two reservoirs and lysis section. They achieved 100% cell lysis for 1000–1500 V/cm electric field application. Also, they found complete cell membrane disruption in cell lysis section at 2000 V/cm electric field application.

**Figure 11.** Microfluidic based flow through electroporation device. Cells from sample reservoir moving to the receiving reservoir and electrical lysis were confined with single cell movement through the lysis section ($W_2$). Permission to reprint obtained from Elsevier [71].

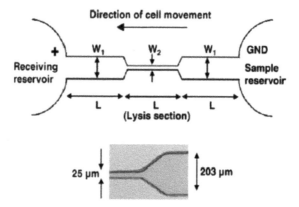

Micro/nanofluidic devices have great ability to analyze the intracellular content after cell lysis by the application of sufficient external electric field. This device can detect and analyze the cell response based on laser induced fluorescence and electrophoresis methods [90–95]. Generally, many biomolecules (protein, metabolites) except nucleic acid cannot amplify. Thus, the fluorescence-based method can detect and analyze of single cell response with high sensitivity.

In 2007, Li *et al.* [94] proposed their microfluidic device for single cell analysis. The chip was fabricated by standard 1-photomask with low cost method. The device consists four reservoirs, four channels and one open region which contain a cell retention chamber. Reservoir one was used for cell introduction and washing, whereas reservoir two was used for reagent delivery. Reservoir three and four were used as waste reservoirs. By using this chip, they quantified dynamic $Ca^{2+}$ mobilization of a single cardiomyocyte during its spontaneous contraction. Also, they monitored successfully dynamic responses from various external stimulation such as daunorubicin (cardiotoxic chemotherapeutic drug), caffeine, and isoliquiritigenin (herbal anticancer). Their results also prove that anticancer drugs have less effect on the $Ca^{2+}$ of the cardiomyocytes. This device has quantified the cellular response of single cardiomyocytes, discovery of heart diseases drug and cardiotoxicity testing.

In 2010, Mellors *et al.* [95] proposed an electrophoretic and electrospray ionization based microfluidic device for single cell analysis. The device was fabricated on corning borosilicate glass substrate by using standard photolithography and wet chemical etching technique. Figure 12 shows the schematic of the microfluidic device, where A was a cell loading reservoir and B was buffer loading, which intersects with the separation channel.

**Figure 12.** Schematic diagram for cell lysis using capillary electrophoresis and mass spectrometry. The arrow indicated direction of electroosmotic flow. Cells flow from cell reservoir (A) to the intersection zone where cells were lysed, then they migrate towards electrospray orifice through separation channel. Figure has been redrawn from reference [95].

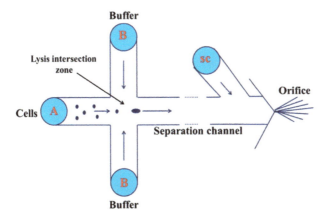

This intersection zone was a cell lysis zone. CS was an electro-osmotic pump which was connected with an electrophoretic separation channel and electrospray orifice. Cells can flow through hydrodynamically or electrically to the intersection zone, where cells were electrically lysed. Then, cells can migrate to electrospray orifice through the separation channel where cells electrospray ionization occurred. This device successfully lysed human erythrocytes with real-time electrophoretic separation. The heme group, $\alpha$ and $\beta$ subunits of hemoglobin were detected from erythrocytes when cells were continuously flowed through the device. This device can analyze 12 c/m.

## 4. Localized Single Cell Membrane Electroporation (LSCMEP)

### 4.1. LSCMEP for Cell Transfection

Localized single cell membrane electroporation can provide better cell transfection with micro/nanofluidic devices compared to single cell electroporation (SCEP) or bulk electroporation (BEP). Because of micro/nanoscale electrode dimension and distance between two electrodes were very small, as a result, electric field can intense in a very small region of the cell membrane compared to single cell dimension. Thus, the local area of the single cell can be affected by a strong electric field, whereas other areas will be unaffected. Due to the effects of small areas of the whole single cell, high cell viability and high transfection rate can be achieved compared to single cell electroporation. However, Boukany *et al.* show localized single cell electroporation by using nano-channel based ion transportation using electrophoresis method with two large electrodes [30]. By fabricating micro/nano electrodes with a micro/nano scale electrode gap, this device can provide some promising parameters such as low voltage and power requirement, lower toxic effect due to negligible ion generation, small sample volume and negligible heat generation. These parameters are essential to achieve high transfection rate and high cell viability. Thus, microfluidic based LSCMEP process can provide a better understanding to analyze intracellular cytosolic compounds compared to SCEP or the bulk electroporation process. Nawarathna *et al.*, demonstrated the AFM based LSCMEP process. Figure 13 shows localized electroporation of a single cell using atomic force microscopy (AFM) technique [29]. For this experiment, they modified AFM tip to act as a nano-electrode to make an intense high electric field near the localized area of the single cell membrane. A boron doped silicon AFM tips ($\sigma = 0.001$ $\Omega$ cm, $k = 1.5$ N/m) was used for LSCMEP process. Before electroporation, the tip was grown with 20 nm $SiO_2$ layer and finally this oxidized tip was sectioned until bare silicon was exposed by focused ion beam (FIB) technique. As a result, a smaller area of bare silicon can cause an intense high electric field on a single cell membrane. They have reduced this bare silicon area down to 0.5 μm in diameter, which was concentrated with an intense electric field on 10 μm diameter of rat fibroblast cell. Figure 13a–h shows the results of LSCMEP technique using AFM tip for electroporation process and Figure 13i demonstrated the AFM tip, which was positioned on top of the single cell for localized single cell membrane electroporation (LSCMEP) process. To make an intense high electric field, 1Vpp with 0.5 Hz pulse was used to transfect rat fibroblast cells. The transfection of single cell was completed within 10 s. This device can perform highly localized electroporation of a sigle cell with concentric electric field on local area of single cell membrane. The experiment can be performed in a friendly environment such as cell culture dishes, *etc.*

**Figure 13.** (**a**) bright field image of atomic force microscopy (AFM) tip and the cell in the electroporation medium (cell A is electroporated while cell B and C are about 20 μm away from cell A); (**b**) Fluorescence image of rat fibroblast cell after electroporation; (**c**) Confocal fluorescence image of an electroporated cell; (**d**)–(**h**) Sequence of real time confocal fluorescence images of rat fibroblast cell after electroporation; (**i**) Calculated spatial distribution of electric field in the vicinity of the cell being electroporated. Permission to reprint obtained from American Institute of Physics (AIP) [29].

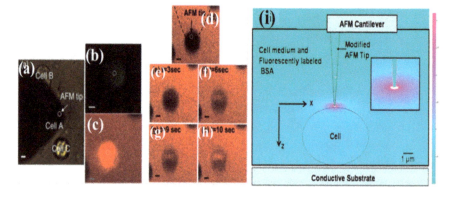

In recent years, Boukany *et al.* [30] showed nanochannel based localized single cell electroporation with a precise amount of biomolecules delivery. In this device, they positioned a single cell in one microchannel by optical tweezers and transfection agent was loaded to another microchannel. These two microchannels were connected by one nanochannel. To apply a very high electric field in between two microchannels, a transfection agent was delivered through the nanochannel using an electrophoretically driven process and finally drugs were delivered inside a single cell through a very small area of the cell membrane. In 2012, Chen *et al.* demonstrated another localized single cell membrane electroporation usimg ITO microelectrode based transparent chip [27]. Figure 14 shows microfluidic localized single cell membrane electroporation device. They deposited ITO films on a covered glass substrate and patterend it by standard lithographic process to form as ITO lines. After that, a thin $SiO_2$ layer was deposited as a passivation layer by plasma enhanced chemical vapor deposition (PECVD) technique. The final ITO lines were cut by the focused ion beam (FIB) technique. The gap between two electrodes were 1 μm and width of each electrode was 2 μm. When single cell was strongly attached in between two electrodes gap, the electric field was intensed in only a 1 μm gap area on single cell membrane. As a result, they demonstrated localized single cell membrane electroporation with microfluidic device. Figure 14a shows localized electroporation process between two micro-electrodes and Figure 14b shows multiple number of electrodes for LSCMEP process. Figure 14 c and d shows the optical microscope image of patterened ITO microelectrodes and scanning electron microscope (SEM) image of ITO microelectrodse with micro-channel. According to their results, they achived 0.93 μm electroporation region with 60% cell viability for $8V_{pp}$ 20 ms pulse application. To reduce the gap between two electrodes, a high transfection rate can be achived by this technique. This device not only control the recovery of cell membranes (reversible electroporation) without cell damage but also it provides clear optical view by using an inverted microscope (ITO based transparent chip).

**Figure 14.** Localized single cell membrane electroporation (LSCMEP) device (**a**) localized electroporation process between two microelectrodes; (**b**) multiple number of microelectrodes for LSCMEP process; (**c**) optical microscope image of ITO microelectrodes; (**d**) scanning electron microscope image of ITO microelectrodes with microchannel. Permission to reprint obtained from Springer [27].

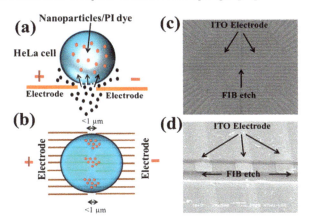

**Figure 15.** (**a**) Schematic diagram with electrical connection of the device and PDMS structure; (**b**) an array of transistors with nanowires and nanoribbons. Figure has been redrawn from reference [77].

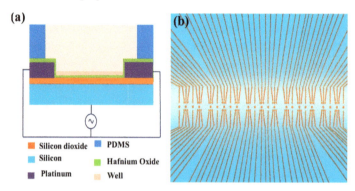

*4.2. LSCMEP for Cell Lysis*

Recently, another LSCMEP based device was proposed by Jokilaakso *et al.* [77] for single cell lysis. They reported a silicon nanowire and nanoribbon based biological field effect transistor for single cell positioning and lysis mechanism. Figure 15a shows the cross sectional view and electric connection with PDMS above the device and Figure 15b shows an array of the transistors with both nanowires and nanoribons. To position the single cell on this device, they used programmable magnetic field for magnetic manipulation of 7.9 μm COOH modified COMPEL magnetic microsphere. After positioning the single cell (HT-29) on top of the transistor, cells were adhered for 30 min prior to electroporation experiment. The applied electric field was 600–900 mV$_{pp}$ (peak to peak) at 10 MHz for 2 ms pulse. This electric field was connected with a shorted source and drain in one terminal and another terminal connected on the gate of the device. The electric field intensity was fringing in nature, which affected the cell membrane integrity leading to cell lysis. This device can perform single cell lysis which is potentially applicable to medical diagnostics and biological cell studies.

**5. Conclusions**

In summary, this article describes the details about bulk electroporation (BEP), single cell electroporation (SCEP), and localized single cell membrane electroporation (LSCMEP) by using micro/nanofluidic devices with their advantages and disadvantages. All of these processes can deliver drugs, DNA, RNA, oligonucleotides, proteins, *etc.* However, to analyze cell to cell behavior with their organelles and intracellular biochemical effect, single cell analysis must be executed. Micro/nanofluidic devices are the potential candidates to analyze single cells, because of their dimension reduction to the dimension of single cell level. These devices provide easy performance such as cell handling, lower power consumption, low toxicity, small sample volume, lower contamination rate, high cell viability, and high transfection rate when compared to conventional electroporation. To reduce the electrode area and gap between two electrodes by using micro/nanofluidic devices, selective and localized drug delivery is possible. This new approach is called localized single cell membrane electroporation (LSCMEP). However, until now this technique is in the development stage. In the future, the LSCMEP process can provide selective and specific single cell manipulation from millions of populations of cells together. Micro/nanofluidic devices can approach this level in the near future, which will be potentially beneficial for medical diagnostics, proteomics analysis and biological studies.

**Acknowledgements**

The authors greatly appreciate for financial support from National Science Council (NSC) of Taiwan ROC through National Nanotechnology and Nanoscience Program under Contract no. (NSC-101-2221-E-007-032-MY3) and (NSC-101-2120-M-007-001).

**Conflicts of Interest**

The authors declare no conflicts of interest.

**References**

1. Zimmermann, U.; Pilwat, G.; Friemann, F. Dielectric breakdown of cell membrane. *Biophy. J.* **1974**, *14*, 881–899.
2. Weaver, J.C.; Chizmadzhev, Y.A. Theory of electroporation: A review. *Bioelectrochem. Bioenerget.* **1996**, *41*, 135–160.
3. Teissie, J.; Golzio, M.; Rols, M.P. Mechanism of cell membrane electropermeabilization: A minireview of our present (lack of ?) knowledge. *Biochim. Biophys. Acta.* **2005**, *1724*, 270–280.
4. Escoffre, J.M.; Porter, T.; Wasungu, L.; Teissie, J.; Dean, D.; Rols, M.P. What is (still not) known of the mechanism by which electroporation mediates gene transfer and expression in cells and tissues. *Mol. Biotechnol.* **2009**, *41*, 286–295.
5. Neu, W.K.; Neu, J.C. Theory of Electroporation. In *Cardiac Bioelectric Therapy*; Efimov, I.R., Kroll, M.W., Tchou, P.J., Eds.; Springer: New York, NY, USA, 2009; pp. 133–134.
6. Ho, S.Y.; Mittal, G.S.; Cross, J.D. Effect of high electric field pulses on the activity of selected enzymes. *J. Food Eng.* **1997**, *31*, 69–84.
7. Prasanna, G.L.; Panda, T. Electroporation: Basic principles, practical consideration and applications in molecular biology. *Bioprocess Eng.* **1997**, *16*, 261–264.
8. Serpersu, E.H.; Tsong, T.Y.; Kinosita, K. Reversible and irreversible modification of erythrocyte membrane permeability by electric field. *Biochim. Biophys. Acta* **1985**, *812*, 779–785.
9. Tsong, T.Y.; Kinosita, K. Use of voltage pulses for the pore opening and drug loading and the subsequent resealing of red blood cells. *Bibliotheca Haematologica* **1985**, *51*, 108–114.
10. Schoenbach, K.H.; Beebe, S.J.; Buescher, E.S. Intracellular effect of ultrashort electrical pulses. *Bioelectromagnetics* **2001**, *22*, 440–448.

11. Chen, N.; Schoenbach, K.H.; Kolb, J.F.; Swanson, R.J.; Garner, A.L.; Yang, J.; Joshi, R.P.; Beebe, S.J. Leukemic cell intracellular responses to nanosecond electric fields. *Biochem. Biophys. Res. Commun.* **2004**, *317*, 421–427.

12. DeBruin, K.A.; Krassowska, W. Modelling electroporation in a single cell. I. Effects of field strength and rest potential. *Boiphys. J.* **1999**, *77*, 1213–1224.

13. DeBruin, K.A.; Krassowska, W. Modelling electroporation in a single cell. II. Effects of ionic concentrations. *Biophys. J.* **1999**, *77*, 1225–1233.

14. Movahed, S.; Li, D. Microfluidics cell electroporation. *Microfluid Nanofluid* **2011**, *10*, 703–734.

15. Chang, D.C.; Chassy, B.M.; Saunders, J.A. *Guide to Electroporation and Electrofusion*; Academic: San Diego, CA, USA, 1992.

16. Tsong, T.Y. Electroporation of cell membranes. *Biophys. J.* **1991**, *60*, 297–306.

17. Neumann, E.; Sowers, A.E.; Jordan, C.A. Electroporation and Electrofusion in Cell Biology. Plenum Press, New York, NY, USA, 1989.

18. Teissie, J.; Rols, M.P. An experimental evalution of the critical potential difference inducing cell membrane electropermeabilization. *Biophys. J.* **1993**, *65*, 409–413.

19. Zimmermann, U. Electric field-mediated fusion and related electric phenomena. *Biochim. Biophys. Acta* **1982**, *694*, 222–227.

20. Stampfli, R. Reversible electric breakdown of the excitable membrane of a Ranvier node. *Ann. Acad. Bras. Cien.* **1958**, *30*, 57–63.

21. Rubinsky, B. Irreversible electroporation in medicine. *Technol. Cancer Res. Treat.* **2007**, *6*, 255–259.

22. Nollet, J.A. *Researches Sur Les Causes Particulieres Des Phenomenes Electriques* (in French); Chez H.L. Guerin & L.F. Delatour: Paris, France, 1754.

23. Fox, M.B.; Esveld, D.C.; Valero, A.; Luttge, R.; Mastwijk, H.C.; Bartels, P.V.; ven den Berg, A.; Boom, R.M. Electroporation of cells in microfluidic devices: A review. *Anal. Bional Chem.* **2006**, *385*, 474–485.

24. Lee, W.G.; Demirci, U.; Khademhosseini, A. Microscale electroporation: Challenges and perspectives for clinical applications. *Integr. Biol.* **2009**, *1*, 242–251.

25. Wang, S.; Lee, L.J. Micro-/Nanofluidics based cell electroporation. **2013**, *7*, doi: 10.1063/1.4774071.

26. Wang, M.; Orwar, O.; Olofsson, J.; Weber, S.G. Single cell electroporation: Review. *Anal. Bional. Chem.* **2010**, *397*, 3225–3248.

27. Chen, S.-C.; Santra, T.S.; Chang, C.-J.; Chen, T.-J.; Wang, P.-C.; Tseng, F.-G. Delivery of molecules into cells using localized single cell electroporation on ITO microelectrode based transparent chip. *Biomed. Microdevices* **2012**, *14*, 811–817.

28. Kim, S.K.; Kim, J.H.; Kim, K.P.; Chung, T.K. Continuous low voltage dc electroporation on a microfluidic chip with polyelectrolytic salt bridges. *Anal. Chem.* **2007**, *79*, 7761–7766.

29. Nawarathna, D.; Unal, K.; Wickramasinghe, H.K. Localized electroporation and molecular delivery into single living cells by atomic force microscopy. *Appl. Phys. Lett.* **2008**, *93*, 153111.

30. Boukany, P.E.; Morss, A.; Liao, W.-C.; Henslee, B.; Jung, H.C.; Zhang, X.; Yu, B.; Wang, X.; Wu, Y.; Li, L.; *et al.* Nanochannel electroporation delivers precise amounts of biomolecules into living cells. *Nat. Nanotecnol.* **2011**, *6*, 747–754.

31. Weaver, J.C. Electroporation of cell and tissues. *IEEE Trans. Plasma Sci.* **2000**, *28*, 24–33.

32. Kinosita, K.; Hibino, M.; Itoh, H.; Shigemori, M.; Hirano, K.; Kirino, Y.; Hayakawa, T. Events of Membrane Electroporation Visualized on a Time Scale from Microsecond to Nanoseconds. In *Guide to Electroporationand Electrofusion*; Chang, D.C., Chassy, B.M., Saunders, J.A., Sowers, A.E., Eds.; Academic Press: Orlando, FL, USA, 1992; pp. 29–46.

33. Neumann, E.; Rosenheck, R. Permeability induced by electric impulsions in vesicular membranes. *J. Membr. Biol.* **1972**, *10*, 279–290.

34. Gabriel, B.; Teissie, J. Direct observation in the millisecond time range of fluorescent molecule asymmetrical interaction with the electropermeabilized cell membrane. *Biophys. J.* **1997**, *73*, 2630–2637.

35. Lundqvist, J.A.; Sahlin, F.; Aberg, M.A.; Strimberg, A.; Eriksson, P.S.; Orwar, O. Altering the biochemical state of individual cultured cells and organelles with ultramicroelectrodes. *Proc. Natl. Acad. Sci. USA* **1998**, *95*, 10356–10360.

36. Valero, A.; Merino, F.; Wolbers, F.; Luttge, R.; Vermes, I.; Andersson, H.; van den Berg, A. Apoptotic cell death dynamics of HL 60 cells studied using a microfluidic cell tarp device. *Lab Chip* **2005**, *5*, 49–55.

37. Suehiro, J.; Yatsunami, R.; Hamada, R.; Hara, M. Quantitative estimation of biological cell concentration suspended in aqueous medium by using dielectrophoretic impedance measurement method. *J. Phys. D Appl. Phys.* **1999**, *32*, 2814–2820.

38. Suehiro, J.; Shutou, M.; Hatano, T.; Hra, M. High sensitive detection of biological cells using dielectrophoretic impedance measurement method combined with electropermeabilization. *Sens. Actuators B* **2003**, *96*, 144–151.

39. Suehiro, J.; Hatano, T.; Shutou, M.; Hra, M. Improvement of electric pulse shape of electropermeabilization-assisted dielectrophoretic impedance measurement for high sensitive bacteria detection. *Sens. Actuators B* **2005**, *109*, 209–215.

40. Loomis-Husselbee, J.W.; Cullen, P.J.; Irvine, R.F.; Dawson, A.P. Electroporation can cause artifacts due to solubilization of cations from the electrode plates. *Biochem. J.* **1991**, *277*, 883–885.

41. Lin, Y.C.; Jen, C.M.; Huang, M.Y.; Wu, C.Y.; Lin, X.Y. Electroporation microchips for continuous gene transfection. *Sens. Actuators B* **2001**, *79*, 137–143.

42. Lin, Y.C.; Li, M.; Fan, C.S.; Wu, L.W. A microchip for electroporation of primary endothelial cells. *Sens. Actuators A* **2003**, *108*, 12–19.

43. Knorr, D.; Angersbach, A.; Eshtiaghi, M.N.; Heinz, V.; Lee, D. Processing concepts based on high intensity electric field pulses. *Trends Food Sci. Technol.* **2001**, *12*, 129–135.

44. Pol, I.E. Pulsed-electric field treatment enhances the bactericidal action of nisin against Bacillus cereus. *App. Enviro. Microbial.* **2000**, *66*, 428–430.

45. Fox, M.B.; Esveld, E.; Luttge, R.; Boom, R. A new pulsed electric field microreactor: Comparison between the laboratory and microscale. *Lab Chip* **2005**, *5*, 943–948.

46. Sedgwick, H.; Caron, F.; Monaghan, P.B.; Kolch, W.; Cooper, J.M. Lab-on-a-chip technologies for proteomic analysis from isolated cells. *J. R. Soc. Interface* **2008**, *5*, S123–S130.

47. De la Rosa, C.; Prakash, R.; Tilley, P.A.; Fox, J.D.; Kaler, K.V. Integrated microfluidic systems for sample preparation and detection of respiratory pathogen bordetella pertussis. *Conf. Proc. IEEE Eng. Med. Biol. Soc.* **2007**, *2007*, 6303–6306.

48. Wang, J.; Bao, N.; Paris, L.L.; Wang, H.Y.; Geahlen, R.L.; Lu. C. Detection of kinase translocation using microfluidic electroporative flow cytometry. *Anal. Chem.* **2008**, *80*, 1087–1093.

49. Wang, H.Y.; Lu, C. Microfluidic electroporation for delivery of small molecules and genes into cells using a common DC power supply. *Biotechnol. Bioeng.* **2008**, *8*, 62–67.

50. Olofsson, J.; Levin, M.; Stromberg, A.; Weber, S.G.; Ryttsen, F.; Orwar, O. Scanning electroporation of selected areas of adherent cell cultures. *Anal. Chem.* **2007**, *79*, 4410–4418.

51. Zudans, I.; Agarwal, A.; Orwar, O.; Weber, S.G. Numerical calculations of single-cell electroporation with an electrolyte-filled capillary. *Biophys. J.* **2007**, *92*, 3696–3705.

52. Agarwal, A.; Zudans, I.; Weber, E.A.; Olofsson, J.; Orwar, O.; Weber, S.G. Effect of cell size and shape on single-cell electroporation. *Anal. Chem.* **2007**, *79*, 3589–3596.

53. Olofsson, J.; Nolkrantz, K.; Ryttsen, F.; Lambie, B.A.; Weber, S.G.; Orwar, O. Single cell electroporation. *Curr. Opin. Biotechnol.* **2003**, *14*, 29–34.

54. Ryttsen, F.; Farre, C.; Brennan, C.; Weber, S.G.; Nolkrantz, K.; Jardemark K.; Chiu, D.T.; Orwar, O. Characterization of single cell electroporation by using patch-clamp and fluorescence microscopy. *Biophys. J.* **2000**, *79*, 1993–2001.

55. Nolkrantz, K.; Farre, C.; Brederlau, A.; Karlsson, R.I.; Brennan, C.; Erikssson, P.S.; Weber, S.G.; Sandberg, M.; Orwar, O. Electroporation of single cells and tissues with an electrolyte filled capillary. *Anal. Chem.* **2001**, *73*, 4469–4477.

56. Fei, Z.; Wang, S.; Xie, Y.; Henslee, B.E.; Koh, C.G.; Lee, L.J. Gene transfection of mammalian cells using membrane sandwich electroporation. *Anal. Chem.* **2007**, *79*, 5719–5722.

57. Fei, Z.; Hu, X.; Choi, H-W.; Wang, S.; Farson, D.; Lee, L.J. Micronozzle array enhanced sandwich electroporation of embryonic stem cells. *Anal. Chem.* **2010**, *82*, 353–358.

58. Vassanelli, S.; Bandiera, L.; Borgo, M.; Cellere G.; Santoni, L.; Bersani, C.; Salamon, M.; Zaccolo M.; Lorenzelli, L.; Girardi, S.; *et al.* Space and time-resolved gene expression experiments on cultured mammalian cells by a single-cell electroporation microarray. *New Biotechnol.* **2008**, *25*, 55–67.

59. Vally, J.K.; Hsu, H.-Y.; Neale, S.; Ohta, A.T.; Jamshidi, A.; Wu, M.C. Assessment of Single Cell Viability Following Light Induced Electroporation through Use of On-Chip Microfluidics. In Proceedings of the IEEE 22nd International Conference on Micro Electro Mechanical Systems, Sorrento, Italy, 25–29 January 2009, 411–414.

60. Valley, J.K.; Neale, S.; Hsu, H.-Y.; Ohta, A.T.; Jamshidi, A.; Wu, M.C. Parallel single-cell light-induced electroporeation and dielectrophoretic manipulation. *Lab Chip* **2009**, *9*, 1714–1720.

61. Brennan, D.; Justice, J.; Corbett, B.; McCarthy, T.; Galvin, P. Emerging optofluidic technologies for point-of-care genetic analysis systems: A review. *Anal. Bioanal. Chem.* **2009**, *395*, 621–636.

62. Lin, Y-H.; Lee, G-B. An optically induced cell lysis device using dielectrophoresis. *Appl. Phys. Lett.* **2009**, *94*,033901.

63. Sott. K.; Eriksson, E.; Petelenz, E.; Goksor, M. Optical system for single cell analysis. *Expert. Opin. Drug Discov.* **2008**, *3*, 1323–1344.

64. Yang, S.-M.; Yu, T.-M.; Huang, H.-P.; Ku, M.-Y.; Hsu, L.; Liu, C.H. Dynamic manipulation and patterning of microparticles and cells by using TiOPc-based optoelectronic dielectrophoresis. *Opt. Lett.* **2010**, *35*, 1959–1961.

65. Yang, S.-M.; Yu, T.-M.; Huang, H.-P.; Ku, M.-Y.; Tseng, S.-Y.; Tsai, C.-L.; Chen, H.P.; Hsu, L.; Liu, C.-H. Light-driven manipulation of pico-bubbles on a TiOPc-based optoelectronic chip. *Appl. Phys. Lett.* **2011**, *98*, 153512.

66. Huang, Y.; Rubinsky, B. Micro-electroporation: Improving the efficiency and understanding of electrical permeabilization of cells. *Biomed. Microdevice.* **1999**, *2*, 145–150.

67. McClain, M.A.; Culbertson, C.T.; Jacobson, S.C.; Allabritton, N.L.; Sims, C.E.; Ramsey, J.M. Microfluidic devices for the high-throughput chemical analysis of cells. *Anal. Chem.* **2003**, *75*, 5646–5655.

68. Gao, J.; Yin, X.F.; Fang, Z.L. Intergation of single cell injection, cell lysis separation and detection of intracellular constituents on a microfluidic chip. *Lab Chip* **2004**. *4*, 47–52.

69. Shin, Y.S.; Cho, K.; Kim, J.K.; Lim, S.H.; Park, C.H.; Lee, K.B.; Park, Y.; Chung, C.; Han, D.-C.; Chang, J.K. Electrotransfection of mammalian cells using microchannel-type electroporation chip. *Anal. Chem.* **2004**, *76*, 7045–7052.

70. Wang, H.-Y.; Lu, C. Electroporation of mammalian cells in a microfluidic channel with geometric variation. *Anal. Chem.* **2006**, *78*, 5158–5164.

71. Wang, H.-Y.; Bhunia, A.K.; Lu, C. A microfluidic flow-through device for high throughput electrical lysis of bacterial cells based on continuous DC voltage. *Biosens. Bioelectron.* **2006**, *22*, 582–588.

72. Ikeda, N.; Tanaka, N.; Yanagida, Y.; Hatsuzawa, T. On-chip single-cell lysis for extracting intracellular material. *Jpn. J. Appl. Phys.* **2007**, *46*, 6410–6414.

73. Valero, A.; Post, J.N.; van Nieuwkasteele, J.W.; Ter Braak, P.M.; Kruijer, W.; van den Berg, A. Gene transfer and protein dynamics in stem cells using single cell electroporation in a microfluidic device. *Lab Chip* **2008**, *8*, 62–67.

74. Lim, J.K.; Zhou, H.; Tilton, R.D. Liposome rupture and contents release over coplanar microelectrodes arrays. *J. Colloid Interface Sci.* **2009**, *332*, 113–121.

75. Zhu, T.; Luo, C.; Huang, J.; Xiong, C.; Quyang, Q.; Fang, J. Electroporation based on hydrodynamic focusing of microfluidics with low DC voltage. *Biomed. Microdevices* **2010**, *12*, 35–40.

76. Qu, B.; Eu, Y.-J.; Jeong, W.-J.; Kim, D.-P. Droplet electroporation in microfluidics for efficient cell transformation with or without cell wall removal. *Lab Chip* **2012**, *12*, 4483–4488.

77. Jokilaakso, N.; Salm, E.; Chen, A.; Millet, L.; Guevara, C.D.; Dorvel, B.; Reddy, B., Jr.; Karlstrom, A.E.; Chen, Y.; Ji, H.; *et al*. Ultra-localized single cell electroporation using silicon nanowires. *Lab Chip* **2013**, *13*, 336–339.

78. Huang, Y.; Rubinsky, B. Microfabricated electroporation chip for single cell membrane permeabilization. *Sens. Actuators A* **2001**, *89*, 242–245.

79. Huang, Y.; Rubinsky, B. Flow through microelectroporation chip for high efficiency single cell genetic manipulation. *Sens. Actuators A* **2003**, *104*, 205–212.

80. Khine, M.; Lau, A.; Ionescu-Zanetti, C.; Seo, J.; Lee, L.P. A single cell electroporation chip. *Lab Chip* **2005**, *5*, 38–43.

81. Suzuki, T.; Yamamoto, H.; Ohoka, M.; Okonogi, A.; Kabata, H.; Kanno, I.; Washizu, M.; Kotera, H. High Throughput Cell Electroporation Array Fabricated by Single Mask Inclined uv Lithography Exposure and Oxygen Plasma Etching. In Proceedings of the IEEE 14th International Conference on Solid-State Sensors, Actuators, and Microsystems, Lyon, France, 10–14 June 2007; pp. 687–690.

82. Ionescu-Zanetti, C.; Blatz, A.; Khine, M. Electrophoresis-assisted single-cell electroporation for efficient intracellular delivery. *Biomed. Microdevic.* **2008**, *10*, 113–116.

83. Gac, S.L.; van den Berg, A. Single cell electroporation using microfluidic devices. *Methods Mol. Biol.* **2012**, *853*, 65–82.

84. Koster, S.; Angile, F.E.; Duan, H.; Agresti, J.J.; Wintner, A.; Schmitz C.; Rowat, A.C.; Merten, C.A.; Pisignano, D.; Griffiths, A.D.; *et al*. Drop-based microfluidic devices for encapsulation of single cells. *Lab Chip* **2008**, *8*, 1110–1115.

85. He, M.; Edgar, J.S.; Jeffries, G.D.M.; Lorenz, R.M.; Shelby, J.P.; Chiu, D.T. Selective encapsulation of single cells and subcellular organelles into picoliter- and femtoliter-volume droplets. *Anal. Chem.* **2005**, *77*, 1539–1544.

86. Luo, C.; Yang, X.; Fu, Q.; Sun, M.; Quyang, Q.; Chen, Y.; Ji, H. Picoliter-volume aqueous droplets in oil: Electrochemical detection and yeast cell electroporation. *Electrophoresis* **2006**, *27*, 1977–1983.

87. Zhan, Y.; Wang, J.; Bao, N.; Lu, C. Electroporation of cells in microfluidic droplets. *Anal. Chem.* **2009**, *81*, 2027–2031.

88. Lu, H.; Schmidt, M.A.; Jensen, K.F. A microfluidic electroporation device for cell lysis. *Lab Chip* **2005**, *5*, 23–29.

89. Wang, H.-Y.; Lu, C. High-throughput and real-time study of single cell electroporation using microfluidics: Effects of medium osmolarity. *Biotechnol. Bioeng.* **2006**, *95*, 1116–1125.

90. Li, X.Y.; Li, P.C.H. Microfluidic selection and retention of a single cardiac myocyte, on-chip dye loading, cell concentration by chemical stimulation, and quantitative fluorescent analysis of intracellular calcium. *Anal. Chem.* **2005**, *77*, 4315–4322.

91. Di Carlo, D.; Aghdam, N.; Lee, L.P. Single cell enzyme concentrations, kinetics, and inhibition analysis using high-density hydrodynamic cell isolation arrays. *Anal. Chem.* **2006**, *78*, 4925–4930.

92. Wheeler, A.R.; Throndset, W.R.; Whelan, R.J.; Leach, A.M.; Zare, R.N.; Liao, Y.H.; Farrell, K.; Manger, I.D.; Daridon, A. Microfluidic device for single-cell analysis. *Anal. Chem.* **2003**, *75*, 3581–3586.

93. Hargis, A.D.; Alarie, J.P.; Ramsey, J.M. Characterization of cell lysis events on a microfluidic device for high-throughput single cell analysis. *Electrophoresis* **2011**, *32*, 3172–3179.

94. Li. X.; Huang, J.; Tibbits, G.F.; Li, P.C. Real-time monitoring of intracellular calcium dynamic mobilization of a single cardiomyocyte in a microfluidic chip pertaining. *Electrophoresis* **2007**, *28*, 4723–4733.

95. Mellors, J.S.; Jorabachi, K.; Smith, L.M.; Ramsey, J.M. Integrated microfluidic device for automated single cell analysis using electrophoretic separation and electrospray ionization mass spectrometry. *Anal. Chem.* **2010**, *82*, 967–973.

# Analysis of Electric Fields inside Microchannels and Single Cell Electrical Lysis with a Microfluidic Device

Bashir I. Morshed, Maitham Shams and Tofy Mussivand

**Abstract:** Analysis of electric fields generated inside the microchannels of a microfluidic device for electrical lysis of biological cells along with experimental verification are presented. Electrical lysis is the complete disintegration of cell membranes, due to a critical level of electric fields applied for a critical duration on a biological cell. Generating an electric field inside a microchannel of a microfluidic device has many advantages, including the efficient utilization of energy and low-current requirement. An ideal microchannel model was compared with a practical microchannel model using a finite element analysis tool that suggests that the overestimation error can be over 10%, from 2.5 mm or smaller, in the length of a microchannel. Two analytical forms are proposed to reduce this overestimation error. Experimental results showed that the high electric field is confined only inside the microchannel that is in agreement with the simulation results. Single cell electrical lysis was conducted with a fabricated microfluidic device. An average of 800 V for seven seconds across an 8 mm-long microchannel with the dimension of 100 μm × 20 μm was required for lysis, with electric fields exceeding 100 kV/m and consuming 300 mW.

Reprinted from *Micromachines.* Cite as: Morshed, B.I.; Shams, M.; Mussivand, T. Analysis of Electric Fields inside Microchannels and Single Cell Electrical Lysis with a Microfluidic Device. *Micromachines* **2013**, *4*, 243-256.

## 1. Introduction

Generating high electric fields inside microchannels are needed for many microfluidic applications, such as lab-on-a-chip (LOC), micro-total-analysis-system (μTAS) and biomedical microelectromechanical systems (bioMEMS) [1,2]. Uniform or non-uniform distribution of the electric fields can be utilized to process biological elements, like cell lysis, electroporation, electrophoresis separation, deoxyribonucleic acid (DNA) detection and separation and electro-osmotic flow generation for electrokinetic (EK) microfluidic pumps [3–5]. Electrical lysis on a portable microfluidic device is critical for point-of-care (POC) devices requiring access to internal contents of the cell. We are motivated to develop a POC device that performs DNA detection within few seconds. Such a development will be valuable for emergency responders, criminal investigators and forensic identification. In this work, electrical lysis of biological cells is investigated with a commonly used microchannel structure, where the electrode with excitation potential is positioned at one end of the microchannel, whereas the electrode at the other end of the microchannel is grounded [5–10]. The novelty of this work is the analysis of the estimation errors of electric fields of typical microfluidic devices used in such experiments and the models to reduce such estimation errors to achieve a high yield, which is critical for single-cell analysis.

The electric potential across the channel caused by the external electrical field can be evaluated with the Laplace equation, $\nabla^2\phi = 0$, where $\phi$ is the external electrical potential [11]. The Poisson-Boltzmann equation is employed to govern the electric potential near the channel wall and in the bulk:

$$\nabla^2\psi = \rho_f = \frac{2n_\infty ze}{\varepsilon}\sinh\left[\frac{ze}{kT}(\psi-\phi)\right] \tag{1}$$

where $\psi$ is the electrical potential, $\rho_f$ is the free charge density, $n_\infty$ is the bulk concentration of the ions, $z$ is the ionic valence, $e$ is the elementary charge, $\varepsilon$ is the dielectric constant of the medium, $k$ is the Boltzmann constant and $T$ is the temperature. The electric field distribution inside the microchannel can be estimated by the Poisson equation, which, for the case of uniform electric charge density in a linear, isotropic and homogeneous medium, becomes:

$$E = \partial V/\partial L \tag{2}$$

This is the most commonly used expression to estimate the electric field strengths inside the microchannels of microfluidic devices [5–9], even though the assumptions involving dielectric constant, fringe field and parallel electrode surface are invalidated. Furthermore, solid-liquid interface develops an electrical double layer (EDL) with the characteristic thickness of the Debye length, which has significant influence on the behavior of ionic conductors. These factors lead to a significant estimation error when Expression (2) is used, which is increasingly critical as the dimensions of the microchannel become smaller—the general trend in microfluidics and nanofluidics.

To accurately determine the electric field distribution, the finite element method (FEM) is more acceptable, as results with higher confidence can be produced through incorporating proper simulation setup, such as boundary conditions and refining of mesh sizes at regions of non-uniformity [8,12]. Using this technique, the analytical expressions developed are design-specific [12–14]. The microchannel structure under consideration has a uniform cross-section throughout its length, and the electrodes are placed at both terminals of the microchannel. There are a number of reports that share this topology [5–10,15]. This work attempts to analyze the estimation error stemming from Expression (2) and proposes two analytical expressions to reduce the error. The findings are applicable for microchannels with uniform electric fields containing physiological solution—a practical scenario.

Single cell electrical lysis experiments were conducted using biological cells with applied electrical excitation. Electrical lysis is a phenomenon of complete cell membrane breakdown under a high electric field of a critical period [8,16–18]. Reports of various types of cell lysis using an electrical field are available, including yeast cells, E. coli [19], cancer cells [20–22], mammalian cells [23], leukocytes [24], erythrocyte [25], red blood cells [8,26] and Chinese hamster ovary cells [6,27]. In this work, non-invasively collected cell debris, i.e., shredded cells, of epidermal tissue from human fingerprints are used as cell-samples.

58

**Figure 1.** Finite element method (FEM) simulations (**a**) without and (**b**) with microchannel structures (microchannels of 100 μm-wide and 20 μm-deep) that depict high electric field distributions inside the microchannel structure, in the latter case away from the electrodes inside the reservoirs with normalized excitation (1 V). A 3D view of a reservoir is shown in the inset. Electric field distributions and electric potentials with the microchannel structure are plotted for five different electrode locations (1 to 5) inside the reservoirs. Note: Electric field distributions inside the fluidic subdomain are only shown in (**b**).

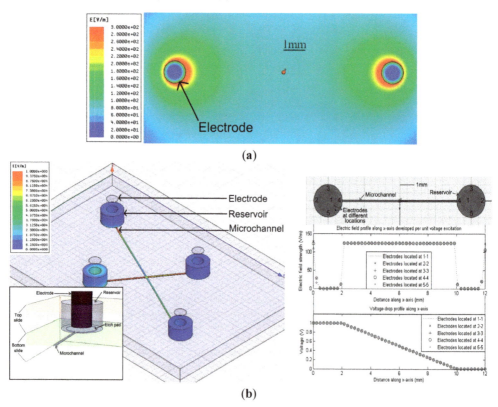

(a)

(b)

## 2. Simulation of Electric Fields inside Microchannels

Before proceeding to a comprehensive analysis of electric fields inside microchannels, a qualitative comparison is depicted through electric field distribution without any microchannel structure (Figure 1a) and with a microchannel structure (Figure 1b). Maxwell3D simulator (Ansoft Corp. acquired by ANSYS Inc., Canonsburg, PA, USA) was used as the FEM tool. Isothermal boundary conditions were applied for the simulation box, whose size was determined iteratively by doubling each dimension until there was no significant change due to the box size in subsequent iterations. The mesh size was manually increased at the corners and inside small features to increase simulation accuracy at locations where a higher gradient is expected. Figure 1a depicts that the electric field distribution without the microchannel was more pronounced around the electrodes, whereas for the case of a microchannel, as depicted in Figure 1b, the higher electric field distribution was concentrated inside the microchannels. Evidently, an advantage of the microchannel structure is that the cell samples placed inside the microchannels away from the electrodes are exposed to high electric fields, thus reducing the possibility of the cell samples being effected by the electrolysis of water that occurs at the interface of the electrodes when a potential is applied. In addition, the use of microchannels lowers the current flow, power dissipation and energy consumption to produce a certain electric field inside the microchannel, due to the confinement of the electron flow-path.

## 2.1. Modeling of an Ideal Microchannel

To begin electric field analysis of the microfluidic device, an ideal model of a microchannel structure is considered, where the microchannel is a "rectangular box" with length, width and height of $l_{ch}$, $w_{ch}$ and $h_{ch}$, respectively. Both electrodes are in contact with the complete cross-sectional areas on both terminals of the microchannel. The microchannel contains physiological buffer fluid (e.g., D-PBS) with the relative permittivity ($\varepsilon_r$) and conductivity ($\sigma_{ch}$) used in the literature (80 and 1.6 S/m, respectively) [28]. The microchannel structure along with the electrodes is enclosed within a large glass substrate. An electric field, $E_{ch}$, develops inside the microchannel as an excitation voltage, $V_{app}$, is applied across the electrode-pair. In this ideal case, the voltage across the microchannel, $V_{ch}$, is the same as $V_{app}$.

For this ideal model of the microchannel, electric flux generated inside the microchannel can be approximated as uniform. Thus, $E_{ch}$ can be expressed using the electric field expression between two parallel electrodes [11], given as:

$$E_{ch} = V_{ch}/l_{ch} \tag{3}$$

Due to the current flow through the buffer fluid, the Columbic power dissipation, $P_d$, inside the microchannel can be expressed as [29]:

$$P_d = V^2_{ch}/R_{ch} \tag{4}$$

where $R_{ch}$ is the electrical resistance of the microchannel. Using the resistivity law [12], $R_{ch}$ for the rectangular box can be expressed as:

$$R_{ch} = \rho_{ch} \times l_{ch}/A_{ch} \tag{5}$$

where $\rho_{ch}$ is the resistivity of the buffer fluid inside the microchannel and $A_{ch}$ ($=w_{ch} \times h_{ch}$) is the cross-sectional area of the microchannel. Hence:

$$P_d = E^2_{ch} \times \Lambda_{ch}/\rho_{ch} \tag{6}$$

where $\Lambda_{ch}$ ($=A_{ch} \times l_{ch}$) is the volume of the microchannel. If $\rho_{ch}$ is a constant, ignoring the effect of localized Joule heating, for a certain buffer fluid, $P_d$ is proportional to the volume of the microchannel for a specific electric field. For microchannel structures, small $\Lambda_{ch}$ would lead to small power dissipation—another advantage of using microchannels for high electric field generation. The temperature increase inside a microchannel with a certain media depends on surface area, conductive heat transfer coefficient and thermal resistance.

The energy density, $u_{ch}$, inside the microchannel due to the electric field can be expressed as [11]:

$$u_{ch} = \tfrac{1}{2}(\varepsilon E^2{}_{ch}) = \tfrac{1}{2}(\varepsilon V^2{}_{ch}/l^2{}_{ch}). \qquad (7)$$

Here, $\varepsilon$ $(=\varepsilon_0\varepsilon_r)$ is the permittivity of the buffer fluid, where $\varepsilon_0$ is the permittivity of the free space and $\varepsilon_r$ is the relative permittivity of the buffer fluid. The total energy stored, $U_{ch}$, can be obtained by integrating $u_{ch}$ over $A_{ch}$ [11]. For this ideal microchannel model, $U_{ch}$ can be expressed by:

$$U_{ch} = \tfrac{1}{2}(\varepsilon E^2{}_{ch}\, A_{ch}) = \tfrac{1}{2}(\varepsilon V^2{}_{ch}\, A_{ch}/l_{ch}) \qquad (8)$$

Hence, for a given electric field and buffer fluid, $U_{ch}$ is proportional to $A_{ch}$. Furthermore, $U_{ch}$ is also proportional to $P_d$ with a proportionality constant of $\varepsilon p_{ch}/2$.

## 2.2. Modeling a Microchannel of the Microfluidic Device

The microfluidic device contains a microchannel that fluidically connects two access holes (reservoirs). To develop an electric field inside the microchannel, electrodes are inserted inside these access holes. Both the microchannel and the access holes contain the physiological buffer fluid (D-PBS) modeled by assigning proper conductivity and permittivity values, as mentioned above. The electrodes were excited with the applied voltage, $V_{app}$. Notice that in this case, $V_{ch}$ is always smaller than $V_{app}$. The microfluidic device was fabricated with two glass slides: top and bottom. The microchannel was created by an etching technique (wet etching with Hydrofluoric acid, HF) on the top surface of the bottom slide. This also created an etch pad at the bottom of the access hole. The two glass slides were thermally fused together, which produces great modification of microchannel height, as compared to other bonding techniques, such as adhesive.

## 2.3. Electric Field Simulations

Both models were simulated for a wide range of microchannel dimensions by using the FEM analysis tool. A script file was written that generated 175 different combinations of microchannel dimensions ($l_{ch}$, $w_{ch}$ and $h_{ch}$). The ranges of $l_{ch}$, $w_{ch}$ and $h_{ch}$ were from 100 to 10,000 μm, from 1 to 1000 μm and from 10 to 1000 μm, respectively. The electrodes of 1 mm diameter were positioned at the middle of the access hole, 0.1 mm above the bottom plate in the practical model, and the dimensions of the access holes, electrodes and etch-holes were kept constant for all combinations. Each structure was simulated for a number of excitation voltages ranging from 1 V to 1000 V. The permittivity and conductivity of the buffer fluid were set to $\varepsilon_r$ = 80 and $\sigma_{ch}$ = 1.6 S m$^{-1}$, respectively, to match those of the physiological solution.

The resultant data shows that the mean values of the practical microchannel significantly deviate from those of the ideal model as $l_{ch}$ becomes smaller or $A_{ch}$ becomes larger. These deviations, resulting in estimation errors if the expressions were derived in the last section for an ideal microchannel are applied for practical microchannels, should be taken under consideration for microfluidic devices involving generation of non-uniform electric fields. This is especially important for small lengths of microchannels, as reported in recent literature [6,8,18–27,30]. Thus, the deviation of the mean values between the ideal and the practical model are of particular interest. To quantify across a range of analysis domain, a metric denoting normalized error ($\delta_{dev}$) is introduced. Subtracting the mean values from the practical model from the ideal model and dividing it by the mean value of the ideal model, the $\delta_{dev}$ is calculated. Mathematically:

$$\delta_{dev} = (\text{Mean}_{ideal} - \text{Mean}_{practical})/\text{Mean}_{ideal} \qquad (9)$$

From the simulation results, the values of $\delta_{dev}$ are always positive, which indicates that the expressions of the ideal model are overestimated. This can be rationalized, due to the fact that $V_{ch}$ is always smaller than $V_{app}$ in practical microchannels, due to parasitics in the reservoir, and the electric field distribution is not uniform throughout the microchannel. As microchannel lengths become smaller, this non-uniformity increases, resulting in the higher value of $\delta_{dev}$. Table 1 lists the range for 10% and 50% overestimations for various parameters and dimension of the practical microchannels. Estimation errors are critical to achieve high yields of lysate from minute cell samples. In practical applications with minute cell samples, low yield might lead to the inability to obtain DNA fragments required for downstream analysis, which is critical for single-cell analysis.

**Table 1.** The overestimation error ranges for a practical microchannels when the expressions for an ideal microchannel are applied.

| Parameter | 10% overestimation range | 50% overestimation range |
|---|---|---|
| $E_{ch}$ | $l_{ch} < 2300$ µm | $l_{ch} < 175$ µm |
| $P_d$ | $A_{ch}/l_{ch} < 0.7$ µm$^2$/µm | $A_{ch}/l_{ch} < 100$ µm$^2$/µm |
| $u_{ch}$ | $l_{ch} < 5000$ µm | $l_{ch} < 400$ µm |
| $U_{ch}$ | $A_{ch}/l_{ch} < 0.7$ µm$^2$/µm | $A_{ch}/l_{ch} < 100$ µm$^2$/µm |

*2.4. Expressions for Error Reduction in Practical Microchannels*

An approach to reduce the estimation errors is to determine $V_{ch}$ for the practical microchannel. To calculate $V_{ch}$, one has to determine the resistance introduced by the access holes that are in series with the microchannel resistance. In this section, two analytical expressions are derived to reduce estimation errors for the electric field. In this analysis, non-uniformity of the electric field distribution inside the microchannel and the capacitive component of the microchannel are neglected, assuming a DC excitation condition and steady state operation.

In this approach, the microchannel resistance ($R_{ch}$) is in series with the two resistances of the access holes external to the microchannel ($R_{ext}$). Ideal microchannel expressions can be applied for $V_{ch}$ and $E_{ch}$; thus:

$$E_{ch} = \frac{V_{ch}}{l_{ch}} = \frac{V_{app}}{l_{ch}} - \frac{2V_{app}R_{ext}}{(R_{ch}+2R_{ext})l_{ch}} = \frac{V_{app}}{l_{ch}}(1-\frac{1}{1+\alpha}) \qquad (10)$$

where $\alpha$ $(=R_{ch}/2\, R_{ext})$ is the ratio of channel resistance to total reservoir resistances. For large $l_{ch}$, $R_{ch}$ is much larger than $R_{ext}$. Hence, for $\alpha \gg 1$, the resulting Expression (10) will approach the expressions for an ideal microchannel. However, for very small $l_{ch}$, $R_{ch}$ is comparable or smaller than $R_{ext}$, thus the second term of the Expression (10) becomes significant. In the extreme cases where $\alpha \ll 1$, $E_{ch}$ diminishes to 0.

A second approach to reduce the estimation errors is to compensate for $\delta_{dev}$. To apply this approach, the $\delta_{dev}$ can be approximated as a linear relationship between $\log(\delta_{dev})$ and $\log(l_{ch})$, which is motivated through careful observation of the data. Thus:

$$\log(\delta_{dev}) = -m\log(l_{ch}) + \log(c)$$
$$\Rightarrow \delta_{dev} = cl_{ch}^{-m}$$
$$\Rightarrow \frac{E_{ideal} - E_{ch}}{E_{ideal}} = \frac{c}{l_{ch}^{m}}$$
$$\Rightarrow E_{ch} = \frac{V_{app}}{l_{ch}}(1 - \frac{c}{l_{ch}^{m}})$$

(11)

where $m$ is the slope of the $\delta_{dev}$ curve, $c$ is a constant and $E_{ideal}$ is the electric field in ideal model.

## 3. Experimental Results

As an experimental platform, a microfluidic device was developed to induce electric lysis of biological cells. The experiments were conducted at the Cardiovascular Devices Division, the University of Ottawa Heart Institute, Ottawa, Canada.

### 3.1. Device Design and Fabrication

The device was designed using the L-edit layout tool (Tanner EDA, CA) and fabricated using the Protolyne fabrication process from Micralyne Inc. (Edmonton, Alberta, Canada). Briefly, the fabricated device consisted of two fused glass slides, with dimensions of 95 mm × 16 mm × 1.1 mm each. Eight predefined access holes (reservoirs) of 2 mm diameter were through-drilled in the top slide. Eight etch-pads of 1.5 mm diameter were etched on the top surface of the bottom slide, such that they align with the access holes. Trenches were also etched on the top surface of the bottom slide, which formed microchannels when both glass slides were fused together. Seven trenches were designed of various lengths ranging from 8 to 17 mm. Here, the length of a microchannel was defined as the intersection of a trench and an access hole. The etch depth, which defined the height of a microchannel, is 20 μm based on fabrication process constraints. The widths of microchannels were 100 μm, a trade-off between free transport of cells and minimized power dissipation. Platinum (Pt) electrodes were inserted inside the access holes for electrical excitation.

### 3.2. Cell-Sample Preparation

Due to the lack of access to proper cell-lines, human fingerprint samples were used as the cell-sample source. Each fingerprint sample was collected from a finger of an individual on a sterile Petri dish. The fingerprint samples contain dead and damaged cells shredded from the epidermal tissue. To collect these cells from the surface of Petri dishes, 20 μL of physiological solution (Dulbecco's Phosphate Buffered Saline, D-PBS) was applied. The D-PBS fluid maintains a pH of 7, required to preserve cell samples from osmotic pressure. The micropipette tip was rubbed on the surface of the Petri dish to detach the cell debris from the surface of the dish and to suspend them into the fluid, which was then collected by the micropipette. Average numbers of debris were calculated by overlapping the Petri dish on a 1 mm-square grid under an optical microscope to count the number of debris under each square, then calculating the average of 25 grids. The average number of debris on the surface for a wet fingerprint before the collection was 41.5 per mm$^2$ and after the collection procedure was 21 per mm$^2$, a collection efficiency of about 50%.

## 3.3. Experimental Procedure

Before each experiment, the microfluidic device was washed with deionized water and dried by blowing warm air. Four microliters of the sample solution were introduced in one access hole, while 4 µL of D-PBS buffer fluid was introduced in an adjacent access hole. A pair of platinum electrodes were introduced in the access holes, and the device was positioned on the stage of an optical microscope (CKX41, Olympus Corp, Westmont, IL, USA) equipped with a CCD (charge-coupled device) camera (Infinity, Lumenera, Ottawa, Canada). The electrode-pair was then connected to a high voltage power supply (FB600, Fisher Scientific, Pittsburgh, PA, USA) and an oscilloscope (Tektronix 2430A, Beaverton, OR, USA) to the electrodes (Channel 1) and across a series resistance, $R_s$, (Channel 2), as schematically shown Figure 2a. Cells migrated through the microchannel when a constant low-electric field gradient was created by applying a voltage of below 200 V through the electrode-pair. When cells were positioned inside the microchannel, the flow was stopped, and a brief high-voltage DC pulse (700 V to 900 V) with a duration up to 9 s was applied through the electrode-pair to lyse the cells. Photographs and video clips (2 fps) were captured through the CCD camera of the optical microscope in phase contrast mode. A photograph of the microfluidic device with electrical connectivity is shown in Figure 2b.

## 3.4. Fluorescence Imaging

Some cell-samples were stained to verify the structures of cells in the samples. Figure 3 shows images of cell debris from a fingerprint sample under optical microscope in phase-contrast mode (a–b) and with staining in bright-field mode (c). The presence of haematoxylin stain indicates the existence of basophilic structures, such as histones, which are present in chromosomes inside the cell nucleus.

Cells were transported from the source reservoir (access hole) towards the waste reservoir through the microchannel by applying a low electric field created with the application of 100 to 200 V across the microchannel, generating a low electric field of a strength below 25 kV/m. As cells are negatively charged, they experience a force pulling them towards the positive electrodes, due to the combined effect of electrophoresis and electro-osmosis phenomena [31,32]. As cells moved inside the microchannel, the applied voltage was withdrawn to position cells inside the microchannel. Such positioning was verified with fluorescent cell marker (Alexa Flour 488 V) and observed under fluorescence microscope. The illuminated cell inside the microchannel, as seen in Figure 4, verified that the cell was positioned inside the microchannel.

64

**Figure 2. (a)** A schematic diagram of the experimental setup of the microfluidic device; **(b)** a photograph of the experimental setup showing the Pexiglass platform, microfluidic device (MFD), spirit level meter and the electrical connections of the platinum (Pt) electrodes inside the access holes.

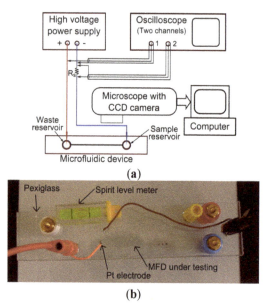

**(a)**

**(b)**

**Figure 3.** Sample cells from a fingerprint observed under **(a)** 10X and **(b)** 40X lens with an optical microscope in phase-contrast mode; **(c)** stained cell-sample with haematoxylin dye clearly showing the cellular structures.

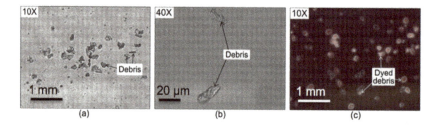

The electrophoretic movement of cells inside the microchannel was not uniform. It was observed that cells tend to adhere to the channel walls while migrating through the microchannel. Two factors might contribute to this type of behavior. Firstly, the surface of the microchannel contained irregularity at the micrometer scale. These irregularities of the channel surfaces were observed with scanning electron microscope (SEM) images, as shown in Figure 5. The irregularities might stem from the chemical etching process of the fabrication technology and the orientation of the crystals. Surface irregularities of the channel walls were more pronounced compared to the channel bed. Secondly, the force developed due to the zeta potential, defined as the electrostatic potential generated by accumulation of surface charges along the silica-based channel surfaces [2], might also contribute to the adherence tendency of the cells. This potential is due to the surface material of the microchannel (silica) and can be alleviated by surface treatment of the microchannel before experiments [2].

**Figure 4.** Cell debris, labeled with Alexa Flour 488 V florescence dye, collected from a fingerprint sample, is positioned inside a microchannel and is observed under a fluorescence microscope. **(a)** Image of the cell with optical microscope with phase-contrast mode; **(b)** image of the cell with 488 nm laser in a fluorescence microscope.

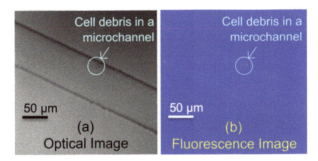

**Figure 5.** SEM photographs of **(a)** a microchannel and **(b)** an exposed trench (top glass slide removed) detailing the surface topography and roughness of the chemically etched microchannels.

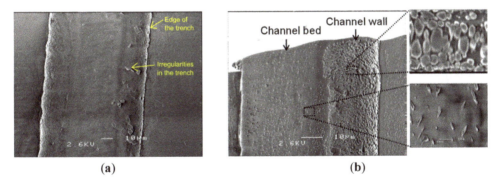

(a)    (b)

*3.5. Single Cell Electrical Lysis Experiments*

A high voltage (700 V to 900 V) was applied to induce electrical lysis of biological cells. The developed electric field was higher than 100 kV/m, a typical electric field for electrical lysis of cells [18,19,25]. Figure 6 shows a temporal sequence of microscopic images captured using the CCD camera of the microscope during an electrical lysis experiment. The sample cell inside the microchannel experienced a high electric field (>100 kV/m) and was lysed in about 6.5 s. The cell marked as "a" is completely lysed, whereas the cell marked as "b" is intact, due to the fact that the electric field developed inside the microchannel is high compared to that inside the reservoir. This experiment clearly demonstrates the difference of electric field inside and outside of the microchannel, which cannot be simply calculated using the electric field Expression (2).

**Figure 6.** Temporal sequence of images of electrical lysis of a single sample cell under a high electric field inside a microchannel captured using an optical microscope. Here, (**a**) is a sample cell inside the microchannel, (**b**) is a cell inside the reservoir, (**c**) is the boundary of the reservoir on the top glass slide, (**d**) is the edge of the microchannel and (**e**) is the boundary of the etching on the bottom glass slide. Eight-hundred volts are applied to the microchannel of 9 mm length. The cell is observed to disappear between 6 and 6.5 s.

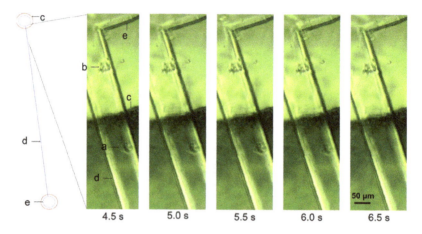

Careful observation of the temporal sequence of photographs in Figure 6 indicates that there was a gradual decrease of the contrast in the images of the sample cell "a" between 5 to 6 s. A logical deduction and explanation is that the electroporation phenomenon [31,32], expected to occur just prior to cell lysis, had caused a reduction of the refractive index difference inside and outside of the cell. The duration of the electroporation was less than 1 s. A very high-applied voltage (>1500 V) resulted in bubble formation through breakdown of the water molecules and produced electric arcs that etched the inner surface of the microchannel, as can be observed in Figure 7. The summaries of data obtained from the experiments of various related parameters are given in Tables 2 and 3.

**Figure 7.** An optical microscope image of a microchannel showing damage of the microchannel surface from electric arcs generated with an applied voltage of 1800 V (electric field over 225 kV/m).

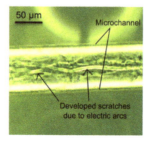

Table 2. Key observations with various electric field strengths.

| Electric field ranges | Observations |
|---|---|
| Below 100 kV/m | Cell movement observed |
| Between 100 to 200 kV/m | Electrical lysis observed |
| Above 200 kV/m | Bubble formation and electric arcs inside microchannels |

Table 3. Results from electrical lysis experiments.

| Parameter | Value |
|---|---|
| Applied potential | Between 700 to 900 V |
| Pulse duration | $7 \pm 2$ s |
| Current flow | ~0.5 mA |
| Power dissipation | <300 mW |

## 4. Conclusions

Electric fields are commonly used in microfluidic devices and LOCs to stimulate, manipulate and analyze biological elements. The macro-scale approximation of electric field expression is still in use. Microscale electric field distribution, however, deviates from this estimation, due to the highly non-linear nature of the distribution pattern. In this work, we have conducted an analysis of electric fields inside the microchannels of an ideal and a practical model. Furthermore, analytical expressions were developed for the practical model to reduce the estimation error. FEM simulations, however, do not account for various factors, such as EDL, localized fluidic flow and vortex due to electrophoresis, thermal and electrical resistivity change due to Joule heating; these lead to new scopes of the refinement of this work.

The experiment shows a mechanism for single cell lysis with electric fields. A sample cell was lysed inside the microchannel of the microfluidic device by applying a high voltage (700 V to 900 V). The time required for lysis and corresponding power consumption were $7 \pm 2$ s and <300 mW, respectively. These results show promise for biological studies and experimentation of single cells with microfluidics and LOC technology that uses electrical lysis inside the microchannel environment to analyze single cell contents or sample preparation that combines with other on-chip biological processes downstream.

## Acknowledgement

This research was conducted at the University of Ottawa Heart Institute and at Carleton University. The authors gratefully acknowledge Canadian Microelectronics Corporation (CMC) towards fabrication of the microfluidic device. The authors would like to thank the anonymous reviewers and editors for their valuable comments, suggestions and insights to improve the quality of this manuscript.

## Conflicts of Interest

The authors declare no conflict of interest.

68

**References**

1. Saliterman, S. *Fundamentals of BioMEMS and Medical Microdevices*; Wiley-Interscience: Bellingham, WA, USA, 2006.
2. Urban, G.A. *BioMEMS*; Springer: Dordrecht, The Netherlands, 2006.
3. Morshed, B.I.; Shams, M.; Mussivand, T. Identifying severity of electroporation through quantitative image analysis. *Appl. Phys. Lett.* **2011**, *98*, 143704, doi:10.1063/1.3575561.
4. Lian, M.; Wu, J. Ultrafast micropumping by biased alternating current electrokinetics. *Appl. Phys. Lett.* **2009**, *94*, 064101, doi:10.1063/1.3080681.
5. Bao, N.; Lu, C. A microfluidic device for physical trapping and electrical lysis of bacterial cells. *Appl. Phys. Lett.* **2008**, *92*, 214103, doi:10.1063/1.2937088.
6. Wang, H.; Bhunia, A.K.; Lu, C. A microfluidic flow-through device for high throughput electrical lysis of bacterial cells based on continuous DC voltage. *Biosens. Bioelectron.* **2006**, *22*, 582–588.
7. Bhagat, A.S.; Dasgupta, S.; Banerjee, R.K.; Papautsky, I. Effects of microchannel cross-section and applied electric field on electroosmotic mobility. In Proceedings of Conference Solid-State Sensors, Actuators and Microsystems, Lyon, France, 10–14 June 2007; pp. 1853–1856.
8. Lee, D.W.; Cho, Y.H. A continuous electrical cell lysis device using a low DC voltage for a cell transport and rupture. *Sens. Actuators B* **2007**, *B 124*, 84–89.
9. Legendre, L.A.; Bienvenue, J.M.; Roper, M.G.; Ferrance, J.P.; Landers, J.P. A simple, valveless microfluidic sample preparation device for extraction and amplification of DNA from nanoliter-volume samples. *Anal. Chem.* **2006**, *78*, 1444–1451.
10. Hong, J.W.; Hagiwara, H.; Fujii, T.; Machida, H.; Inoue, M.; Seki, M.; Endo, I. Separation and Collection of a Specified DNA Fragment by Chip-based CE System. In *Micro Total Analysis Systems 2001*; Publisher: Dordrecht, The Netherlands, 2001; pp. 113–114.
11. Ulaby, F.T.; Michielssen, E.; Ravaioli, U. *Fundamentals of Applied Electromagnetics*; Pearson Prentice Hall: Upper Saddle River, NJ, USA, 2010.
12. Jenkins, A.; Chen, C.P.; Spearing, S.; Monaco, L.A.; Steele, A.; Flores, G. Design and modelling of a microfluidic electro-lysis device with controlling plates. In Proceedings of 2006 International MEMS Conference, Singapore, 9–12 May 2006; pp. 620–625.
13. Linderholm, P.; Seger, U.; Renaud, P. Analytical expression for electrical field between two facing strip electrodes in microchannel. *Electron. Lett.* **2006**, *42*, 145–146.
14. Chatterjee, A.N.; Aluru, N.R. Combined circuit/device modeling and simulation of integrated microfluidic system. *J. Microelectromech. Syst.* **2005**, *14*, 81–95.
15. Koh, C.G.; Tan, W.; Zhao, M.; Ricco, A.J.; Fan, Z.H. Integrating polymerase chain reaction, valving, and electrophoresis in a plastic device for bacterial detection. *Anal. Chem.* **2003**, *75*, 4591–4598.
16. Lodish, H.; Berk, A.; Zipursky, S.L.; Matsudaira, P.; Baltimore, D.; Darnell, J. *Molecular Cell Biology*; W. H. Freeman and Co.: New York, NY, USA, 2003.
17. Malacinski, G.M. *Essentials of Molecular Biology*; Jones and Bartlett Publishers: Burlington, MA, USA, 2005.

18. Ikeda, N.; Tanaka, N.; Yangida, Y.; Hatsuzawa, T. On-chip single-cell lysis for extracting intracellular material. *Jpn. J. Appl. Phys.* **2007**, *46*, 6410–6414.
19. Lee, S.W.; Tai, Y. A micro cell lysis device. *Sens. Actuators A* **1999**, *73*, 74–79.
20. Huang, Y.; Rubinsky, B. Microfabricated electroporation chip for single cell membrane permeabilization. *Sens. Actuators A* **2001**, *89*, 242–249.
21. Huang, Y.; Rubinsky, B. Micro-electroporation: Improving the efficiency and understanding of electrical permeabilization of cells. *Biomed. Microdevices* **1999**, *2*, 145–150.
22. Huang, Y.; Rubinsky, B. Flow-through micro-electroporation chip for high efficiency single-cell manipulation. *Sens. Actuators A* **2003**, *104*, 205–212.
23. Han, F.; Wang, Y.; Sims, C.E.; Bachman, M.; Chang, R.; Li, G.P.; Allbritton, N.L. Fast electrical lysis of cells for capillary electrophoresis. *Anal. Chem.* **2003**, *75*, 3688–3696.
24. Lu, K.; Wo, A.M.; Lo, Y.; Chen, K.; Lin, C.; Yang, C. Three dimensional electrode array for cell lysis via electroporation. *Biosens. Bioelectron.* **2006**, *28*, 24–33.
25. Gao, J.; Yin, X.; Fang, Z. Integration of single cell injection, cell lysis, separation and detection of intercellular constituents on a microfluidic chip. *Lab Chip* **2004**, *4*, 47–52.
26. Lee, D.W.; Cho, Y. A continuous cell lysis device using focused high electric field and self-generated electroosmotic flow. In Proceedings of the 19th IEEE International Conference on Micro Electro Mechanical Systems, Istanbul, Turkey, 22–26 January 2006; pp. 426–429.
27. Wang, H.; Lu, C. High-throughput and real-time study of single cell electroporation using microfluidic: Effects of medium osmolarity. *Biotechnol. Bioeng.* **2006**, *95*, 1116–1125.
28. Joshi, R.P.; Schoenbach, K.H. Electroporation dynamics in biological cells subjected to ultrafast electrical pulses: A numerical simulation study. *Phys. Rev. E* **2000**, *62*, 1025–1033.
29. Nilsson, J.W.; Riedel, S.A. *Electric Circuits*; Prentice-Hall: Upper Saddle River, NJ, USA, 2000.
30. Bhagat, A.S.; Dasgupta, S.; Banerjee, R.K.; Papautsky, I. Effects of microchannel cross-section and applied electric field on electroosmotic mobility. In Proceedings of 2007 International Solid-State Sensors, Actuators and Microsystems Conference, Lyon, France, 10–14 June 2007; pp. 1853–1856.
31. Weaver, J.C. Electroporation of cells and tissues. *IEEE Trans. Plasma Sci.* **2000**, *28*, 24–33.
32. Dev, S.B.; Rabussay, D.P.; Widera, G.; Hofmann, G.A. Medical applications of electroporation. *IEEE Trans. Plasma Sci.* **2000**, *28*, 206–223.

70

# Review on Impedance Detection of Cellular Responses in Micro/Nano Environment

**Kin Fong Lei**

**Abstract:** In general, cell culture-based assays, investigations of cell number, viability, and metabolic activities during culture periods, are commonly performed to study the cellular responses under various culture conditions explored. Quantification of cell numbers can provide the information of cell proliferation. Cell viability study can understand the percentage of cell death under a specific tested substance. Monitoring of the metabolic activities is an important index for the study of cell physiology. Based on the development of microfluidic technology, microfluidic systems incorporated with impedance measurement technique, have been reported as a new analytical approach for cell culture-based assays. The aim of this article is to review recent developments on the impedance detection of cellular responses in micro/nano environment. These techniques provide an effective and efficient technique for cell culture-based assays.

Reprinted from *Micromachines*. Cite as: Lei, K.F. Review on Impedance Detection of Cellular Responses in Micro/Nano Environment. *Micromachines* **2014**, *5*, 1-12.

## 1. Introduction

Cell culture, which cultures cells as a monolayer on a surface of a cell culture vessel (e.g., Petri dish or multi-well microplate) is widely used in life science research for the investigation of cellular behavior. It has the advantage of simplicity in terms of operations and observations. In general cell culture-based assays, monitoring of cell number, viability, and metabolic activity are commonly performed to provide information of cellular responses under a specific culture condition studied. Conventionally, counting cells microscopically, quantifying indicative cellular components (e.g., DNA), live/dead fluorescent dye staining, and analysis of indicative metabolites synthesized by the cultured cells are adopted. These analytical methods have become standard protocols for the cell culture-based assays. However, these approaches are normally labor-intensive and time-consuming, limiting the throughput of the cell culture-based assay works like drug screening or toxin testing. In addition, analysis of the indicative cellular components and fluorescent dye staining normally need to sacrifice the cultured cells and thus hamper the observation of the subsequent cellular responses. Therefore, alternative analytical methods are crucial in need for achieving both effective and efficient detections.

In the past decade, microfluidic system, also called "lab-on-chip (LOC)", "bio-chip", or "micro-total-analysis-system (μTAS)", has attracted attention because of its capability of combining engineering and life science [1–3]. Therefore, it is often interpreted as a miniaturized and automatic version of a conventional laboratory. Due to their miniaturization and automation, there are a number of advantages of using microfluidic systems, such as less sample/reagent consumption, reduced risk of contamination, less cost per analysis, lower power consumption, enhanced sensitivity and specificity, and higher reliability. Microfluidic systems have been developed for various biological analytical applications, such as DNA analysis [4–8], immunoassay [9–13], and cell analysis [14–18]. Moreover, a number of demonstrations showed that cell culture can be performed on the microfluidic systems to achieve higher throughput and more reliable results [19,20]. For example, a microfluidic device for culturing cells inside an array of microchambers with continuous perfusion of medium was reported to provide a cost-effective and automated cell culture [21]. Each circular microchamber was 40 μm in height and surrounded by multiple narrow perfusion channels of 2 μm in height. The high aspect ratio between the microchamber and the perfusion channels offered a stable and homogenous microenvironment for cell growth. Human carcinoma (HeLa) cells were cultured in $10 \times 10$ microfluidic cell culture array and able to grow to confluency after eight days. Moreover, a fully automated cell culture screening system was developed and demonstrated on maintaining cell viability for weeks [22]. Individual culture conditions in 96 independent culture chambers can be customized in terms of cell seeding density, composition of culture medium, and feeding schedule. Each chamber was imaged with time-lapse microscopy to perform quantitative measurements of the influence of transient stimulation schedules on cellular activities. In these excellent demonstrations, optical imaging was utilized to quantify cellular activities. However, this measurement technique is time-consuming and may induce large tolerance. Alternatively, impedance measurement was proposed to be one of the promising techniques to quantify cellular responses during culture on the microfluidic systems. The detection results are represented by electrical signals, which can easily interface with miniaturized devices. Typically, a pair of electrodes as an electrical transducer is utilized to measure the impedance change caused by the existence of the biological substances. Literature has demonstrated the use of the similar principle for the detection of various biological substances such as enzymes [23], antibodies and antigens [10,24–26], DNA [27,28], and cells [17,29–33]. This technique provides a non-invasive and label-free measurement, and is found practically useful for the detection of substances in miniaturized analytical devices like microfluidic systems.

The aim of this article is to review recent developments on the impedance detection of cellular responses in micro/nano environment. Cell number and cell viability are the important characteristics during cell culture, and can be monitored by various impedance measurement techniques. Moreover, as a microfluidic system is an integrated system for multi-purposes, monitoring of metabolic activities of cells with cell stimulation is also significant for cell culture-based studies. Literature review and in-depth discussion of the impedance measurement will be presented. Microfluidic systems incorporated with impedance measurement technique provide an effective and efficient technique for cell culture-based assays.

## 2. Electrical Equivalent Circuit

Generally, an electrical equivalent circuit is used to curve fit the experimental data for the explanation of the characteristics of the impedance detection system. A number of electrical equivalent circuits were proposed to describe the cellular detection [34]. In order to have an easier understanding, a simplified electrical equivalent circuit and its impedance spectrum were reported and are shown in Figure 1 [31]. It is generally suggested that two identical double layer capacitances at each electrode ($C_{dl}$) are connected to the medium resistance ($R_{sol}$) in series, and the dielectric capacitance of the medium ($C_{di}$) is introduced in parallel with these series elements. In the equivalent circuit, there are two parallel branches, which are $C_{di}$ and $C_{dl} + R_{sol} + C_{dl}$. The impedance of each branch could be expressed with the following equations:

$$|Z_1| = \sqrt{R_{sol}^2 + \frac{1}{(\pi f C_{dl})^2}} \quad \text{(for branch } C_{dl} + R_{sol} + C_{dl})$$  (1)

$$|Z_2| = \sqrt{\frac{1}{(2\pi f C_{di})^2}} \quad \text{(for branch } C_{di})$$  (2)

**Figure 1. (a)** Electrical equivalent circuit of impedance measurement system with interdigitated electrode. **(b)** Typical impedance spectrum. $C_{dl}$ is the double layer capacitance at each electrode. $R_{sol}$ is the resistance of the medium. $C_{di}$ is the dielectric capacitance of the medium. (Copyright 2004. Reprinted from [22] with permission from Elsevier).

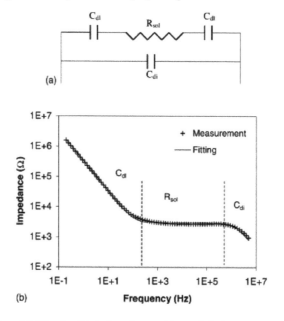

At a frequency below 1 MHz, the $C_{di}$ is inactive and is modeled as an open circuit. Current could not pass through the branch of dielectric capacitance and the total impedance is expressed as $Z_1$. Both $C_{dl}$ and $R_{sol}$ are included in this frequency region, and they dominate at different frequencies, as shown in the impedance spectrum. At a low frequency range, the spectrum shows capacitive characteristics, which is contributed by the $C_{dl}$. The impedance decreases with increasing frequencies. Up to a certain frequency (depending on the electrode dimensions, and the conductivity and permittivity of the medium), the $C_{dl}$ offer no impedance. The total impedance is contributed by the $R_{sol}$ and is frequency-independent (resistive characteristics). When cells are present in the system, the presence of the electrically insulated cell membranes influences the $C_{dl}$ as biological cells are very poor conductors at frequencies below 10 kHz [32]. The conductivity of the cell membrane is around $10^{-7}$ S/m, whereas the conductivity of the interior of a cell can be as high as 1 S/m [35]. Therefore, cell proliferation can be estimated by the total impedance at low frequency region.

## 3. Monitoring of Cell Number

### 3.1. Detection of Cells Adhered on the Electrode Surface

If cells adhere and proliferate on the surface of the measurement electrodes, the electrode surface area is effectively reduced and the total impedance across the electrodes is, hence, increased for the detection of the presence of cells. Most of the impedance biosensors are based on this principle. A pioneer work of cellular monitoring with an applied electric field was reported in 1984 [36]. Later, impedance measurement of cell concentration, growth, and the physiological state of cells was demonstrated [32]. An interdigitated electrode was utilized to demonstrate on-line and real-time cellular monitoring. Long-term cellular behavior was clearly shown by the impedance change of the electrodes. This detection principle was also applied to detect *Salmonella typhimurium* in mike samples [31]. An interdigitated microelectrode was utilized as impedance sensors to measure the bacterial growth curve at four frequencies (10 Hz, 100 Hz, 1 kHz, and 10 kHz). Illustration of the experimental setup is shown in Figure 2. The most significant change in impedance was observed at 10 Hz. The biosensor can detect the bacterial concentration of $10^5-10^6$ CFU/mL. Moreover, in order to detect cells specifically, antibodies are utilized to capture cells and provide selectivity to the sensor. Microelectrode array biosensors, with surface functionalization, were reported for the detection of *Escherichia coli* O157:H7 [37] and *Legionella* pneumophila [17]. The sensor surface was functionalized for bacterial detection using immobilized antibodies to create a biological sensing surface. The bacteria suspended in liquid samples were captured on the sensor surface and the impedance change was measured over a frequency range of 100 Hz–10 MHz. The sensors were able to determinate cellular concentrations of $10^4-10^7$ CFU/mL and $10^5-10^8$ CFU/mL, respectively. Another approach was to use magnetic nanoparticle-antibody conjugates (MNAC) to capture the specific cells. A microfluidic flow cell with embedded gold interdigitated array microelectrode was developed for rapid detection of *Escherichia coli* O157:H7 in ground beef samples [38]. MNAC were used to separate and concentrate the target bacteria from the samples. The cells of *E. coli* O157:H7 inoculated in a food sample were first captured by the MNAC, separated and concentrated by applying a magnetic field, washed and suspended in solution, injected through the microfluidic flow cell, and attracted by magnetic field on the active layer for impedance measurement. This impedance biosensor was able to detect as low as $1.6 \times 10^2$ and $1.2 \times 10^3$ cells of *E. coli* O157:H7 cells present in pure culture and ground beef samples, respectively.

### 3.2. Detection of Suspended Cells

When cells suspend in the liquid buffer, impedance measurement can also be used to determine cell number in the buffer. However, the impedance spectroscopic responses are very dependent on the conductivity of the buffer used in the systems. The detection of *Salmonella* cell suspensions was demonstrated in deionzed (DI) water and phosphate buffered saline (PBS), respectively [39]. It showed that bacterial cell suspensions in DI water with different concentrations can result in different electrical impedance spectral responses; conversely, cell suspensions in PBS cannot. The impedance spectra are shown in Figure 3. It was reported that the impedance of the cell suspensions in DI water decreased with the increasing cell concentration. It was suggested that the cell wall charges and the release of ions or other osmolytes from the cells caused the proportional impedance change.

**Figure 2.** Experimental setup of the impedance measurement with the interdigitated electrodes for the detection of cells. (Copyright 2004. Reprinted from [22] with permission from Elsevier).

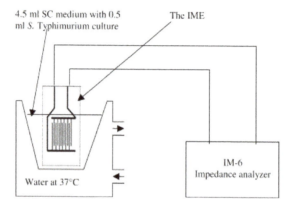

**Figure 3.** Impedance spectra of *Salmonella* suspensions in (**A**) DI water and (**B**) PBS with the cell concentrations in the range of $10^4$ to $10^9$ cfu/mL, along with water and PBS as controls. Frequency range: 1 Hz–100 kHz. Amplitude: ±50 mV. (Copyright 2008. Reprinted from [27] with permission from Elsevier).

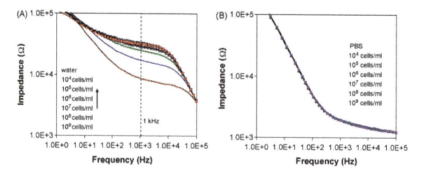

## 4. Monitoring of Cellular Viability

Cell death leads to the release of cells from the surface of the measurement electrode. That induces the decrease of the impedance measured across the electrodes. Real-time evaluation of targeted tumor cells treated with a combination of targeted toxin and particular plant glycosides was demonstrated [40]. HeLa cells were seeded onto interdigitated electrode and treated with targeted toxin. The impedance was directly correlated with the cell viability and able to trace the temporal changes of cell death during treatment. The above demonstration utilized a two-electrode system (*i.e.*, interdigitated electrode) for the measurement. A three-electrode system was also demonstrated for the monitoring of cell growth with the treatment of potentially cytotoxic agents [41]. It has the advantage of better reproducibility than traditional two-electrode impedance measurement. The cell chip consisted of an eight-well cell culture chamber incorporated with a three-electrode system on each well, as shown in Figure 4. Human hepatocellular carcinoma cells (HepG2) were cultured in the chamber and toxic effects on the HepG2 cells was monitored. The impedance was decreased after treatments with several toxicants, such as tamoxifen and menadione, indicating the detachment of dead cells. Moreover, a $10 \times 10$ micro-electrode array was used to monitor the culture behavior of mammalian cancer cells and evaluate the chemosensitivity of anti-cancer drugs using impedance spectroscopy [42]. Human oesophageal cancer cells were cultured on the surface of the electrodes and then treated with anti-cancer drug. Morphology changes during cells adhesion, spreading, proliferation, and chemosensitivity effects on cells can be monitored by impedimetric analysis in a real-time and non-invasive way. Recently, commercial cell analyzers are available to monitor the cellular responses. Although they are not designed for microfluidic environment, but impedance measurement shows a promising tool for cellular analyses. Real-time detection of cell death in a neuronal cell line of immortalized hippocampal neurons (HT-22 cells), neuronal progenitor cells (NPC), and differentiated primary cortical neurons was demonstrated using the system [43]. Schematic overview of the measurement principle is shown in Figure 5. These excellent demonstrations showed that impedance measurement is a convenient and reliable technique for real-time monitoring of cellular responses.

**Figure 4.** (**A**) Configuration of the microfabricated cell chip: RE, reference electrode; WE, working electrode; CE, counter electrode. (**B**) Fabricated cell chip. (Copyright 2005. Reprinted from [29] with permission from Elsevier).

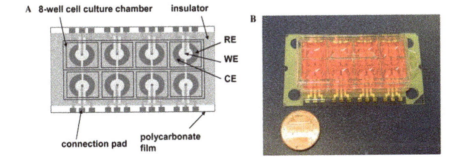

**Figure 5.** Schematic overview of the measurement principle of cellular impedance. (**A**) Each well of the culture dish features a bottom with embedded gold-electrodes. The electrode array has a minimal distance of 30 µm between the electrodes. The right picture shows an upright view of the electrode array. (**B**) Cells were seeded on top of the electrode-covered surface of the culture dish. After attaching to the bottom of the well, the cells partially insulate the electrodes, causing a rise in impedance. With an increasing cell density, the cells have a greater overall insulating capacity, showing in a further increase in impedance. Inflicting cellular damage and cell death causes changes in membrane morphology, cellular shrinkage, and detachment, resulting in a decrease of the cellular impedance. (Copyright 2012. Reprinted from [31] with permission from Elsevier).

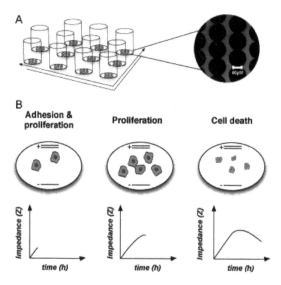

## 5. Monitoring of the Metabolic Activity of Cells

Monitoring of the metabolic activity during cell culture is very important for the study of cell physiology. A microfluidic chamber was reported to enable the real-time measurement of extracellular lactate of single heart cell under simultaneous electrical stimulation [44]. This device is comprised of one pair of pacing microelectrodes, used for field-stimulation of the cell, and three other microelectrodes configured as an electrochemical lactate micro-biosensor. Single heart cell was stimulated at pre-determined rates and its metabolic conditions were explored under the "working" situation. Moreover, monitoring of cell medium by comparing the rates of glucose and oxygen before and after contact with cells was demonstrated [45]. Two arrays of glucose and oxygen electrochemical sensors were fabricated at the inlet and outlet microchannels of the microfluidic cell culture chip, as shown in Figure 6. Real-time monitoring of glucose and oxygen was shown and the chip was utilized to the study of transient effluxes of these species during cell culture.

**Figure 6. (a)** Cross-section and **(b)** general schematic view of the developed biochip composed of two arrays of glucose and oxygen electrochemical microsensors integrated at the inlet and outlet microchannels of a PDMS microfluidic chamber. (Copyright 2008. Reprinted from [33] with permission from Elsevier).

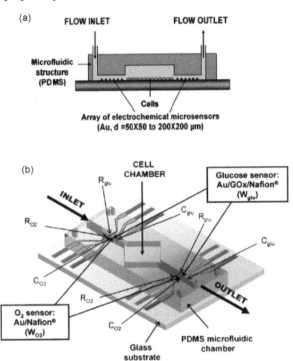

## 6. Cell Monitoring from 2D to 3D Cell Culture Format

Impedimetric cell monitoring in 2D cell culture format in microfluidic systems has been discussed and showed an effective and efficient technique for cell culture-based assays. 2D cell culture is widely adopted because of its simplicity in terms of operations and observations of cellular behavior. More recently, 3D culture format was proposed to provide a better approximation of the *in vivo* conditions in some cases [46,47]. Three-dimensional cell culture is that cells are encapsulated in a 3D polymeric scaffold material and can mimic the native cellular microenvironment since animal cells inhabit environments with very 3D features [46]. Thus, that might provide a more physiologically meaningful culture condition for cell-based assays. However, since cells are encapsulated in the scaffold, direct observation of cellular behavior cannot be practically performed. Destructive methods, such as detection of indicative cellular components and fluorescent dye staining are commonly used for the cell analysis. Alternatively, impedance measurement technique was reported to provide a real-time and non-invasive way to monitor cellular response in the 3D scaffold [33]. A microfluidic chip integrated with a pair of vertical electrodes in the 3D culture chamber was developed for quantifying cell number in the 3D scaffold. The impedance change was directly proportional to the cell number from $10^3$ to $10^7$ cells/mL in the 3D scaffold. This demonstration showed that the impedance measurement can be extended to monitor cellular responses from 2D to 3D cell culture format. It is expected that more demonstrations for real-time and non-invasive cellular monitoring will be reported.

## 7. Conclusions

With the rapid development of impedance measurement technique, commercial cell analyzers have been launched recently to provide convenient and reliable equipment for life science research and pharmaceutical development. In this article, impedance detection of cellular response in micro/nano environment has been discussed. The microfluidic systems incorporated with impedance measurement technique provide non-invasive and label-free monitoring of cellular responses in 2D and 3D culture format. More importantly, these systems are miniaturized and automatic. A sterile and homogenous microenvironment for cell culture can be created for precise monitoring. It is believed that more cell culture-based assays will be reported using the microfluidic cell culture systems.

## Acknowledgment

Author would like to thank the National Science Council, Taiwan for the financial support (project no. NSC101-2221-E-182-003-MY3).

## Conflicts of Interest

The author declares no conflict of interest.

## References

1.  Lei, K.F. Microfluidic systems for diagnostic applications: A review. *J. Lab. Autom.* **2012**, *17*, 330–347.
2.  Andersson, H.; van den Berg, A. Microfluidic devices for cellomics: A review. *Sens. Actuators B* **2003**, *92*, 315–325.
3.  Zhang, C.; Xu, J.; Ma, W.; Zheng, W. PCR microfluidic devices for DNA amplification. *Biotech. Advances* **2006**, *24*, 243–284.
4.  Erickson, D.; Liu, X.; Krull, U.; Li, D. Electrokinetically controlled DNA hybridization microfluidic chip enabling rapid target analysis. *Anal. Chem.* **2004**, *76*, 7269–7277.
5.  Wang, L.; Li, P.C.H. Microfluidic DNA microarray analysis: A review. *Anal. Chim. Acta.* **2011**, *687*, 12–27.
6.  Weng, X.; Jiang, H.; Li, D. Microfluidic DNA hybridization assays. *Microfluid. Nanofluid.* **2011**, *11*, 367–383.
7.  Lei, K.F.; Cheng, H.; Choy, K.Y.; Chow, L.M.C. Electrokinetic DNA concentration in micro systems. *Sens. Actuators A* **2009**, *156*, 381–387.
8.  He, Y.; Tsutsui, M.; Fan, C.; Taniguchi, M.; Kawai, T. Gate manipulation of DNA capture into nanopores. *ACS Nano.* **2011**, *5*, 8391–8397.

9. Diercks, A.H.; Ozinsky, A.; Hansen, C.L.; Spotts, J.M.; Rodriguez, D.J.; Aderem, A. A microfluidic device for multiplexed protein detection in nano-liter volumes. *Anal. Biochem.* **2009**, *386*, 30–35.

10. Lei, K.F. Quantitative electrical detection of immobilized protein using gold nanoparticles and gold enhancement on a biochip. *Meas. Sci. Technol.* **2011**, *22*, doi:10.1088/0957-0233/22/10/105802.

11. Hervas, M.; Lopez, M.A.; Escarpa, A. Electrochemical immunosensing on board microfluidic chip platforms. *TrAC Trends Anal. Chem.* **2012**, *31*, 109–128.

12. Ng, A.H.C.; Uddayasankar, U.; Wheeler, A.R. Immunoassays in microfluidic systems. *Anal. Bioanal. Chem.* **2010**, *397*, 991–1007.

13. Bhattacharyya, A.; Klapperich, C.M. Design and testing of a disposable microfluidic chemiluminescent immunoassay for disease biomarkers in human serum samples. *Biomed. Microdevices* **2007**, *9*, 245–251.

14. Van den Brink, F.T.G.; Gool, E.; Frimat, J.P.; Borner, J.; van den Berg, A.; Le Gac, S. Parallel single-cell analysis microfluidic platform. *Electrophoresis* **2011**, *32*, 3094–3100.

15. Zare, R.N.; Kim, S. Microfluidic platforms for single-cell analysis. *Annu. Rev. Biomed. Eng.* **2010**, *12*, 187–201.

16. Wu, M.H.; Huang, S.B.; Lee, G.B. Microfluidic cell culture systems for drug research. *Lab Chip* **2010**, *10*, 939–956.

17. Lei, K.F.; Leung, P.H.M. Microelectrode array biosensor for the detection of *Legionellapneumophila*. *Microelectron. Eng.* **2012**, *91*, 174–177.

18. Lei, K.F.; Wu, M.H.; Liao, P.Y.; Chen, Y.M.; Pan, T.M. Development of a micro-scale perfusion 3D cell culture biochip with an incorporated electrical impedance measurement scheme for the quantification of cell number in a 3D cell culture construct. *Microfluid. Nanofluid.* **2012**, *12*, 117–125.

19. Meyvantsson, I.; Beebe, D.J. Cell culture models in microfluidic systems. *Ann. Rev. Anal. Chem.* **2008**, *1*, 423–449.

20. Ni, M.; Tong, W.H.; Choudhury, D.; Rahim, N.A.A.; Iliescu, C.; Yu, H. Cell culture on MEMS platforms: A review. *Int. J. Mol. Sci.* **2009**, *10*, 5411–5441.

21. Hung, P.J.; Lee, P.J.; Sabounchi, P.; Aghdam, N.; Lin, R.; Lee, L.P. A novel high aspect ratio microfluidic design to provide a stable and uniform microenvironment for cell growth in a high throughput mammalian cell culture array. *Lab Chip* **2005**, *5*, 44–48.

22. Gomez-Sjoberg, R.; Leyrat, A.A.; Pirone, D.M.; Chen, C.S.; Quake, S.R. Versatile, fully automated, microfluidic cell culture system. *Anal. Chem.* **2007**, *79*, 8557–8563.

23. Saum, A.G.E.; Cumming, R.H.; Rowell, F.J. Use of substrate coated electrodes and ac impedance spectroscopy for the detection of enzyme activity. *Biosens. Bioelectron.* **1998**, *13*, 511–518.

24. Grant, S.; Davis, F.; Law, K.A.; Barton, A.C.; Collyer, S.D.; Higson, S.P.J.; Gibson, T.D. Label-free and reversible immunosensor based upon an ac impedance interrogation protocol. *Anal. Chem. Acta* **2005**, *537*, 163–168.

25. Chiriaco, M.S.; Primiceri, E.; D'Amone, E.; Ionescu, R.E.; Rinaldi, R.; Maruccio, G. EIS microfluidic chips for flow immunoassay and ultrasensitive cholera toxin detection. *Lab Chip* **2011**, *11*, 658–663.

26. Gupta, S.; Kilpatrick, P.K.; Melvin, E.; Velev, O.D. On-chip latex agglutination immunoassay readout by electrochemical impedance spectroscopy. *Lab. Chip* **2012**, *12*, 4279–4286.

27. Ma, K.S.; Zhou, H.; Zoval, J.; Madou, M. DNA hybridization detection by label free *versus* impedance amplifying label with impedance spectroscopy. *Sens. Actuators B* **2006**, *114*, 58–64.

28. Javanmard, M.; Davis, R.W. A microfluidic platform for electrical detection of DNA hybridization. *Sens. Actuators B* **2011**, *154*, 22–27.

29. Mishra, N.N.; Retterer, S.; Zieziulewicz, T.J.; Isaacson, M.; Szarowski, D.; Mousseau, D.E.; Lawrence, D.A.; Turner, J.N. On-chip micro-biosensor for the detection of human CD4$^+$ cells based on AC impedance and optical analysis. *Biosens. Bioelectron.* **2005**, *21*, 696–704.

30. Krommenhoek, E.E.; Gardeniers, J.G.E.; Bomer, J.G.; van den Berg, A.; Li, X.; Ottens, M.; van der Wielen, L.A.M., van Dedem, G.W.K.; van Leeuwen, M.; van Gulik, W.M.; *et al.* Monitoring of yeast cell concentration using a micromachined impedance sensor. *Sens. Actuators B* **2006**, *115*, 384–389.

31. Yang, L.; Li, Y.; Griffis, C.L.; Johnson, M.G. Interdigitated microelectrode (IME) impedance sensor for the detection of viable *Salmonella typhimurium*. *Biosens. Bioelectron.* **2004**, *19*, 1139–1147.

32. Ehret, R.; Baumann, W.; Brischwein, M.; Schwinde, A.; Stegbauer, K.; Wolf, B. Monitoring of cellular behavior by impedance measurements on interdigitated electrode structures. *Biosens. Bioelectron.* **1997**, *12*, 29–41.

33. Lei, K.F.; Wu, M.H.; Hsu, C.W.; Chen, Y.D. Real-time and non-invasive impedimetric monitoring of cell proliferation and chemosensitivity in a perfusion 3D cell culture microfluidic chip. *Biosens. Bioelectron.* **2014**, *51*, 16–21.

34. Varshney, M.; Li, Y. Interdigitated array microelectrodes based impedance biosensors for detection of bacterial cells. *Biosens. Bioelectron.* **2009**, *24*, 2951–2960.

35. Pethig, R.; Markx, R.H. Applications of dielectrophoresis in biotechnology. *Trends Biotechnol.* **1997**, *15*, 426–432.

36. Giaever, I.; Keese, C.R. Monitoring fibroblast behavior in tissue culture with an applied electric field. *Proc. Natl. Acad. Sci. USA* **1984**, *81*, 3761–3764.

37. Radke, S.M.; Alocilja, E.C. A high density microelectrode array biosensor for detection of *E. coli* O157:H7. *Biosens. Bioelectron.* **2005**, *20*, 1662–1667.

38. Varshney, M.; Li, Y.; Srinivasan, B.; Tung, S. A label-free, microfluidics and interdigitated array microelectrode-based impedance biosensor in combination with nanoparticles immunoseparation for detection of *Escherichia coli* O157:H7 in food samples. *Sens. Actuators B* **2007**, *128*, 99–107.

39. Yang, L. Electrical impedance spectroscopy for detection of bacterial cells in suspensions using interdigitated microelectrodes. *Talanta* **2008**, *74*, 1621–1629.

40. Thakur, M.; Mergel, K.; Weng, A.; Frech, S.; Gilabert-Oriol, R.; Bachran, D.; Melzig, M.F.; Fuchs, H. Real time monitoring of the cell viability during treatment with tumor-targeted toxins and saponins using impedance measurement. *Biosens. Bioelectron.* **2012**, *35*, 503–506.

41. Yeon, J.H.; Park, J.K. Cytotoxicity test based on electrochemical impedance measurement of hepg2 cultured in microfabricated cell chip. *Anal. Biochem.* **2005**, *341*, 308–315.

42. Liu, Q.; Yu, J.; Xiao, L.; Tang, J.C.O.; Zhang, Y.; Wang, P.; Yang, M. Impedance studies of bio-behavior and chemosensitivity of cancer cells by micro-electrode arrays. *Biosens. Bioelectron.* **2009**, *24*, 1305–1310.

43. Diemert, S.; Dolga, A.M.; Tobaben, S.; Grohm, J.; Pfeifer, S.; Oexler, E.; Culmsee, C. Impedance measurement for real time detection of neuronal cell death. *J. Neurosci. Methods* **2012**, *203*, 69–77.

44. Cheng, W.; Klauke, N.; Sedgwick, H.; Smith, G.L.; Cooper, J.M. Metabolic monitoring of the electrically stimulated single heart cell within a microfluidic platform. *Lab Chip* **2006**, *6*, 1424–1431.

45. Rodrigues, N.P.; Sakai, Y.; Fujii, T. Cell-based microfluidic biochip for the electrochemical real-time monitoring of glucose and oxygen. *Sens. Actuators B* **2008**, *132*, 608–613.

46. Abbot, A. Cell culture: Biology's new dimension. *Nature* **2003**, *424*, 870–872.

47. Cukierman, E.; Pankov, R.; Stevens, D.R.; Yamada, K.M. Taking cell-matrix adhesions to the third dimension. *Science* **2001**, *294*, 1708–1712.

# Polydimethylsiloxane (PDMS) Sub-Micron Traps for Single-Cell Analysis of Bacteria

Christopher Probst, Alexander Grünberger, Wolfgang Wiechert and Dietrich Kohlheyer

**Abstract:** Microfluidics has become an essential tool in single-cell analysis assays for gaining more accurate insights into cell behavior. Various microfluidics methods have been introduced facilitating single-cell analysis of a broad range of cell types. However, the study of prokaryotic cells such as *Escherichia coli* and others still faces the challenge of achieving proper single-cell immobilization simply due to their small size and often fast growth rates. Recently, new approaches were presented to investigate bacteria growing in monolayers and single-cell tracks under environmental control. This allows for high-resolution time-lapse observation of cell proliferation, cell morphology and fluorescence-coupled bioreporters. Inside microcolonies, interactions between nearby cells are likely and may cause interference during perturbation studies. In this paper, we present a microfluidic device containing hundred sub-micron sized trapping barrier structures for single *E. coli* cells. Descendant cells are rapidly washed away as well as components secreted by growing cells. Experiments show excellent growth rates, indicating high cell viability. Analyses of elongation and growth rates as well as morphology were successfully performed. This device will find application in prokaryotic single-cell studies under constant environment where by-product interference is undesired.

Reprinted from *Micromachines.* Cite as: Santra, T.S.; Tseng, F.G. Micro/Nanofluidic Devices for Single Cell Analysis. *Micromachines* **2013**, *4*, 357-369.

## 1. Introduction

Single-cell analysis is a promising field for researchers from various disciplines as it holds potential for unraveling the intrinsic mechanisms of life with high accuracy. Investigations are performed on a single-cell basis rather than using typical bulk and average based measurements, which may mask conspicuous phenomena on the single-cell level. Therefore, microfluidics has become an essential part of the study of living microorganisms at small scale with spatial and temporal resolution, which would not be possible with conventional cytometric methods such as fluorescent activated cell sorting (FACS) and coulter counter.

Microfluidic single-cell analysis assays can be divided into two main categories, namely studying either the whole cell (growth [1], morphology [2], or fluorescent bioreporters [3,4]) or its lysate (genome, transcriptome, proteome and metabolome) [5]. Emerging technologies such as genetically encoded bioreporters have extended the toolbox for noninvasive whole-cell single-cell analysis and have been applied to measure metabolic states such as intercellular pH [6] and product formation [3].

Recently, two main microfluidic cultivation principles for single cells were exploited, namely:

(i)   the cultivation of single mother cells growing into discrete isogenic microcolonies [2,7,8] and

(ii)  arrays of physically separated individual cells and cell tracks [9,10].

In microcolonies, individual cells may be exposed to extracellular stimuli from neighboring cells, for example due to secreted metabolites or environmental gradients within the microcolony [11]. However, when performing perturbation studies to analyze single-cell responses, avoiding such community effects becomes essential.

Various physical principles have been applied to immobilize individual cells by means of, for example, single droplets [12,13], acoustic waves [14], electrophoretic forces [15–20], optical tweezers [21] or mechanical objects and structures [22]. Most of these single-cell trapping methods require laborious setups and may impact on the entrapped cells through temperature gradients or the formation of oxygen radicals [23], for example.

Alternatively, mechanical barriers and trapping structures inducing hydrodynamic forces on the cell enable the fast and reliable immobilization of hundreds of cells in parallel [9]. Single cells were entrapped in arrays of cup-shaped barrier structures with the openings facing towards the flow direction. Simultaneous cell pairing and the fusion of large arrays of cells were realized in [10] using the same passive cell-trapping approach. Instead of barrier structures, single cells can also be immobilized using rejoined gaps, where a meander-shaped channel is interconnected at multiple points by narrow junctions along its length [24]. The difference in the hydraulic resistance of the channels forces single cells into the narrow channels, where they become entrapped. The immobilization realized by both approaches is a statistical process and does not allow for a specific cell to be taken out of the flow or released again. More active control over the immobilization was achieved by applying negative pressure in order to pull cells into narrow channels arranged along the channel walls [25–28]. Throughput is typically decreased by better spatial control over the single cells.

Despite the many advantages of these methods, all of them share the same limitation concerning cell size and shape. Previous work was carried out mainly with large mammalian cells or spherical eukaryotic cells such as yeast. Efforts have been made to apply identical concepts for immobilizing bacteria, for example *Escherichia coli*. Obviously, their small size (10 times smaller than yeast) and typically rod-shaped morphology make it difficult to immobilize them precisely [29]. Most concepts lack the possibility of removing the surplus of daughter cells once a single mother cell divides, leading to larger colonies after cell division. As microbial growth is often faster than eukaryotic cell growth, a reliable microbial single-cell analysis system necessitates the continuous removal of daughter cells.

To enable long-term analysis, the so-called "mother machine" was utilized to immobilize and cultivate hundreds of *E. coli* mother cells in narrow dead-end channels with a height of 1 μm [30]. At the end of each channel, the proliferating mother cell was observed over several hours as well as multiple generations of its descendants before cells were pushed out of the channel and flushed away. The mother machine concept is well suited for cell aging studies as the old pole mother cell remains at a fixed position. However, accumulation of secreted products inside the dead-end channels and concentration gradients might still cause cell–cell heterogeneity in more complex assays. A similar approach was reported by [11,31] in which parallel growth channels with two openings facing the media supply streams were used to cultivate single cells. As single cells grew towards both openings of the tracks, the device was not suited for cell aging studies. In contrast, a balanced culture was maintained over multiple generations. Instead of PDMS, [11] applied porous agarose as chip material to allow diffusion between each of the growth channels. Indeed, this was proven through the successful co-cultivation of two dependent *E. coli* auxotrophs that can complement the amino acid deficiencies of one another [11]. Due to the agarose material, concentration gradients may lead to inhomogeneous cultivation conditions. Inoculation of mother cells was achieved by simply pipetting a cell suspension onto the bottom glass slide of the device, before placing the agarose perfusion chip with incorporated growth channels on top of it. Instead, [31] applied PDMS as chip material, not facilitating diffusion between the growth channels. However, cell–cell interactions and accumulation of secreted products may occur inside the densely packed growth channels. In [31], device cell seeding was achieved by an imbalance of the two media volume flows inside the main channels actively pushing the mother cells into the tracks.

This article outlines the fabrication and characterization of sub-micron sized single-cell traps for the cultivation and analysis of individual bacteria located inside a continuous media flow. High-resolution electron-beam-written photolithography masks were utilized to fabricate SU-8 molds with 300–400 nm structural resolution with the approximate size of typical bacteria and smaller. Polydimethylsiloxane (PDMS) replication was performed to fabricate single-use chip devices, thereby replicating the sub-micron SU-8 trapping structures well. *E. coli* MG1655 cells were immobilized simply by flow inside the single-cell traps, cultivated, and observed by time-lapse microscopy over several hours. Division times at 20 min demonstrated excellent cell viability. Due to the fast media flow towards and around the traps, side products secreted by the cells were rapidly washed away without affecting any other cells further downstream. Supporting flow profile analysis was performed using computational fluidic dynamics. The present system will be used for single-bacteria perturbation studies.

## 2. Experimental

### 2.1. Soft Lithography

A video-based description of a comparable fabrication method can be found in [32]. Microfluidic master molds were fabricated using the negative photoresist SU-8 (MicroChem, Newton, MA, USA). Prior to resist deposition, a 4-inch silicon wafer was cleaned with piranha solution followed by hydrofluoric acid and rinsed with DI water. After dry spinning, the substrate was dehydrated for 20 min at 200 °C. For the first layer of photoresist, a mixture of two different SU-8 photoresists was used to achieve the designated height of 1 µm. The photoresists SU-8 2000.5 and SU-8 2010 were mixed in a ratio of 24:88, with a total weight of 60 g. This mixture was spin-coated onto the substrate at 500 rpm with an acceleration of 100 rpm/s for 10 s and at 2000 rpm with an acceleration of 300 rpm/s for 30 s. Soft bake was performed at 65 °C for 90 s, at 95 °C for 90 s and at 65 °C for 60 s. Afterwards, the substrate was exposed (7 mW/cm²) for 3 s using a mask aligner

(MA-6, SUSS MicroTec, Garching, Germany) and an electron-beam-written chromium dark-field mask. Post-exposure bake was carried out at 65 °C for 60 s and 95 °C for 60 s. Unexposed parts of the photoresist were dissolved by immersing the substrate in developer solution (mr-DEV 600, micro resist technology GmbH, Berlin, Germany) for 60 s, then again in fresh developer solution for 40 s, and dipping it in isopropanol for 20 s. Developed substrates were dried and hard-baked for 10 min at 150 °C.

The second layer was coated with the negative photoresist SU-8 2010 at 500 rpm with an acceleration of 100 rpm/s for 10 s and 4000 rpm with an acceleration of 300 rpm/s for 30 s. After the deposition, the substrate was baked at 65 °C for 15 min and at 95 °C for 60 min. The photoresist was exposed (7 mW/cm²) for 12 s using a mask aligner (MA-6, SUSS MicroTec, Garching, Germany) and an electron-beam-written chromium dark-field mask. Post-exposure bake was carried out at 65 °C for 5 min and at 95 °C for 3 min. The development was carried out as described for the first layer. Finally, the structures were hard-baked for 6 h at 150 °C.

PDMS replicas were fabricated by pouring a 10:1 mixture of PDMS (Sylgard 184, Dow Corning, Midland, MI, USA) onto the wafer and baking it at 80 °C for 90 min. Next, the PDMS slab was peeled off the wafer and cut into separate chips. The chips were washed in n-pentane for 90 min to remove monomer residue and then transferred to an acetone bath for 90 min to remove the n-pentane. The chips were dried overnight. Prior to the experiments, each chip was thoroughly cleaned with acetone, isopropanol and, after drying, with scotch tape to remove any dust particles that may have clung to it. For high-resolution microscopy, a cleaned chip was bonded onto a 170 µm thin glass cover slip using an oxygen plasma generator (Diener electronic GmbH, Ebhausen, Germany).

*2.2. Sample Preparation*

*E. coli* (MG1655) was pre-cultured in 20 mL of fresh LB medium in 100 mL shake flasks and cultivated at 37 °C and 150 rpm overnight. 25 µL of the overnight culture was transferred to 20 mL of fresh LB and grown until an optical density (OD 600, BioPhotometer plus, Eppendorf AG, Hamburg, Germany) of 1 was reached. Afterwards, 100 µL of the main culture was diluted in 900 µL of fresh LB medium prior to inoculation into the microfluidic device.

*2.3. Experimental Procedure*

*E. coli* cells were inoculated into single-cell trapping arrays and cultivated for 4 h. Cells were entrapped by infusing the cell suspension through the main channel until the traps were filled with single cells. Afterwards, the main channel was continuously flushed with fresh growth medium (200 nL/min) to remove excessive cells and ensure constant environmental conditions. Cells were grown at 37 °C using an in-house developed incubator mounted to a motorized microscope (Ti Eclipse, Nikon, Tokyo, Japan). Time-lapse images of immobilized cells were taken at 5 min intervals and analyzed using the commercially available software suit NIS-Elements.

86

## 3. Results and Discussion

### 3.1. Trap Layout and Geometry

Due to the typical size of *E. coli* (≈500 nm diameter and ≈2 μm length), the various concepts for the immobilization of single eukaryotic cells that have been demonstrated in other studies do not work properly for *E. coli*. However, [9] laid the foundation for microfluidic barrier trapping structures. In a first approach, we miniaturized the existing concepts for barrier structures down to the size of single *E. coli*. Our microfluidic device incorporates two key elements, namely:

(i) the main channels for cell suspension and growth media supply, with a height of 10 μm (Figure 1a), and

(ii) the cultivation area containing barrier structures for cell entrapment with a height between 800 nm and 1 μm, as depicted in Figure 1b.

A cell suspension was flushed through the main channel to inject single bacteria into the traps. The barrier structures developed by [9] allowed fluid flow to pass over the structures between PDMS and glass. This principle was not possible in our approach as bacteria tend to grow into narrow gaps [33].

Initial experiments with this newly developed single-cell trapping method revealed that clogging occurred through unspecific adhesion of the cells during the filling process as well as during cultivation (Figure 1c). Cells became trapped before reaching the gap of the trapping region or adhered to the glass slide inside the 1 μm channel. This shows that systems which were initially developed for eukaryotic cells cannot simply be scaled down to match conditions for single-bacteria analysis. In particular, the handling of different shapes and the removal of daughter cells that appear have to be considered.

In a second approach, the trapping region was improved by reducing the plateau area to minimize clogging and unspecific adhesion, enabling cells to flow by without getting stuck (Figure 2a). Nevertheless, further experiments showed that this alteration did not prevent the adhesion of cells outside of the barrier structures. Finally, the trapping region was reduced to a round pillar with a height of 9 μm and a diameter of 17 μm (Figure 2b). This change allowed the successful immobilization of single *E. coli* cells without undesirable adhesion during the filling process and during cell growth. After division, daughter cells were immediately removed from the trapping region and washed away with the media stream.

Single-cell studies presented in this paper were carried out using two types of barrier structures as depicted in Figure 3. The first design allows one cell at a time to be immobilized (Figure 3a) inside a 1.5 μm wide gap formed by three rectangular barriers with a width of 2 μm and a height of 1 μm.

The second design allows two cells to be trapped simultaneously, increasing the throughput compared to the first structure, which allows single-cell trapping only. The gap between the barrier structures is 1 μm in width and 1 μm in length. The constriction at the end of each gap is 500 nm in width (Figure 3b).

**Figure 1. (a)** Immobilization of single bacteria into a trapping array. **(b)** SEM images of trapping region containing several trapping structures for the immobilization of single bacteria. **(c)** Unspecific adhesion of *E. coli* leading to crowded growth in first single-cell trapping concept.

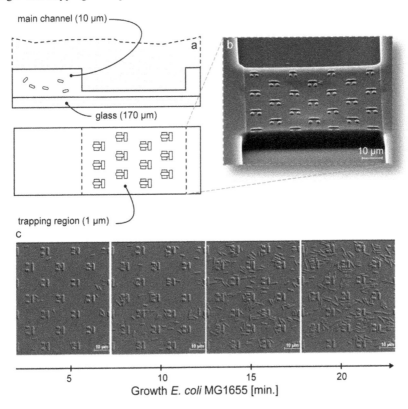

**Figure 2. (a)** SEM image of single-cell trapping structures with partially reduced trapping area. **(b)** SEM image of final trapping structure.

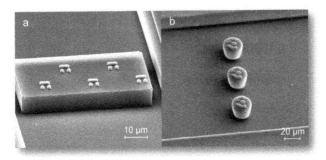

In contrast to previously published single-bacteria analysis devices by [11,30,31], our system facilitates fast and efficient inoculation by simply injecting the cell suspension. In fact, within a few seconds of perfusion, a good number of traps were inoculated, each with a single cell. The current proof-of concept chip contained 45 single traps and 42 double traps resulting in a loading capacity of individual 129 bacteria. As shown in Figure 3b, 60% of the single-traps and 87% of the double-traps were occupied within 20 s.

Experiments showed that despite the small dimensions between the barrier structures of design (a), *E. coli* was still able to grow through the barrier structure. Better results were achieved with design (b), where the additional constriction of 500 nm at the end of each gap restricted growth to the front inlet direction.

**Figure 3.** (a) Sub-micron single-cell trapping structures used for the successful immobilization and cultivation of *E. coli*. (b) Comparison of the number of trapped cells in single and double cell traps. After flushing the device with the cell suspension for a couple of seconds, 60% of the single traps and 87% of double traps were filled.

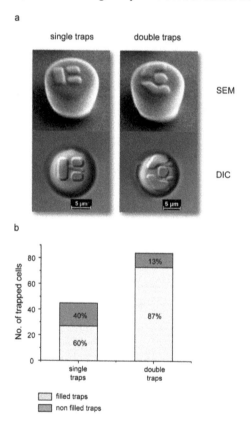

*3.2. Numerical Simulation*

Numerical simulations were conducted using COMSOL Multiphysics to analyze the fluid flow inside and around the single-cell trapping structures. Figure 4a shows the model geometry used in all simulations with a total length of 100 μm, width of 100 μm and height of 10 μm. The inlet boundary was defined to have a volumetric velocity of $16.67 \times 10^{-12}$ m$^3$/s, corresponding to a flow rate of 1000 nL/min in our system, which equals the flow rate used for cell inoculation during experiments. The outlet boundary was set to a gauge pressure of 0 Pa. All other surfaces of the geometry were defined as walls with a no-slip condition.

Reduction of the channel height (1 µm) near the trapping structure led to a drastic 1000 fold increase in the hydraulic resistance and much lower velocity inside the traps (Figure 4c) compared to the neighboring regions of the channel with an overall height of 10 µm (Figure 4b). Once a single cell is trapped, the flow is forced to diverge and flow around the trapping structure instead of flowing through the structure, and cannot trap any additional cells. This guarantees that only one cell at a time is trapped. Due to the reduced area of the shallow space surrounding the trapping structure, no additional cells can be caught in front. Furthermore, due to a higher convective flow around the trapping structure, by-products and surplus cells are washed away continuously, maintaining constant conditions over time.

**Figure 4. (a)** Geometry used for numerical simulation with an inlet flow rate of 1000 nL/min, outlet gauge pressure 0 Pa and walls defined as no-slip walls. **(b)** Flow profile and velocity distribution along the whole microfluidic channel. **(c)** Distribution of flow velocity in the shallow region surrounding the trapping structure.

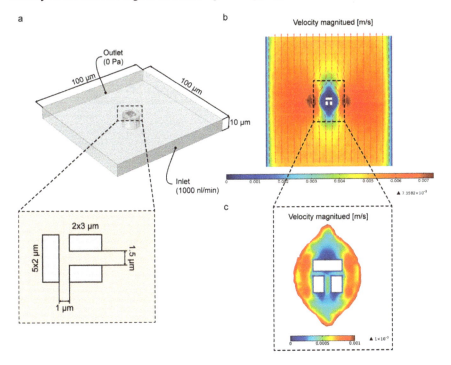

## 3.3. Single Cell Cultivation

Growth and morphology are key viability indicators in microbiology [34]. Single-cell growth assays analyzing division time and morphology were used in the present approach to validate our device. As shown in Figure 5a, we measured the cell length from one individual *E. coli* over

300 min cultivation by manually analyzing recorded time-lapse images. Division times as well as cell elongation rates were obtained. For analysis, a linear curve was fitted to the cell length over each generation period as illustrated in Figure 5d. The slope of each fit represents the respective elongation rate, as shown in Figure 5b.

**Figure 5. (a,b)** Single-cell traces (cell length, division time and elongation rate) of one distinct *E. coli* mother cell. **(c)** Time-lapse image series showing the successful removal of a "daughter" cell from the trap during cultivation. **(d)** Cell length over the 30 min of cultivation describing the determination of the division time as well as the elongation rate.

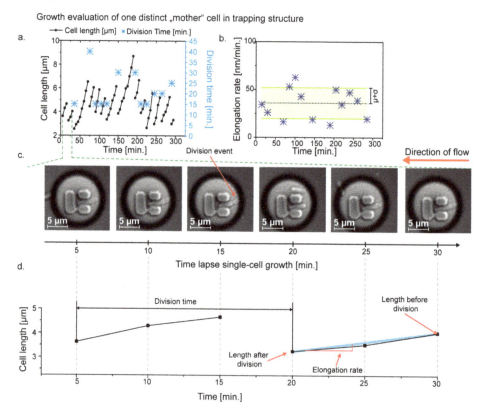

By averaging the division time of single cells in multiple single-cell trapping arrays (Figure 5b), we derived a 20 min division time of *E. coli*, which corresponds well to previously reported results [11,30]. Division times were derived by manual image analysis, as depicted Figure 5c,d. The time-lapse image in which both cells were apparently separated by a visible septum, was considered as the division end. Obviously, the higher the image frequency during time-lapse microscopy, the more accurate the division time could be evaluated. In our experiments, we found the time-lapse imaging frequency of 5 min as a reasonable compromise between total throughput and accuracy of analysis.

The mean division time and standard deviation were calculated over at least 9 generations from five traps, respectively (Figure 6a). Longer division times can be explained by the appearance of filaments, a well-known phenomenon in many microbial organisms often induced by cell stress [35]. Filamentation leads to much longer cells and delays the division event. However, by evaluating cell length before ($L_{Before}$) and after ($L_{After}$) division, we observed an almost Gaussian distribution (Figure 6b). Filamentation only occurred in a few instances and was mainly observed directly after the seeding of the single-cell trapping structures. After the first division, the filamentous cells reverted to normal growth behavior with an average $L_{Before} = 5$ μm and $L_{After} = 3$ μm. The Gaussian distribution was validated by using the Kolmogorov-Smirnov test (goodness of fit). As it can be seen in Figure 6b, for a significance level of $\alpha = 0.05$ and a critical value $d = 0.174$ ($n = 61$) it was found that $D_{after} = 0.094$ ($p$-value $= 0.643$) and $D_{before} = 0.085$ ($p$-value $= 0.781$). Since both values are smaller than the critical value $d$, we concluded that they are evenly distributed. Thus, we can presume that our newly developed method is suitable for the cultivation and analysis of single-cells such as *E. coli*.

**Figure 6.** (a) Average division time of 20 min derived from 5 single-cell trapping structures over the whole cultivation period of 300 min. (b) Average cell length distribution before ($L_{Before} \approx 5$ μm) and after ($L_{After} \approx 3$ μm) division of all analyzed traps, showing a nearly Gaussian distribution.

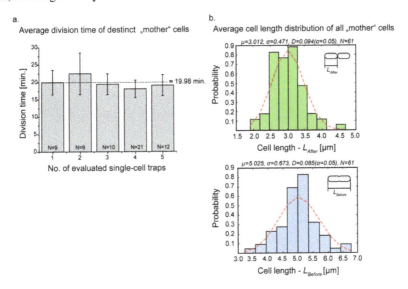

## 4. Conclusions

Microfluidics has emerged as a powerful tool in single-cell analysis, with a wide spectrum of different applications. However, many microfluidic systems for single whole-cell analysis are restricted by the size of the organisms (mammalian cells or eukaryotic cells such as yeast) that can be cultivated. In the present article, we presented a microfluidic device containing sub-micron sized single-cell traps for the immobilization and cultivation of individual bacteria, successfully demonstrated with *E. coli*. Furthermore, a simple loading procedure was established in which simply the cell suspension is perfused through the media supply channel filling the traps with a good efficiency and reproducibility within a few seconds. Barrier structures with sub-micron sized channel geometry allowed for the trapping of single rod-shaped *E. coli*. The layout ensured that neighboring cells and by-products were continuously removed by a fast media flow maintaining constant conditions. We cultivated *E. coli* cells over several hours showing constant division times and typically rod-shaped morphology, indicating good viability. Our findings form the basis for further single-bacteria analysis under constant environmental conditions without neighboring cells affecting each other. In future applications, our device is going to be applied for analyzing extracellular and intracellular responses of single bacteria due to short term fluctuations in pH, temperature, carbon sources and others. This will be achieved, e.g., by the application of genetically encoded fluorescence sensors [3,4]. The layout can be applied to many other types of typically rod-shaped bacteria of similar size.

**Acknowledgments**

This work was performed in part at the Helmholtz Nanoelectronic Facility (HNF) of Forschungszentrum Jülich GmbH. The authors would like to thank all those at HNF for their help and support.

**Conflicts of Interest**

The authors declare no conflict of interest.

**References**

1. Grünberger, A.; van Ooyen, J.; Paczia, N.; Rohe, P.; Schiendzielorz, G.; Eggeling, L.; Wiechert, W.; Kohlheyer, D.; Noack, S. Beyond growth rate 0.6: Corynebacterium glutamicum cultivated in highly diluted environments. *Biotechnol. Bioeng.* **2013**, *110*, 220–228.
2. Grunberger, A.; Paczia, N.; Probst, C.; Schendzielorz, G.; Eggeling, L.; Noack, S.; Wiechert, W.; Kohlheyer, D. A disposable picolitre bioreactor for cultivation and investigation of industrially relevant bacteria on the single cell level. *Lab Chip* **2012**, *12*, 2060–2068.
3. Mustafi, N.; Grünberger, A.; Kohlheyer, D.; Bott, M.; Frunzke, J. The development and application of a single-cell biosensor for the detection of l-methionine and branched-chain amino acids. *Metab. Eng.* **2012**, *14*, 449–457.
4. Schendzielorz, G.; Dippong, M.; Grünberger, A.; Kohlheyer, D.; Yoshida, A.; Binder, S.; Nishiyama, C.; Nishiyama, M.; Bott, M.; Eggeling, L. Taking control over control: Use of product sensing in single cells to remove flux control at key enzymes in biosynthesis pathways. *ACS Synth. Biol.* **2013**, doi:10.1021/sb400059y.
5. Yin, H.; Marshall, D. Microfluidics for single cell analysis. *Curr. Opin. Biotech.* **2012**, *23*, 110–119.

6. Miesenbock, G.; de Angelis, D.A.; Rothman, J.E. Visualizing secretion and synaptic transmission with pH-sensitive green fluorescent proteins. *Nature* **1998**, *394*, 192–195.

7. Prindle, A.; Samayoa, P.; Razinkov, I.; Danino, T.; Tsimring, L.S.; Hasty, J. A sensing array of radically coupled genetic "biopixels". *Nature* **2012**, *481*, 39–44.

8. Groisman, A.; Lobo, C.; Cho, H.; Campbell, J.K.; Dufour, Y.S.; Stevens, A.M.; Levchenko, A. A microfluidic chemostat for experiments with bacterial and yeast cells. *Nat. Meth.* **2005**, *2*, 685–689.

9. Di Carlo, D.; Aghdam, N.; Lee, L.P. Single-cell enzyme concentrations, kinetics, and inhibition analysis using high-density hydrodynamic cell isolation arrays. *Anal. Chem.* **2006**, *78*, 4925–4930.

10. Skelley, A.M.; Kirak, O.; Suh, H.; Jaenisch, R.; Voldman, J. Microfluidic control of cell pairing and fusion. *Nat. Methods* **2009**, *6*, 147–152.

11. Moffitt, J.R.; Lee, J.B.; Cluzel, P. The single-cell chemostat: an agarose-based, microfluidic device for high-throughput, single-cell studies of bacteria and bacterial communities. *Lab Chip* **2012**, *12*, 1487–1494.

12. Brouzes, E.; Medkova, M.; Savenelli, N.; Marran, D.; Twardowski, M.; Hutchison, J.B.; Rothberg, J.M.; Link, D.R.; Perrimon, N.; Samuels, M.L. Droplet microfluidic technology for single-cell high-throughput screening. *P. Natl. Acad. Sci.* **2009**, *106*, 14195–14200.

13. Choi, K.; Ng, A.H.C.; Fobel, R.; Wheeler, A.R. Digital Microfluidics. *Annu. Rev. Anal. Chem.* **2012**, *5*, 413–440.

14. Ding, X.; Lin, S.-C.S.; Kiraly, B.; Yue, H.; Li, S.; Chiang, I.-K.; Shi, J.; Benkovic, S.J.; Huang, T.J. On-chip manipulation of single microparticles, cells, and organisms using surface acoustic waves. *P. Natl. Acad. Sci.* **2012**.

15. Chiou, P.Y.; Ohta, A.T.; Wu, M.C. Massively parallel manipulation of single cells and microparticles using optical images. *Nature* **2005**, *436*, 370–372.

16. Dusny, C.; Fritzsch, F.S.O.; Frick, O.; Schmid, A. Isolated microbial single cells and resulting micropopulations grow faster in controlled environments. *Appl. Environ. Microbiol.* **2012**, *78*, 7132–7136.

17. Fritzsch, F.S.O.; Rosenthal, K.; Kampert, A.; Howitz, S.; Dusny, C.; Blank, L.M.; Schmid, A. Picoliter nDEP traps enable time-resolved contactless single bacterial cell analysis in controlled microenvironments. *Lab Chip* **2013**, *13*, 397–408.

18. Hsu, H.-y.; Ohta, A.T.; Chiou, P.-Y.; Jamshidi, A.; Neale, S.L.; Wu, M.C. Phototransistor-based optoelectronic tweezers for dynamic cell manipulation in cell culture media. *Lab Chip* **2010**, *10*, 165–172.

19. Kortmann, H.; Chasanis, P.; Blank, L.M.; Franzke, J.; Kenig, E.Y.; Schmid, A. The envirostat—A new bioreactor concept. *Lab Chip* **2009**, *9*, 576–585.

20. Kim, S.H.; Yamamoto, T.; Fourmy, D.; Fujii, T. Electroactive microwell arrays for highly efficient single-cell trapping and analysis. *Small* **2011**, *7*, 3239–3247.

21. Ramser, K.; Hanstorp, D. Optical manipulation for single-cell studies. *J. Biophotonics* **2010**, *3*, 187–206.

22. Johann, R.M. Cell trapping in microfluidic chips. *Anal. Bioanal Chem* **2006**, *385*, 408–412.

23. Svoboda, K.; Block, S.M. Biological applications of optical forces. *Annu. Rev. Biophys. Biomed. Struct.* **1994**, *23*, 247–285.

24. Kobel, S.; Valero, A.; Latt, J.; Renaud, P.; Lutolf, M. Optimization of microfluidic single cell trapping for long-term on-chip culture. *Lab Chip* **2010**, *10*, 857–863.

25. Khine, M.; Lau, A.; Ionescu-Zanetti, C.; Seo, J.; Lee, L.P. A single cell electroporation chip. *Lab Chip* **2005**, *5*, 38–43.

26. Lee, P.J.; Hung, P.J.; Shaw, R.; Jan, L.; Lee, L.P. Microfluidic application-specific integrated device for monitoring direct cell–cell communication via gap junctions between individual cell pairs. *Appl. Phys. Lett.* **2005**, *86*, 223902, doi:10.1063/1.1938253.

27. Valero, A.; Post, J.N.; van Nieuwkasteele, J.W.; ter Braak, P.M.; Kruijer, W.; van den Berg, A. Gene transfer and protein dynamics in stem cells using single cell electroporation in a microfluidic device. *Lab Chip* **2008**, *8*, 62–67.

28. Zhu, Z.; Frey, O.; Ottoz, D.S.; Rudolf, F.; Hierlemann, A. Microfluidic single-cell cultivation chip with controllable immobilization and selective release of yeast cells. *Lab Chip* **2012**, *12*, 906–915.

29. Kim, M.-C.; Isenberg, B.C.; Sutin, J.; Meller, A.; Wong, J.Y.; Klapperich, C.M. Programmed trapping of individual bacteria using micrometre-size sieves. *Lab Chip* **2011**, *11*, 1089–1095.

30. Wang, P.; Robert, L.; Pelletier, J.; Dang, W.L.; Taddei, F.; Wright, A.; Jun, S. Robust growth of escherichia coli. *Curr. Biol.* **2010**, *20*, 1099–1103.

31. Long, Z.; Nugent, E.; Javer, A.; Cicuta, P.; Sclavi, B.; Cosentino Lagomarsino, M.; Dorfman, K.D. Microfluidic chemostat for measuring single cell dynamics in bacteria. *Lab Chip* **2013**, *13*, 947–954.

32. Gruenberger, A., Probst, C., Heyer, A., Wiechert, W., Frunzke, J., Kohlheyer, D. Microfluidic picoliter bioreactor for microbial single-cell analysis: Fabrication, system setup and operation. *J. Vis. Exp.* **2013**, doi:10.3791/50560.

33. Männik, J.; Driessen, R.; Galajda, P.; Keymer, J.E.; Dekker, C. Bacterial growth and motility in sub-micron constrictions. *P. Natl. Acad. Sci.* **2009**, *106*, 14861–14866.

34. Lecault, V.; White, A.K.; Singhal, A.; Hansen, C.L. Microfluidic single cell analysis: From promise to practice. *Curr. Opin. Chem. Biol.* **2012**, *16*, 381–390.

35. Justice, S.S.; Hunstad, D.A.; Cegelski, L.; Hultgren, S.J. Morphological plasticity as a bacterial survival strategy. *Nat. Rev. Micro.* **2008**, *6*, 162–168.

# Hydrodynamic Cell Trapping for High Throughput Single-Cell Applications

Amin Abbaszadeh Banaeiyan, Doryaneh Ahmadpour, Caroline Beck Adiels and Mattias Goksör

**Abstract:** The possibility to conduct complete cell assays under a precisely controlled environment while consuming minor amounts of chemicals and precious drugs have made microfluidics an interesting candidate for quantitative single-cell studies. Here, we present an application-specific microfluidic device, cellcomb, capable of conducting high-throughput single-cell experiments. The system employs pure hydrodynamic forces for easy cell trapping and is readily fabricated in polydimethylsiloxane (PDMS) using soft lithography techniques. The cell-trapping array consists of V-shaped pockets designed to accommodate up to six *Saccharomyces cerevisiae* (yeast cells) with the average diameter of 4 µm. We used this platform to monitor the impact of flow rate modulation on the arsenite (As(III)) uptake in yeast. Redistribution of a green fluorescent protein (GFP)-tagged version of the heat shock protein Hsp104 was followed over time as read out. Results showed a clear reverse correlation between the arsenite uptake and three different adjusted low = 25 nL min$^{-1}$, moderate = 50 nL min$^{-1}$, and high = 100 nL min$^{-1}$ flow rates. We consider the presented device as the first building block of a future integrated application-specific cell-trapping array that can be used to conduct complete single cell experiments on different cell types.

Reprinted from *Micromachines*. Cite as: Banaeiyan, A.A.; Ahmadpour, D.; Adiels, C.B.; Goksör, M. Hydrodynamic Cell Trapping for High Throughput Single-Cell Applications. *Micromachines* **2013**, *4*, 414-430.

## 1. Introduction

Single cell analysis techniques emerging in the past decade have proposed numerous novel and fascinating prospects in the area of life sciences. This involves not only biologists but also scientists from the fields of engineering, physics, and chemistry to join forces in resolving some of the sophisticated and fundamental problems of stochastic cellular behavior. This would have not been possible without the creation and development of some clever and state-of-the-art platforms forming the foundations of the research. Lab-on-Chip devices [1–3] for example have been one of the main tools employed to realize such possibilities. No doubts, these systems have brought about the potential of studying individual cells in such detail that for instance our knowledge have penetrated into the covert voids of—as it seems—totally stochastic fluctuations of gene expression [4,5]. Investigating such heterogeneities in clonal cell populations has provided invaluable information about intracellular signaling events and cell-to-cell communication phenomena, which was not possible to obtain through the traditional, well established biological techniques, such as Western blotting [6] and real time PCR [7]. Briefly, single cell analysis approaches have offered the possibility to extract detailed information on inherent cell-to-cell variations in large populations thus providing a deeper understanding of cell dynamics and producing high-quality statistical data for modeling and systems biology resolutions [8,9].

Numerous microfluidic devices have been developed to provide a controlled environment where single cells can be captured, immobilized, cultured, exposed to selected stimuli, and specific intracellular events can be detected by time-lapse microscopy techniques [10]. For example, techniques employing gravity forces have been reported to capture cells in microwell arrays [11–13]. Although the throughput of such devices is high and many cells can be trapped in an array-based format, precise geometrical optimizations are required in designing the microwells to achieve a high trapping efficiency [12]. In this method cells are not actively held inside the traps and the following chemical rinsing step may remove the cells from the bottom of the microwells. Several other methods have also been coupled with microfluidics for cell immobilization and conducting controlled, complete cell assays. Flow-based active cell trapping by using control valves [14,15], non-invasive optical trapping [16–18], dielectrophoresis [19–21], surface chemistry modification techniques [22,23], arrays of physical barriers [24], cell trapping by negative pressure [25,26], and hydrodynamic methods [27–29] are some of these successfully established techniques.

In our previous work, we developed an experimental platform combining a microfluidic chamber with optical tweezers and advanced time-lapse microscopy [17,30,31], which has vastly been used to identify the underlying mechanisms of different signaling pathways in *Saccharomyces cerevisiae* (budding yeast) cells. Cells were trapped by the optical tweezers and positioned precisely in an array format at the bottom of the microfluidic chamber. Prior to the experiments, the microfluidic system was treated with a concanavalin A solution to immobilize the cells when pressed to the bottom surface. Thereafter, immobilized cells were exposed to the specific concentrations of intended solutions. The great potential of this system in changing the cellular environment rapidly and reversibly provided a pronounced understanding of the single cell dynamics. However, a limitation with this system was that precise cell positioning with optical tweezers demanded careful measures and thus, the number of the cells that could be trapped and positioned in an appropriate time period was limited. In addition, due to the limited number of cells in each experimental run, the information extracted lacked the statistical significance. Under the ideal experiment conditions the maximum number of cells that could be positioned in an array was constricted to 25–50 cells. To address the need for an easy-to-operate system capable of providing high-throughput single cell data with substantial statistical relevance we designed and fabricated a versatile and reliable platform, being referred to as cellcomb. Our device exploited hydrodynamic forces to direct the cells into a trapping area where single cells were held steadily inside V-shaped pockets by streamlines of the flow. After a successful cell-trapping step, controlled extracellular environmental changes were applied using a minute amount of intended stimuli and the intracellular events could be followed over time by means of time-lapse bright field and fluorescence microscopy. By employing the cellcomb platform we could conduct single cell experiments with up to 624 cells per run without forfeiting the spatial and temporal resolutions.

We demonstrated the functionality of this device for trapping yeast cells and showed that the device could successfully be used for single-cell applications. We optimized the flow rates in the system to actively modulate the uptake of arsenite (As(III)) in yeast. Sodium arsenite and YNB

(Yeast Nitrogen Base) were infused into the microchannels and redistribution of a green fluorescent protein (GFP)-tagged version of the heat shock protein Hsp104 was recorded over time as readout. Arsenite promotes protein misfolding, causing protein aggregations. Hsp104, which is otherwise evenly distributed in cytosol co-sediments with arsenite induced protein, aggregates and therefore relocalizes to distinct foci (aggregates) [32]. The Hsp104-GFP relocalization occurs in an arsenite concentration dependent manner [32] and here was employed as readout indicating the cellular arsenite uptake. As described by Jacobsson *et al.* [32], the formation of aggregates is somewhat a slow response and once formed, it requires about three hours until cells can clear the cytosol from protein aggregates. This therefore, provides a suitable temporal resolution for all the filled pockets along the device to be sequentially imaged. Moreover, the arsenite-induced aggregates can be precisely quantified with the single cytosolic Hsp104-GFP reporter without a need for introducing further reporters.

## 2. Experimental Procedure

### 2.1. Microfluidic System Design and Fabrication

Our microfluidic device was designed to hydrodynamically trap cells in a high throughput manner and keep them in position for the subsequent chemical exposure step. The cellular responses to the imposed perturbations could then be followed over time by fluorescence microscopy imaging. Figure 1a shows the overview of the device with cell inlets, reagent inlets and the outlets. The device comprised three adjacent channels, referred to as the main channel and the two side channels. The main channel was 20 μm wide and included the trapping zone of the chip. Cells were loaded into the device from the inlets "b" and "c" and inlet "a" was used to introduce the intended stress substance to the system. Inlets "d" and "f" are the main side inlets used for the cell loading step or introduction of stimuli via the side channels. Inlets "e" and "g" can be used as sheath flow inlets or to introduce additional reagents in the side channels. The two 60 μm-wide side channels were connected to the main channel via the V-shaped pockets with the dimensions of 10 μm × 10 μm and confinement openings with the width of 2 μm as shown in Figure 1b. The pockets were designed to trap up to six yeast cells with an average diameter of 4 μm. The entire system had a height profile of 4.8 μm to realize a single layer cell accommodation. The 2-μm openings acted like flow nuzzles and created a jet flow at the bottom of the confinement openings. A fraction of the fluid drawn into the pockets dragged the floating cells with it and confined them inside the traps consequently. Microfluidic devices were designed in a CAD program (AutoCAD 2012, Autodesk Inc., San Francisco, CA, USA) and photomasks were fabricated with e-beam lithography. SU8 (MicroChem Corp., Newton, MA, USA) was used as the negative photoresist and the pattern of the microchannels was transferred from the photomasks to the silicon substrates in a photolithography step. PDMS was then cast onto the SU8 masters to fabricate the microfluidic chips. SU8-5 was spin-coated on a 3-inch (100) silicon wafer at 3000 rpm, for 30 s, to achieve a film thickness of 5 μm according to the photoresist manufacturer data sheet. The thickness of the photoresist film was verified by using Dektak 150 surface profiler (Veeco instruments Inc., Plainview, NY, USA). The measured height of the microchannels was 4.8 μm (surface profiler data not shown).

Photoresist-coated wafers were soft-baked on a hot plate for 2 min at 65 °C and 5 min at 95 °C, and then were exposed to the UV light with the dose of 6 mJ/s cm$^2$ for 18 seconds in a conventional mask aligner (KS MJB3-DUV, SussMicrotech, Garching, Germany). A post exposure bake (PEB) was applied according to the instructions from the resist manufacturer for 1 min at 65 °C and 3 min at 95 °C. Wafers were developed in mr-Dev 600 (Micro resist technology GmbH, Berlin, Germany) for 7 min to dissolve the unexposed photoresist. Patterned wafers were then hard-baked in a closed-cover hotplate at 160 °C for 10 min. A 10:1 PDMS (polydimethylsiloxane) and curing agent mix was cast onto the masters and cured in the oven at 90 °C for 2 h. Microfluidic chips were cut and gently released from the masters, inlet and outlet holes were punched and PDMS replicas were irreversibly bonded on coverslips (Thickness no. 1.5 (0.16 to 0.19 mm), VWR, Stockholm, Sweden) by oxygen plasma treatment (PDC-32G/32G-2 (115/230V), Harrick Plasma, Ithaca, NY, USA) at 18 W RF power for 30 s. To increase the surface wettability and reduce the risk of bubble formation inside the channels, sealed microfluidic devices underwent an extended oxygen plasma treatment step for 5 min before performing the experiments [33]. Detailed fabrication procedure has been described by Sott *et al.* [34].

*2.2. Numerical Simulations Using COMSOL Multiphysics*

A series of fluid dynamic simulations were performed in COMSOL Multiphysics (COMSOL Inc., Burlington, MA, USA) to identify the fluid flow inside the individual traps. Microfluidics module was used with the single-phase, laminar flow approximations and the simulations were built upon stationary incompressible Navier-Stokes equations and the continuity equation, under the assumption of the constant fluid density and the mass conservation:

$$\rho\left(\frac{\delta\mu}{\delta t}+\mu\times\nabla\mu\right)=-\nabla p+\eta\nabla^2\mu+f \tag{1}$$

$$\nabla\mu=0 \tag{2}$$

Here, $\mu$ is the flow velocity, $\rho$ and $\eta$ are the density and the dynamic viscosity of the fluid, respectively. $p$ is the pressure and f denotes the other body forces e.g., gravity or magnetic forces. Simulations were performed under the condition of body forces equal to "zero". Flows were assumed to be Newtonian and incompressible *i.e.*, the viscosity of the fluid ($\eta$) being independent of the flow velocity and the density of the fluid ($\rho$) independent of the pressure. No-slip boundary condition (flow velocity at all solid boundaries is "zero") was selected for the channel walls and shallow-channel approximation applied for all three channels with the height of 4.8 μm. More details of the simulations can be found in [17], as described by Eriksson *et al.* [17].

*2.3. Cell Preparation*

The *Saccharomyces cerevisiae* (yeast cells) strain used in this study is *HSP104-GFP* in BY4741 background. The cells were grown on filtered minimal SC (synthetic complete) medium (0.67% yeast nitrogen base) supplemented with auxotrophic requirements and 2% glucose as carbon source, at 30 °C on a shaker (220 rpm). The cells were then collected at $OD_{600} = 0.5–1.0$, and were diluted in the same filtered medium to obtain the desired cell densities prior to the experiments.

**Figure 1. (a)** Overview of the microfluidic device with inlets and outlets. Inlets "*a*", "*b*", and "*c*" were connected to the main channel and used to inject the cells and stress substances into the device. Inlets "*d*" and "*f*" were used as the side inlets for hydrodynamic cell loading and reagent injection into the side channels. Inlets "*e*" and "*g*" were sheath flow inlets. Close-up view shows the trapping zone of the device and the flow direction in the main channel. **(b)** Device dimensions engineered for experiments with yeast cells.

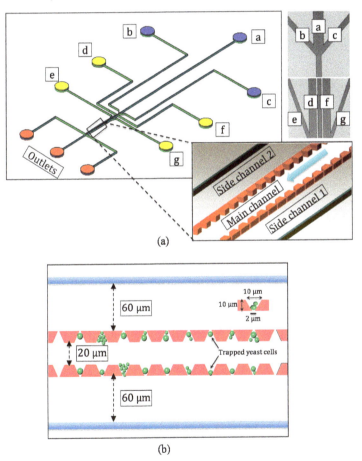

(a)

(b)

## 2.4. Sodium Arsenite Solution Preparation

Sodium arsenite ($NaAsO_2$) was dissolved in mili-Q water. A 10 mM solution was prepared and was diluted to achieve the final concentration of 0.5 mM.

## 3. Experimental Setup, Data Acquisition and Analysis

### 3.1. Microfluidic System Operation

The microfluidic chips were adapted to be used with an inverted epifluorescence microscope stage (DMI 6000B, Leica Microsystems, Wetzlar, Germany). Microfluidic chips were set on the motorized XYZ stage and time-lapse microscopy was exploited to gather the cell response data, e.g., subcellular relocation or aggregation of a reporter protein upon stimuli exposure. Before preparation of each experiment, microfluidic systems were treated with oxygen plasma and flushed with culture medium to maintain the hydrophilicity before starting the cell experiments and to remove air bubbles or PDMS residues in the microchannels. The intended solutions were injected into the microfluidic chips via 250 µL glass syringes that were connected to the channel inlets by needles and polytetrafluoroethylene (PTFE) tubing (Cole-Parmer, Vernon Hills, IL, USA). The syringes were mounted on conventional syringe pumps (CMA 400, CMA Microdialysis, Solna, Sweden) and all flow rates were manually set to 2.5 nL min$^{-1}$ before starting the automated image acquisition and pump control software. Bright field and fluorescence images were obtained by using an EM-CCD camera (C9100-12, Hamamatsu Photonics, Shizuoka, Japan) and a HCX plan fluotar 100× oil immersion objective with a numerical aperture of 1.3 (Leica Microsystems). We used a 15 W high-pressure mercury lamp (EL6000, Leica Microsystems) with 200 ms exposure time for fluorescence excitation. All equipment were controlled automatically by the multifunction imaging software OpenLab (PerkinElmer, Waltham, MA, USA). After preparing the syringes with the intended solutions, the microfluidic system was fixed on a metallic holder and positioned firmly on the microscope stage. Tubing were connected to the inlet channels and the cells were loaded into the device with fast pulses of the syringe pumps. The cell-loading step was easy and quick and the system could be flushed several times through the side channels in case cell loading was not successful or if cells or air bubbles clogged the microchannels. After this rinsing step, the cell loading was repeated. The cell concentrations were experimentally optimized (starting OD = 0.6, diluted twice in YNB) to make the cell loading as facile as possible and so that the microchannels will not be jammed by excessive cell accumulation.

### 3.2. Image Acquisition and Analysis

The microfluidic system was divided in 13 segments lengthways, with each segment containing eight V-shaped pockets, which fitted in one field of view of the microscope. All segments of the trapping zone were imaged in sequence and the stage was moved to the next segment until all of the filled traps were imaged. Bright field images were taken first to follow the cells in time and to control the focus of the imaging and compensate for the drift in the axial direction. In order to cover the whole volume of the cells, 9 stacks of bright field images were taken in z direction. The imaging state was then switched to fluorescence and 9 stacks of fluorescent images were taken. The whole experiment time was set to 45 min and images were captured in time intervals of 30 s between each two neighboring segments. All imaging data was transferred to the open source image analysis custom software for single cell analysis CellStress [35] for processing. Captured images of all fields of view of the microscope were cropped and prepared so that the software could identify and find the cell contours. After the cells were distinguished from the background, the fluorescent images for each segment were analyzed. The aggregates were found based on an algorithm to pinpoint the areas with higher intensities amongst all the image layers in all time points during the whole experiment period.

## 4. Results and Discussion

### 4.1. Velocity Field Simulations

The velocity field inside the microchannels was simulated for three different flow rate settings in the main channel. In all simulations the flow rates in the two side channels were kept at 5 nL min$^{-1}$ and the low, moderate and high flow rates in the main channel were set to 25 nL min$^{-1}$, 50 nL min$^{-1}$, and 100 nL min$^{-1}$, respectively. Laminar flow boundary conditions were applied for the inlet nodes. The outlet nodes were set to pressure, no viscous stress ($p_0 = 0$ Pa) boundary conditions. Results of the simulations are shown in Figure 2. It can be seen that in all three flow rate settings a portion of the flow in the main channel was diverged into the V-shaped pockets and created a jet flow at the confinement openings. Streamlines of the flow denote that floating cells will be dragged into the traps at high flow velocities and kept at the bottom of the confinement openings as long as the high flow rate conditions are maintained in the main channel. The velocity field reached its maximum at the confinement openings of the two first traps and decreased while moving downstream the channels due to the flow escape to the side channels according to the laws of physics. In the actual experiments the trapped cells blocked the confinement openings and the high-velocity zone shifted alongside the channels.

### 4.2. Cell Loading Efficiency

One of the main advantages of our device is that for the cell-loading there is no need for precise control on the flow rates. As the cells are sucked into the pockets based on the pressure difference between the two sides of the confinement openings, the only requirement is to fill the side channels with YNB to avoid bubble formation and then infuse the cells into the main channel with fast pulses of the syringe pump. The loading process takes less than 30 s, and we wait for 5 min to allow the system to return to its equilibrium before starting the experiments. The pockets were designed to accommodate a single layer of up to six yeast cells with the average diameter of 4 μm. Cells were collected at an OD of 0.6 and were diluted to different concentrations to decide the final cell densities. To investigate the single-cell trapping efficiency, freshly harvested Hsp104-GFP cells were loaded into the device with the final OD of 0.1. We observed that at this cell concentration single yeast cells occupied close to 60% (±3%) of the pockets (Figure 3a,b). We also observed that cell concentrations higher than OD = 0.1 will lead to multiple cells inside the pockets. For concentrations lower than OD = 0.1 the cell loading turned out not to be successful. To employ the full capacity of the system we optimized the cell density to have an OD of 0.3 and infused the cells into the device. We managed to successfully fill 80% (±4%) of the pockets with one to six yeast cells without clogging the main channel (Figure 3a,c). We did not detect any significant differences in cell trapping efficiency for cell densities higher than OD = 0.3. Infusing the device with the initial cell concentration (OD = 0.6) resulted in cell clogging in the main channel.

## 4.3. Effect of Flow Rate Modulation on Arsenite Uptake in Yeast

We conducted several experiments with GFP tagged *HSP104* yeast cells to follow the redistribution of Hsp104-GFP in the cytosol upon the exposure to sodium arsenite.

For accurately imaging of the trapping zone, the height of the device was tailored precisely to accommodate a single layer of cells inside the traps. By preventing the cells from stacking on top of each other a clear single-cell signal could be read from the trapped cells. With the engineered dimensions of the traps, cells with a diameter larger than 3 μm got trapped in the trapping zone while smaller buds were guided to the waste chambers of the system. Prior to the experiments the plasma treated devices were primed with YNB and mounted on the microscope stage.

**Figure 2.** Simulation results for the velocity field under the three different main flow rate conditions. The side flow rates in all cases were kept at 5 nL·min$^{-1}$. Jet flows were formed at the bottom of the flow nozzles. The flow velocity reached its maximum at the bottom of trap 1 and trap 2 and decreases along the channel due to the partial leakage of the flow to the side channels. Streamlines of the velocity field show the portion of the flow diverged from the main channel to the side channels. (**a**) The flow rate in the main channel was 25 nL min$^{-1}$ and the maximum flow velocity was 8.2 mm/s; (**b**) the flow rate in the main channel was 50 nL min$^{-1}$ and the maximum flow velocity was 16.4 mm/s; and (**c**) the flow rate in the main channel was 100 nL·min$^{-1}$ and the maximum flow velocity was 32.5 mm/s.

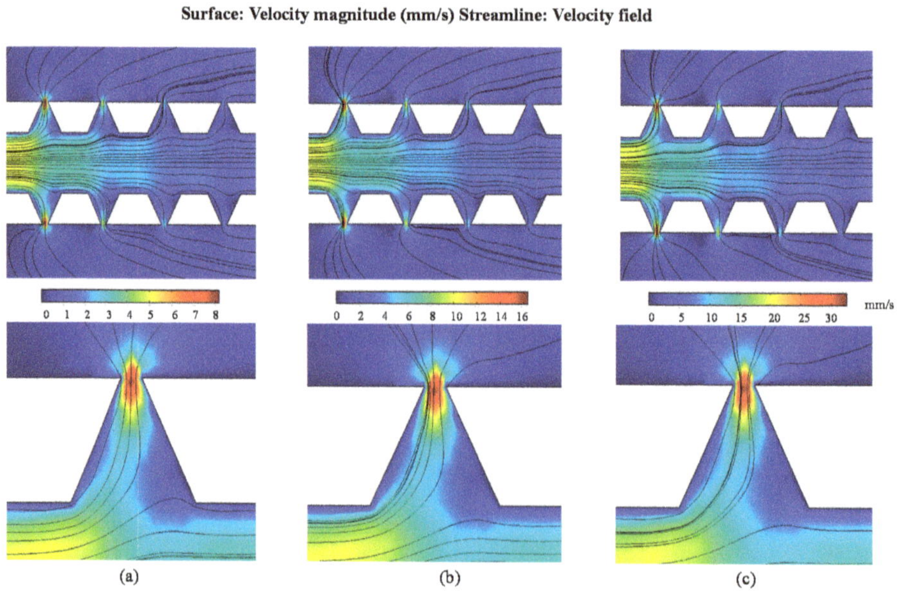

Surface: Velocity magnitude (mm/s) Streamline: Velocity field

(a)   (b)   (c)

**Figure 3.** Trapping efficiency in cellcomb microfluidic system. (**a**) Percentage of occupied pockets with two experimentally adjusted cell concentrations. Results indicate that by changing the cell density from OD = 0.1 to OD = 0.3, trapping efficiency increases significantly; (**b**) at lower cell density (OD = 0.1) single cells occupy 60% of the traps; and (**c**) in higher cell concentration (OD = 0.3) multiple cells are trapped in *ca.* 80% of the pockets. Scale bar is 10 μm.

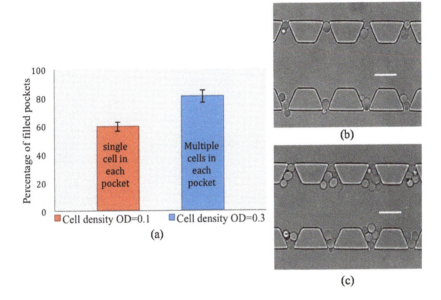

The prepared cell syringes were connected to the inlets "b" and "c" and cells were loaded into the device by several fast pulses of the syringe pumps. As control, we first monitored the cells under the normal condition while YNB was flowed over the trapped cells for 45 min. YNB was infused from inlet "a" in the main channel and the trapping area was scanned and imaged as described earlier. Our data showed no Hsp104-GFP redistribution (aggregate formation) under this experiment condition. To investigate the effect of different arsenite flow rates on the single yeast cells we defined a scenario where we performed separate experiments in separate microfluidic devices. We modulated the stimulus flow rates in the main channel from 100 to 50 nL min$^{-1}$ and 25 nL min$^{-1}$ as high, moderate, and low flow rates, respectively. In each case, the cells were exposed to the final concentration of 0.5 mM sodium arsenite. Interestingly, we found that both the time of aggregate formation and the number of aggregates in the studied cells were affected by the change of the flow rates. Our data clearly showed that when the flow rate was decreased from 100 to 25 nL min$^{-1}$ Hsp104-GFP aggregates appeared earlier and the total number of induced aggregates increased significantly. The uptake of arsenite in the presence of glucose into the yeast cells is mediated by a plasma membrane protein, Fps1 [36]. Fps1 is an aquaglyceroporin and facilitates passive diffusion of arsenite down the concentration gradient into the yeast cells [37,38]. Therefore, it is expected that arsenite passive diffusion occurs more efficiently in the condition of lower flow rate in which cells are in closer and longer contact with the arsenite molecules. Figure 4 demonstrates the comparison of the mean number of aggregates per cell for the three different arsenite flow rates. The values were obtained by averaging the total number of aggregates over the total number of trapped viable cells. Total numbers of aggregates were counted separately in all occupied segments of the device for both the first and last time points. As described earlier in microfluidic system operation, images from subsequent trapping segments were acquired in 30 s time intervals from the adjacent segments. Each imaging time point we have referred to, consisted of images for all occupied segments during one whole scanning of the trapping zone. For example the data shown for the 25 nL min$^{-1}$ arsenite flow rate was obtained for 12 occupied segments, thus, the first time-point cluster included images taken at time points $t = 0$–5.5 min. The final time-point cluster included images at time points $t = 38$–44 min. The ratios are shown for the first and the final time-point clusters of each experiment (Figure 4).

**Figure 4.** Effect of the flow rate modulation on arsenite uptake by yeast cells in the microfluidic system. Three different flow rates of 25, 50 and 100 nL min$^{-1}$ were investigated. To determine the arsenite exposure effect on relocalization of the Hsp 104-GFP protein and for the sake of comparison "number of aggregates per cell" measure was calculated in the three different cases. The number of aggregates/cell values in the first imaging time-point cluster (when the arsenite treatment is initiated) are 0.06, 0.04 and 0.035 while these values in the last imaging time-point cluster increase to 2.13, 1.24 and 0.45 for the 25, 50 and 100 nL·min$^{-1}$ flow rates, respectively (44 min of arsenite treatment).

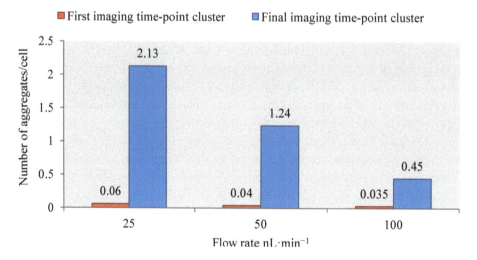

Localization of Hsp104-GFP is demonstrated in one field of view of the device under the 25 nL min$^{-1}$ flow rate condition. As seen in Figure 5, the number of aggregates increased during the experiment time.

In order to show the stochasticity in the behavior of the individual cells we used software, "Tableau" (Tableau Software Inc., Seattle, WA, USA) to plot the single-cell data. We chose the data from the experiment with the 25 nL min$^{-1}$ arsenite flow rate where we got the maximum number of aggregates in the cells. Total number of viable trapped cells was 312 at the beginning of the experiment and 334 at the final time point (new buds were considered in cell counting). We demonstrated the single-cell data for three time-point clusters of the experiment with the most significant changes observed:

The initial time-point cluster (time points $t = 0$–5.5 min), the middle time-point cluster (time points $t = 19$–24.5 min), and the final time-point cluster (time points $t = 38$–44 min).

**Figure 5.** Trapped cells were exposed to the 25 nL min$^{-1}$ flow rate of arsenite. (**a**) Bright field microscope image of one trapping segment; (**b**) first fluorescence image of the segment at the treatment initiation at $t = 60$ s; images (**c–f**) were taken from the same field of view at different time points with 6-minute time intervals; image (**f**) was the last image taken at the final time point. The increase in the number of aggregates is clearly shown in the image sequence. The image sequence at the bottom from the same image series (**b–f**) shows the aggregate formation for the cells trapped in one of the pockets [pocket in image (**a**) inside the white rectangle].

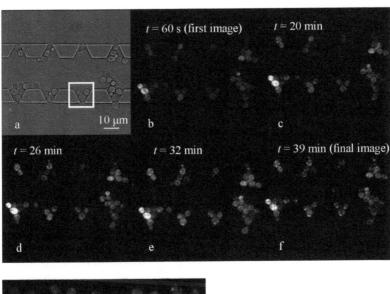

Results are illustrated in Figure 6, with the three time-point clusters being separated by solid black lines. Data is shown for all 12 occupied segments of the device. To increase the readability of the data, individual cells are grouped together based on the number of aggregates. The color bars in the figure denote the percentage out of all trapped cells in each segment having a certain number of aggregates. Monitoring the cellular responses in time revealed that the formation of aggregates in individual cells followed a totally random pattern with some of the cells being disturbed drastically while other groups showing a trivial affection or not responding to the treatment at all. Data also clearly showed an increasing trend in the number of aggregates with time.

**Figure 6.** Single-cell responses to the arsenite stress under the 25 nL min$^{-1}$ flow rate condition. Results represent the formation of Hsp 104-GFP aggregates in individual cells in three significant time-point clusters during the experiment. The time-point clusters (**a–c**) are separated by black solid lines. A clear increase in the number of aggregates under the influence of the treatment was observed in exposed cells. The color code designates the number of aggregates per cell. Color bars in the figure denote the percentage out of all trapped cells in each segment having a certain number of aggregates. For instance, in segment 3, cluster (**a**), around 8% of the cells have one, 5% have two and the rest show no aggregates. In cluster (**b**) these values increase to 10.3% of the cells with one, 8% with two, 2.6% with four and the rest with zero aggregates. Number of aggregates per cells in cluster (**c**) climbs up to 24.4% with one, 17% with two, 17% with three, 14.6% with four, 2.5% with five, 5% with six, and the rest with no aggregates.

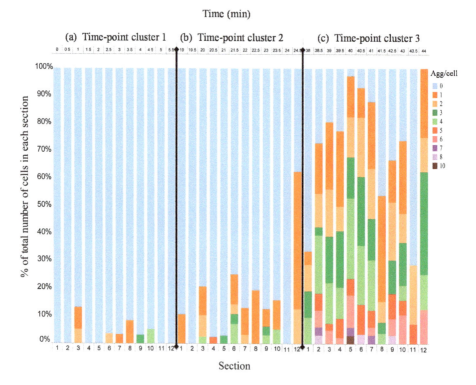

## 4.4. Discussion

The microfluidic platform that we presented in this work was employed to obtain high quality quantitative data on the single cell basis. The special design of the device allowed for trapping hundreds of cells inside V-shaped pockets that were fully covered and exposed to selected stress substances. The flow behavior inside the microchannels was simulated to ensure the predicted functionality of the device, especially to discover the direction of the flow at the confinement openings of the trapping zone. Simulation results indicated that a jet flow was created at the 2-μm wide confinement openings of the device, which could act as the force to trap and immobilize the cells inside the pockets. We showed, as an example, that how the arsenite flow rate modulation could affect the substance uptake by yeast cells. We monitored the relocalization of GFP-tagged Hsp104 protein in individual yeast cells upon continuous exposure to sodium arsenite. Intracellular responses were followed by means of bright field and fluorescence time-lapse microscopy. The data revealed that the arsenite uptake increased noticeably at lower flow rates of the stimulus. This can be attributed to a more efficient passive diffusion of arsenite molecules due to the closer and longer contact with the cells. The experiment time was set to 45 min in this case as the clear effect of the arsenite on Hsp104-GFP aggregate formation was observed in this time period. However the system can be used to conduct long-term experiments for hours or days depending on the specific requirements of the study. It is also worth mentioning that the automatic flow rate control, image acquisition, and microscope stage drive provides a sustainable experimental platform, which is robust, easy to use, and flexible for different experimental conditions. The 60 μm-wide side channels were mainly intended for creating the low-pressure region in the device to drag the floating cells into the traps. Buds smaller than the size of the confinement openings passed to the side channels and were guided to the waste chambers of the device. Additionally, the platform can be used for studying cell-to-cell communication events, thanks to the special design of the device. The two side channels can be employed to reach the trapped cells from the confinement openings and locally expose the cells to the selected stimuli. This way it will be possible to follow the intercellular signaling amongst the cell clusters sitting tightly together.

The device was sensitive to the flow rates in the side channels and flow variations were automatically controlled to maintain the symmetrical behavior of the device. The main advantage of the device for the cell-loading step is that no precise flow rate control is needed. Cells can be infused into the channels by rapid pulses of the syringe pump in less than 30 s. However the density of the cell suspension had to be controlled carefully as it played a major role in the cell-loading step. In order to capture single yeast cells in each pocket we diluted the cell suspension with the initial OD of 0.6, 6 times and infused the device. At this concentration, single cells occupied nearly 60% (±3%) of the pockets. To achieve the full trapping capacity of the device we increased the cell density and managed to successfully fill *ca.* 80% (±4%) of the traps with one to six cells without blocking the main channel at the OD = 0.3. High cell densities (OD > 0.6) blocked the 20-μm-wide mid-channel of the device and a huge mass of cells could be flushed out of the channel with difficulty. The empty trapping sites were found at the downstream of the device. Cells tended to pass the pockets and continue with the flow towards the outlets. We attribute this phenomenon to the pressure drop along the main channel, which leads to the change in the behavior of the flow inside the V-shaped pockets and results in a decreased fraction of the flow passing through the traps. Prior to the experiments or to reuse the system, microchannels were flushed and rinsed with buffer solution or YNB via the side channels. Rapid flushing pulses in the side channels effectively removed the dirt and bubbles in all channels. The height of the system was adjusted to be in the order of the average diameter of a single yeast cell. This feature of the device was of a great significance since it prevented the trapped cells from assembling on top of each other and a clear fluorescent read out signal could be detected from a single layer of cells.

## 5. Conclusions

Here, we present an application-specific microfluidic platform, cellcomb, for high-throughput single-cell applications. The device is intended for cell capturing, chemical exposure and time-lapse imaging. Cell capturing mechanism is based on hydrodynamic forces imposed on suspended cells inside the microchannels, resulting in cell immobilization in the tailored trapping zone of the device. The trapping zone consists of 104 V-shaped pockets with the dimensions of 10 μm × 10 μm and confinement openings with the width of 2 μm. The pockets are designed to accommodate up to six yeast cells with the average diameter of 4 μm. In a fully operational device, 624 cells can be trapped and undergo various extracellular environmental changes and chemical exposures. Dynamic cellular responses, such as specific reporter protein migrations or aggregations, can be followed over time by bright field and fluorescence microscopy imaging. Compared to previous designs, our new platform allows for conducting single-cell experiments with noticeably increased number of cells, providing valuable statistical data with a high spatiotemporal resolution. We have exploited the power of this system to investigate the effect of flow rate modulations on arsenite uptake in *Saccharomyces cerevisiae* cells. By experimentally optimizing the flow rates we demonstrated that arsenite uptake by the cells increased significantly as we lowered the flow rate from 100 to 25 nL min$^{-1}$. We foresee that this robust, easy-to-operate, and flexible platform will be used for several applications. Cell signaling pathways are particularly of a great interest and this device can provide the opportunity of experimentally studying their modes of function and regulation. Intercellular communication events are also considered a suitable target area where our system can offer a great deal of opportunities. Another point of strength is that the device is adaptable for different cell types and can be employed, for instance, to run experiments with mammalian cells. From the initial tests with NIH/3T3 cells we expect that the device can be used for long-term on-chip cell proliferation under the controlled gas and temperature conditions. Subsequent investigations, such as drug screening in cancer cells or studying signaling pathways can be performed accordingly.

## Acknowledgments

Authors acknowledge the financial support from Swedish Research Council (VR), Carl Trygger foundation for Scientific Research and the European Commission program UNICELLSYS.

We would like to acknowledge Markus J. Tamás, Stefan Hohmann and Peter Dahl for kindly providing the yeast cell strain. We thank Fraunhofer Chalmers Research Center Industrial Mathematics (Gothenburg, Sweden) for the Cellstat software. We also thank Martin Adiels (Mathematical Sciences, Chalmers University of Technology, Gothenburg, Sweden) for the precious assistance with organizing and demonstration of single-cell data in "Tableau" software.

## Conflicts of Interest

The authors declare no conflict of interest.

## References

1   Figeys, D.; Pinto, D. Lab-on-a-chip: A revolution in biological and medical sciences. *Anal. Chem.* **2000**, *72*, 330A–335A.
2   Haeberle, S.; Zengerle, R. Microfluidic platforms for lab-on-a-chip applications. *Lab Chip* **2007**, *7*, 1094–1110.
3   Squires, T.M.; Quake, S.R. Microfluidics: Fluid physics at the nanoliter scale. *Rev. Mod. Phys.* **2005**, *77*, 977–1026.
4   Elowitz, M.B.; Levine, A.J.; Siggia, E.D.; Swain, P.S. Stochastic gene expression in a single cell. *Sci. Signal.* **2002**, *297*, 1183–1186.
5   Kærn, M.; Elston, T.C.; Blake, W.J.; Collins, J.J. Stochasticity in gene expression: From theories to phenotypes. *Nat. Rev. Genet.* **2005**, *6*, 451–464.
6   Burnette, W.N. "Western blotting": Electrophoretic transfer of proteins from sodium dodecyl sulfate-polyacrylamide gels to unmodified nitrocellulose and radiographic detection with antibody and radioiodinated protein a. *Anal. Biochem.* **1981**, *112*, 195–203.
7   Dorak, M.T. *Real-Time PCR*; Taylor & Francis: New York, NY, USA, 2006.
8   Svahn, H.A.; van den Berg, A. Single cells or large populations? *Lab Chip* **2007**, *7*, 544–546.
9   Breslauer, D.N.; Lee, P.J.; Lee, L.P. Microfluidics-based systems biology. *Mol. Biosyst.* **2006**, *2*, 97–112.
10  Muzzey, D.; van Oudenaarden, A. Quantitative time-lapse fluorescence microscopy in single cells. *Ann. Rev. Cell Dev. Biol.* **2009**, *25*, 301–327.
11  Jen, C.-P.; Hsiao, J.-H.; Maslov, N.A. Single-cell chemical lysis on microfluidic chips with arrays of microwells. *Sensors* **2011**, *12*, 347–358.
12  Rettig, J.R.; Folch, A. Large-scale single-cell trapping and imaging using microwell arrays. *Anal. Chem.* **2005**, *77*, 5628–5634.
13  Yamamura, S.; Kishi, H.; Tokimitsu, Y.; Kondo, S.; Honda, R.; Rao, S.R.; Omori, M.; Tamiya, E.; Muraguchi, A. Single-cell microarray for analyzing cellular response. *Anal. Chem.* **2005**, *77*, 8050–8056.
14  Irimia, D.; Toner, M. Cell handling using microstructured membranes. *Lab Chip* **2006**, *6*, 345–352.
15  Wheeler, A.R.; Throndset, W.R.; Whelan, R.J.; Leach, A.M.; Zare, R.N.; Liao, Y.H.; Farrell, K.; Manger, I.D.; Daridon, A. Microfluidic device for single-cell analysis. *Anal. Chem.* **2003**, *75*, 3581–3586.
16  Ashkin, A.; Dziedzic, J.; Yamane, T. Optical trapping and manipulation of single cells using infrared laser beams. *Nature* **1987**, *330*, 769–771.
17  Eriksson, E.; Scrimgeour, J.; Graneli, A.; Ramser, K.; Wellander, R.; Enger, J.; Hanstorp, D.; Goksör, M. Optical manipulation and microfluidics for studies of single cell dynamics. *J. Opt. A Pure Appl. Opt.* **2007**, *9*, S113, doi:10.1088/1464-4258/9/8/S02.

18  Ramser, K.; Hanstorp, D. Optical manipulation for single-cell studies. *J. Biophotonics* **2010**, *3*, 187–206.

19  Taff, B.M.; Voldman, J. A scalable addressable positive-dielectrophoretic cell-sorting array. *Anal. Chem.* **2005**, *77*, 7976–7983.

20  Gascoyne, P.; Mahidol, C.; Ruchirawat, M.; Satayavivad, J.; Watcharasit, P.; Becker, F.F. Microsample preparation by dielectrophoresis: Isolation of malaria. *Lab Chip* **2002**, *2*, 70–75.

21  Gagnon, Z.R. Cellular dielectrophoresis: Applications to the characterization, manipulation, separation and patterning of cells. *Electrophoresis* **2011**, *32*, 2466–2487.

22  Falconnet, D.; Csucs, G.; Michelle Grandin, H.; Textor, M. Surface engineering approaches to micropattern surfaces for cell-based assays. *Biomaterials* **2006**, *27*, 3044–3063.

23  Lim, J.Y.; Donahue, H.J. Cell sensing and response to micro-and nanostructured surfaces produced by chemical and topographic patterning. *Tissue Eng.* **2007**, *13*, 1879–1891.

24  Di Carlo, D.; Wu, L.Y.; Lee, L.P. Dynamic single cell culture array. *Lab Chip* **2006**, *6*, 1445–1449.

25  Zhu, Z.; Frey, O.; Ottoz, D.S.; Rudolf, F.; Hierlemann, A. Microfluidic single-cell cultivation chip with controllable immobilization and selective release of yeast cells. *Lab Chip* **2012**, *12*, 906–915.

26  Van den Brink, F.T.; Gool, E.; Frimat, J.P.; Bomer, J.; van den Berg, A.; le Gac, S. Parallel single-cell analysis microfluidic platform. *Electrophoresis* **2011**, *32*, 3094–3100.

27  Tan, W.-H.; Takeuchi, S. A trap-and-release integrated microfluidic system for dynamic microarray applications. *Proc. Natl. Acad. Sci. USA* **2007**, *104*, 1146–1151.

28  Kobel, S.; Valero, A.; Latt, J.; Renaud, P.; Lutolf, M. Optimization of microfluidic single cell trapping for long-term on-chip culture. *Lab Chip* **2010**, *10*, 857–863.

29  Chung, K.; Rivet, C.A.; Kemp, M.L.; Lu, H. Imaging single-cell signaling dynamics with a deterministic high-density single-cell trap array. *Anal. Chem.* **2011**, *83*, 7044–7052.

30  Eriksson, E.; Enger, J.; Nordlander, B.; Erjavec, N.; Ramser, K.; Goksör, M.; Hohmann, S.; Nyström, T.; Hanstorp, D. A microfluidic system in combination with optical tweezers for analyzing rapid and reversible cytological alterations in single cells upon environmental changes. *Lab Chip* **2006**, *7*, 71–76.

31  Eriksson, E.; Sott, K.; Lundqvist, F.; Sveningsson, M.; Scrimgeour, J.; Hanstorp, D.; Goksör, M.; Granéli, A. A microfluidic device for reversible environmental changes around single cells using optical tweezers for cell selection and positioning. *Lab Chip* **2010**, *10*, 617–625.

32  Jacobson, T.; Navarrete, C.; Sharma, S.K.; Sideri, T.C.; Ibstedt, S.; Priya, S.; Grant, C.M.; Christen, P.; Goloubinoff, P.; Tamás, M.J. Arsenite interferes with protein folding and triggers formation of protein aggregates in yeast. *J. Cell Sci.* **2012**, *125*, 5073–5083.

33  Tan, S.H.; Nguyen, N.-T.; Chua, Y.C.; Kang, T.G. Oxygen plasma treatment for reducing hydrophobicity of a sealed polydimethylsiloxane microchannel. *Biomicrofluidics* **2010**, *4*, 32204, doi:10.1063/1.3466882.

34  Sott, K.; Eriksson, E.; Goksör, M. Acquisition of Single Cell Data in an Optical Microscope. In *Lab on a Chip Technology: Biomolecular Separation and Analysis*; Caister Academic Press: Norfolk, UK, 2009; pp. 151–166.

35  Smedh, M.; Beck, C.; Sott, K.; Goksör, M. Cellstress-Open Source Image Analysis Program for Single-Cell Analysis. In Proceedings of SPIE 7762, Optical Trapping and Optical Micromanipulation VII, 77622N, San Diego, CA, USA, 27 August 2010; International Society for Optics and Photonics: Bellingham, WA, USA, 2010; doi:10.1117/12.860403.

36  Wysocki, R.; Chéry, C.C.; Wawrzycka, D.; van Hulle, M.; Cornelis, R.; Thevelein, J.M.; Tamás, M.J. The glycerol channel fps1p mediates the uptake of arsenite and antimonite in *Saccharomyces cerevisiae*. *Mol. Microbiol.* **2001**, *40*, 1391–1401.

37  Tamás, M.J.; Karlgren, S.; Bill, R.M.; Hedfalk, K.; Allegri, L.; Ferreira, M.; Thevelein, J.M.; Rydström, J.; Mullins, J.G.; Hohmann, S. A short regulatory domain restricts glycerol transport through yeast fps1p. *J. Biol. Chem.* **2003**, *278*, 6337–6345.

38  Maciaszczyk-Dziubinska, E.; Migdal, I.; Migocka, M.; Bocer, T.; Wysocki, R. The yeast aquaglyceroporin Fps1p is a bidirectional arsenite channel. *FEBS Lett.* **2010**, *584*, 726–732.

# Ultrasound-Induced Cell–Cell Interaction Studies in a Multi-Well Microplate

**Martin Wiklund, Athanasia E. Christakou, Mathias Ohlin, Ida Iranmanesh, Thomas Frisk, Bruno Vanherberghen and Björn Önfelt**

**Abstract:** This review describes the use of ultrasound for inducing and retaining cell-cell contact in multi-well microplates combined with live-cell fluorescence microscopy. This platform has been used for studying the interaction between natural killer (NK) cells and cancer cells at the level of individual cells. The review includes basic principles of ultrasonic particle manipulation, design criteria when building a multi-well microplate device for this purpose, biocompatibility aspects, and finally, two examples of biological applications: Dynamic imaging of the inhibitory immune synapse, and studies of the heterogeneity in killing dynamics of NK cells interacting with cancer cells.

Reprinted from *Micromachines*. Cite as: Wiklund, M.; Christakou, A.E.; Ohlin, M.; Iranmanesh, I.; Frisk, T.; Vanherberghen, B.; Önfelt, B. Ultrasound-Induced Cell–Cell Interaction Studies in a Multi-Well Microplate. *Micromachines* **2014**, *5*, 27-49.

## 1. Introduction

Dynamic studies of single cells are important for our understanding of cell function and behavior [1]. Cells are complex biological systems that respond to different kinds of stimuli over time periods ranging from fractions of a second [2] to several days [3]. Even if the stimulus is kept constant in a certain measurement, the cellular response may vary over time and from cell to cell [4]. In standard bulk-based assays, such variations are not resolved since the measured parameter is typically the average signal from many cells [1]. Thus, there is a need for screening methods where an individual cell's properties are measured. One such established and very efficient screening method is flow cytometry, or fluorescence-activated cell sorting (FACS) [5]. This method is based on a serial screening where fluorescence and/or scattered light are measured from individual cells at high throughputs. However, flow cytometry in its standard format is not compatible with dynamic monitoring, and therefore, only instantaneous cell properties are measured. On the contrary, live-cell fluorescence microscopy is a suitable tool for measuring dynamic cell properties [6]. Today, many different fluorescent probes exist for monitoring a variety of cellular functions, processes and status. Examples include live/dead assays, cell cycle assays and metabolic assays [7]. However, in order to combine both dynamic and single-cell monitoring, a tool for keeping track of each cell over time is needed. For this purpose, multi-well microplates can be used. In general, microplates have long been used in many different types of assays (e.g., in enzyme-linked immunosorbent assays (ELISAs)) [8]. However, in this review we focus on the use of microplates for live-cell microscopy imaging of individual cells [9].

When studying single cells in multi-well microplates, there are two different strategies that can be employed. One strategy is to dispense one cell per well for keeping track of each individual property of each single cell. This method has been used for e.g., single-cell culture and proliferation studies [10]. An alternative strategy is to dispense several cells per well and then to study individual interactions between two or more cells. This has been used for studying interaction between natural killer cells and different types and numbers of target cells [9,11–14], and also for migration studies [15].

Although microplates combined with live-cell fluorescence microscopy is a powerful tool for parallel and dynamic single-cell studies, it is still problematic when studying cell-cell interactions. The reason is that the time to cell–cell contact may vary depending on cell type, environment and microplate design [11]. In addition, there is a stochastic distribution in time to contact between different wells. This puts very high requirements on the imaging system and data analysis. Furthermore, it may also be of interest to study the effects of forced interaction and compare with spontaneous interaction. For these reasons, we have during the last few years developed and implemented ultrasonic particle manipulation technology into a microplate device designed for high-resolution live-cell fluorescence microscopy [16–18]. In this review, we summarize our work on the use of ultrasound as a tool for inducing and retaining cell–cell contacts in such multi-well microplates. The review discusses basic principles of ultrasonic manipulation technology and design criteria for such microdevices (Section 2), how to design a biocompatible manipulation system (Section 3), and finally an example of a biological application of the platform where the interaction between natural killer (NK) cells and cancer cells are studied (Section 4).

## 2. Method and Device

### 2.1. Method: Ultrasonic Manipulation of Cells

Ultrasonic manipulation of suspended particles is based on the time-averaged acoustic radiation force. This forces origins from a non-linear effect in the acoustic pressure field and was first described by Lord Rayleigh [19] and later nicely summarized in a review paper by Beyer [20]. In 1962, a very useful theoretical model was presented by Gor'kov [21]. This model is valid for arbitrary sound fields and a single, spherical particle with known material properties. Gor'kov's generalized equation can be rewritten into the acoustic radiation force, $\mathbf{F}$, dependent on the sound field, $p$ and material properties [22]:

$$\mathbf{F}(p) = -\frac{V_p \beta_f}{4} \nabla \left( f_1 p^2 - \frac{3}{2k^2} f_2 (\nabla p)^2 \right) \tag{1a}$$

with

$$f_1 = 1 - \frac{\beta_p}{\beta_f} \quad \text{and} \quad f_2 = 2\frac{(\rho_p - \rho_f)}{2\rho_p + \rho_f} \tag{1b}$$

here, $p$ is the acoustic pressure amplitude, $V_p$ is the volume of the particle, $\beta = 1/(\rho c^2)$ is the compressibility (defined by the density, $\rho$, and the sound speed, $c$), $k = \omega/c$ is the wave number, and $f_1$ and $f_2$ are the acoustic contrast factors defined by the compressibility $\beta$ and the density $\rho$. The index "f" denotes "fluid" and the index "p" denotes "particle". From the equation, we conclude that the radiation force drives suspended particles in a direction parallel with the gradient of the acoustic field and has a direction and magnitude defined by the contrast factors $f_1$ and $f_2$. The magnitude is also dependent on the particle volume, $V_p$, and sound frequency (via $k = \omega/c$). Since steeper field gradients result in stronger forces, standing-wave fields are most often utilized. In a standing-wave field, the radiation force drives most suspended particles either to the pressure nodes or the pressure anti-nodes, depending on the signs of the contrast factors $f_1$ and $f_2$. In principle, particles stiffer than the suspension medium are driven to the pressure nodes (defined by the first term in Equation (1a)), while particles denser than the suspension medium are driven to the velocity antinodes (defined by the second term in Equation (1a)). In simple standing-wave fields (such as a one-dimensional field), the pressure nodes and the velocity antinodes are co-located. Although the standing-wave field in the multi-well plate is of more complex type, experimental observations confirm that the cells used in our work are driven to the positions of the numerically calculated pressure nodes [16].

When several particles are driven to a pressure node, they tend to aggregate in tight clusters. In one-dimensional (1D) standing-wave fields, the clusters typically take the form of flat monolayers in the pressure nodal planes. The reason for this is the particle-particle interaction force, sometimes called the Bjerknes force [23]. However, in 2D or 3D standing-wave fields, the cluster shapes are more complicated to predict or control [24].

The theoretical model above (Equation (1)) is valid for spherical particles with well-known material properties (density and compressibility) suspended in an inviscid fluid. However, the method reviewed in this paper is designed for cell applications. Generally, cells have unknown material properties, or if known, their material properties have a wider distribution than for synthetic particles (e.g., polystyrene). In addition, the material properties of cells are also dependent on many external and internal factors. Altogether, this makes it difficult to predict the contrast factors $f_1$ and $f_2$ for cells. Nevertheless, attempts have been made to estimate the contrast factors and corresponding radiation forces acting on different cell types. For example, Barnkob et al. [25] used two types of particles (polystyrene and melamine resin) for calibrating the radiation forces from a known acoustic field, and used this data for measuring the contrast factors for two different cell types: White blood cells and DU145 prostate cancer cells. They concluded that the radiation force was about one order of magnitude smaller for these cells, relative polystyrene particles of equal size. A similar approach was carried out by Hartono et al. [26], who concluded that the radiation force was 1.5 times smaller for red blood cells, and between 2 and 4 times smaller for different types of cancer cells relative to the force on equally sized polystyrene. Furthermore, Mishra et al. [27] concluded from numerical modeling that for biological cells, the radiation force was less dependent on shape but more dependent on internal structures and inhomogeneity. For example, the force on a cell with nucleus was predicted to be approx. twice the force of a non-nucleated cell of similar size. In summary, we may expect the acoustic radiation force in a given acoustic field to be roughly a few times smaller for cells than for polystyrene particles of similar size, and that the corresponding trapping time is expected to be a few times longer.

*2.2. Device: Ultrasonic Manipulation in a Multi-Well Micro-Plate*

For the design of the multi-well microplate used for ultrasonic cell manipulation, the following criteria have been prioritized [12]: The microplate should be compatible with high-resolution optical microscopy, and it should be biocompatible allowing long-term cellular assays. In addition, it should also be easy to use by a non-technically skilled operator. An illustration of the microplate fabrication process is shown in Figure 1. A complete description of the fabrication process is given in Ref. [12]. In summary, silicon wafers with diameter 100 mm and thickness 300 μm (Figure 1a) were used for processing of nine individual microplates per wafer, where each final microplate is 22 × 22 mm$^2$ (Figure 1h). Each microplate has 10 × 10 wells, where each well is 300 μm deep and with horizontal cross section 300 × 300 μm$^2$, or 350 × 350 μm$^2$, and with 100 μm wall thickness between individual wells. After spinning photo resist on the silicon wafer (Figure 1b) and defining the well geometry by lithography (Figure 1c), the wells were etched through the 300 μm silicon layer by deep reactive-ion etching (DRIE) (Figure 1d). Care was taken to optimize the process so that the wells had a constant cross section through the depth of the silicon layer. This was confirmed by scanning electron microscopy (SEM) after the etching process and with a silicon layer that was diced across the wells [12]. Following the deep-etching of the wells and stripping of the photo resist and oxide mask (Figure 1e), the silicon wafers were furnace wet-oxidized to a surface oxide thickness of approx. 200 nm (Figure 1f). This important step was performed for improving the biocompatibility [12], and also for enabling cleaning and re-usage of the microplates. Finally, a 175 μm thick borosilicate glass layer was anodically bonded to each processed silicon layer (Figure 1g), and the silicon-glass stack was diced into square-shaped microplates (Figure 1h).

Two different designs have been used for the ultrasonic actuation system for the microplates. The original design [16,18] used a wedge-transducer [22,28] (Figure 2a). In the upgraded version of the ultrasonic actuation system, the wedge transducer was replaced by a ring transducer, which was fully integrated into the microplate holder [17] (Figure 2b). This device is more robust and simple to use, but requires higher driving voltages. The wedge-transducer device (Figure 2a) consists of an ultrasonic transducer made by a piezoceramic plate (1) and a titanium wedge (2). The transducer is positioned on top of the multi-well microplate (5), and it is reversibly glued with a thin layer of water-soluble adhesive gel. The cell suspension sample is pipetted from above over the wells and stored within a rectangular frame made in PDMS (4), which can be closed by a glass cover slip (3) to minimize evaporation. The other device, the ring-transducer chip (Figure 2b), has the same general function including parts (3)–(5), but here the ultrasonic coupling is accomplished from below via a larger ring-shape piezoceramic plate (6). This design is more robust and reliable since it is not dependent on how the transducer is positioned relative to the chip. Furthermore, it is also more temperature-stable when driven at higher voltages (>20 Vpp) and therefore more suitable for applications requiring higher radiation forces, faster response times and long assay times (up to several days). Both designs shown in Figure 2a,b are relatively broadband, which is useful for the employed ultrasonic actuation method described below.

116

**Figure 1.** Schematic outline of the silicon-glass microplate fabrication process. (**a**) Oxidized silicon wafer, 100 mm in diameter, 300 μm thick; (**b**) Spin coating of wafer with positive photoresist; (**c**) Masked UV-exposure of photoresist layer; (**d**) Plasma etching of the oxidized silicon wafer; (**e**) Removal of photoresist and oxide mask; (**f**) Oxidation of the wafer after the strip of the photoresist and oxide mask; (**g**) The anodic bonding of the 175 μm thick glass bottom to the silicon "grid"; (**h**) Dicing to individual chips, 9 per wafer, where each final chip is 22 × 22 mm². Based on a figure in Ref. [12].

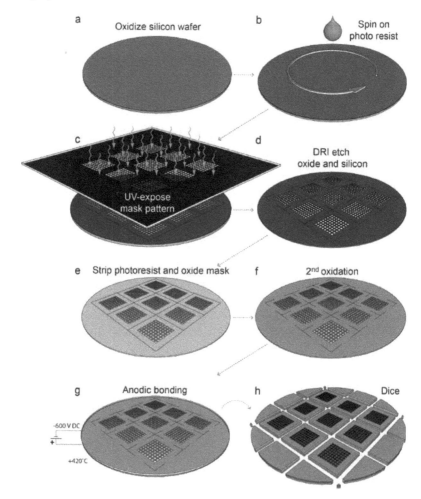

**Figure 2.** The two different designs of ultrasonic actuation system used for the multi-well microplate: The wedge-transducer device [18] (**a**) and the ring-transducer device [17] (**b**). (1) Piezoceramic plate; (2) Titanium wedge; (3) Glass lid; (4) PDMS frame; (5) Multi-well microplate; (6) Ring-shaped piezoceramic plate.

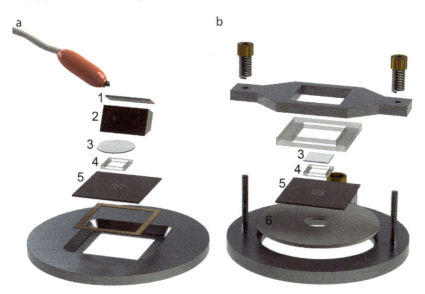

The purpose of the ultrasonic actuation in the multi-well microplate is to create an acoustic resonance in each well, so that suspended particles or cells are aggregated and positioned by the acoustic radiation force described by Equation (1). The trapping position is in most cases the pressure node of the standing wave formed in the fluid cavity (*i.e.*, the well) by the acoustic resonance. In a two-dimensional rectangular cavity with dimensions $L_x$ and $L_y$, the acoustic pressure, $p$, is described by [29]:

$$p(x,y,t) = p_0 \cos(k_x x)\cos(k_y y)\sin(\omega t) \tag{2a}$$

$$k_x = \frac{n_x \pi}{L_x}; \quad k_y = \frac{n_y \pi}{L_y} \tag{2b}$$

where $k_x$ and $k_y$ are the wavenumbers for each horizontal direction ($x$ and $y$) in the cavity, and $n_x$, $n_y$ = 0, 1, 2, 3, ..., are the numbers of half wavelengths along the $x$- and $y$-directions, respectively. Note that in Equation (2), we have neglected any (vertical) $z$-dependence of the pressure. In practice, this is valid for three-dimensional cavities having short $L_z$-dimensions (relative the acoustic wavelength). Given an acoustic resonance in the fluid cavity described by Equation (2), the resonance frequency of mode ($n_x$, $n_y$) is [29]:

$$f_{(n_x,n_y)} = \frac{c}{2\pi}\sqrt{k_x^2 + k_y^2} = \frac{c}{2\pi}\sqrt{\left(\frac{n_x \pi}{L_x}\right)^2 + \left(\frac{n_y \pi}{L_y}\right)^2} \tag{3}$$

where $c$ is the sound velocity in the fluid. If the purpose is to trap the particles in the center of each well, one should use the lowest possible resonance mode. The wells used in our multi-well microplate have square-shaped horizontal cross-sections (*cf.* Figures 1, 3 and 4). For a square-shaped cavity ($L_x = L_y$), the lowest possible mode is either the (1,0)-mode or the (0,1)-mode. According to Equation (3), these two modes have identical frequencies, and it is therefore not clear how the pressure field can be described at this frequency. However, due to differences in boundary conditions and properties/shapes of the supporting structures around the wells, the two modes are often slightly degenerated. Thus, for a given excitation frequency, only one of the two modes exists. In our multi-well microplate, where a complex acoustic interaction between all 100 wells occurs, the result is a pressure field inside each well having a node oriented as shown in the simulated pressure field in Figure 3a (and described more thoroughly in Ref. [16]). As seen from the simulation, the node of the half-wave resonance in each well is not a pure (1,0)- or (0,1)-mode, but rather something in between. If the excitation frequency is slightly changed, the node orientation changes (primarily it rotates). For this reason, a simple method for generating point-shaped pressure nodes in the center of each well is to quickly average a set of such single-frequency resonances. We have realized this by cycling linear frequency sweeps around the nominal (1,0)- or (0,1)-resonance frequency. The simulation result of this frequency modulation scheme is shown in Figure 3b. The simulated acoustic resonances in Figure 3a,b are experimentally confirmed using the wedge-transducer device in Figure 3c,d, respectively. Here, the pressure field is visualized by the shapes and positions of 5 μm polyamide particle aggregates driven to the pressure nodes by the acoustic radiation force. Experimentally, frequency modulation actuation is realized by sawtooth-modulation with a center frequency corresponding to the (1,0) or (0,1) resonance (which is around 2.5 MHz for a 300 × 300 μm² well) and a typical bandwidth of 100 kHz and a cycling rate of 1 kHz. This modulation function is very simple to implement since it is a built-in function in most signal generators. The modulation bandwidth is difficult to predict theoretically and needs instead to be optimized experimentally for each microplate device. The cycling rate is typically chosen as a rate being above the threshold for aggregate movement (*i.e.*, time for reconfiguration of the aggregate between different single- frequency resonances within the sweep). We have concluded that a rate of 1 kHz is well above this threshold. Finally, a similar experimental verification for the ring-transducer device is shown in Figure 4. Here, we used a microplate with well size 350 × 350 μm² actuated with center frequency 2.30 MHz and modulation bandwidth of 200 kHz. When using a lower concentration of 10 μm particles, it is clear from the experiments that particle trapping and aggregation work for both single-frequency actuation (blue aggregates) and frequency-modulation actuation (red aggregates). However, the accurate positioning of aggregates in the center of each well can only be accomplished by frequency-modulation actuation. In addition, frequency modulation also provides more compact aggregates [17].

A limiting factor for the trapping performance in any acoustophoretic device is acoustic streaming [30]. In the multi-well microplate, acoustic streaming causes the trapped particles or cells to be flushed away upwards if very high actuation voltages are used (approx. 100 Vpp or more) [17]. One reason for this streaming is that it is not an accurate approximation to model the wells in the microplate as 2D cavities (*cf.* Equations (2) and (3)). Thus, Equations (2) and (3) are useful for qualitative understanding of how resonances are built up in the system and for predicting trapping positions of cells, but for accurate quantitative modeling including acoustic streaming, a 3D model is needed. This is a challenge for future work. Still, it should be mentioned that the frequency-modulation methods tends to suppress acoustic streaming when comparing with single-frequency actuation [30,31]. Thus, for moderate actuation voltages using the frequency modulation method, acoustic streaming is not causing any problem for the trapping efficiency and trapping stability over time.

**Figure 3.** Comparison between modeling (**a,b**) and experiments (**c,d**) for the wedge-transducer device. Simulation of the time-averaged pressure squared ($p^2$) for single-frequency actuation at 2.60 MHz (**a**) and for the average of 50 single frequencies between 2.55 and 2.65 MHz (**b**). Both plots are normalized individually and shown in logarithmic scale. The predicted trapping locations (*i.e.*, the minima of $p^2$) are indicated in yellow (in **a**) and in dark blue (in **b**). Experimental confirmation of the simulations using 5 µm particles at single-frequency actuation (**c**) and with frequency-modulated actuation (**d**) using the same frequency intervals as (**a**) and (**b**). Scale bar is indicated by the wells (300 µm wide squares).The figure is reproduced from Ref. [16] with permission from RSC.

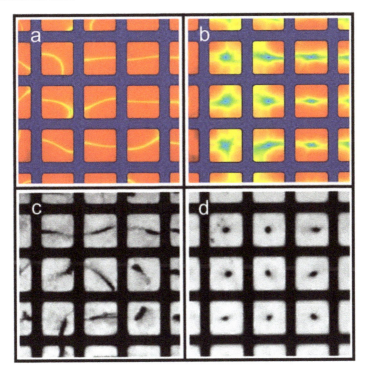

**Figure 4.** Detailed experimental evaluation of the trapping and positioning performance of 10 μm particles in the ring-transducer device. Scale bar is indicated by the wells (350 μm wide squares with slightly rounded walls). The actuation frequency is 2.30 MHz (single-frequency, blue aggregates) and $2.30 \pm 50$ kHz at the modulation rate 1 kHz (frequency-modulation, red aggregates). The figure is based on results presented in Ref. [17].

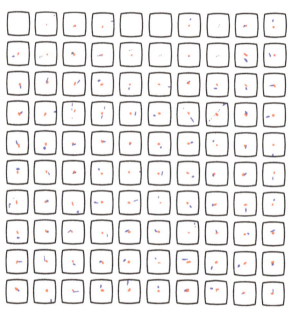

For the practical handling of the device with a cell suspension sample, the method is summarized in Figure 5. The fluid reservoir within the PDMS frame shown in Figure 5a has the purpose of providing a controlled environment of temperature- and $CO_2$-regulated cell medium. The cell medium volume (50 μL) needs to be large enough for enabling cell culturing over long terms (hours to days) and also for the practical handling (*i.e.*, enough to avoid sample evaporation). To this primed volume of cell medium, a small aliquot of cell suspension is pipetted from above (see Figure 5b) before closing the device with the glass lid (*cf.* item #3 in Figure 2). The seeding of cells into the wells is based on gravitational settlement (see Figure 5c). The strength of this method, besides simplicity, is the ability to study different numbers of cells per well interacting. Thus, the average number of cells per well is controlled by the cell concentration in the added drop (*cf.* Figure 5b), and the seeding principle causes a stochastical distribution around this average. Finally, when ultrasound is applied with the frequency-modulation method presented in Figure 3, the cells are aggregated and positioned in the center of each well where they can be monitored over time by high-resolution fluorescence microscopy. If confocal microscopy is used, it is a benefit to know the exact locations of the 100 cell aggregates. Since confocal microscopy is a relatively slow method, only the small area where the cells are located needs to be scanned, instead of the whole microplate.

**Figure 5.** Schematic illustration (not to scale) of the different steps of the cell handling method. For simplicity, only three out of a hundred wells are shown (vertical cross-section view), and only the PDMS frame and the multi-well microplate (item #4 and #5 in Figure 2). (**a**) The microplate is first primed with cell medium shown in blue; (**b**) The cell suspension is added as a small drop from a pipette tip; (**c**) Cells sediment by gravity down into the wells. The average number of cells per well is controlled by the cell concentration in the added drop in (**b**). In this example, there is on average 1 red cell and 2.33 green cells per well; (**d**) When ultrasound is turned on according to the procedure described in Figure 3, cells are trapped, aggregated and centrally positioned in each well.

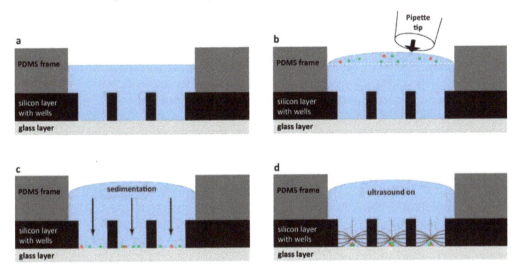

*2.3. Quantifying Acoustic Energy Density, Acoustic Pressure Amplitude, Acoustic Radiation Forces and Acoustic Streaming*

In order to fully characterize the device, it is important to be able to measure the properties of the acoustic field including the acoustic radiation forces and acoustic streaming acting on the particles, cells and the fluid, respectively. In a resonant acoustic field, there is no clear propagation direction of the wave. For that reason, acoustic energy density is a commonly used measure. This energy density can be translated into, e.g., acoustic pressure amplitude or acoustic radiation force (*cf.* Ref. [17]). Thus, knowing these acoustic field properties is important for estimating the trapping efficiency of cells, but also for estimating the risk of having cavitation in the sample (see Section 3). It is very difficult to measure the acoustic field properties by direct methods in an acoustofluidic device. However, there are different indirect methods available. Here, we will present three different methods used in our lab: Light intensity, particle tracking and particle image velocimetry (PIV). The methods are based on translating a measured property (i.e., light intensity, particle position or particle velocity) into acoustic energy density or acoustic pressure. All methods are based on one-dimensional (1D) geometries, but can be used for 2D geometries for order-of-magnitude estimations of the energy, pressure and forces.

The first method, light intensity, has been developed in collaboration with Rune Barnkob and Henrik Bruus (Denmark Technical University, Copenhagen, Denmark) [28,32]. This method is specifically designed for acoustofluidic chips that are optically transparent and compatible with standard bright-field microscopy [6]. One strength of the light intensity method is that the chips do not need to be compatible with high-resolution microscopy. For example, individual particles do not need to be resolved, and relatively high particle concentrations (up to $10^9$ beads/mL) can be used. In brief, the method is based on measuring the total transmitted light intensity passing through a certain part of a microchannel or a microchamber during the focusing process of suspended particles. When particles are focused and trapped in the pressure node, the fluid cavity gradually becomes more transparent for light. A detailed description of the method is found in Ref. [32], but here it is sufficient to show an example of what the method can be used for. In Figure 6, we demonstrate quantification of the acoustic energy density in a microchannel when it is operated at a single (optimal) frequency, and we compare with the corresponding energy density for the same (center) frequency, but with the frequency-modulation function active (100 kHz bandwidth and 1 kHz rate). As seen in the diagram, the average energy density is just slightly lower for frequency-modulation relative single-frequency actuation. This result is important since it means that there is no compromise between positioning accuracy and radiation forces when using frequency- modulation actuation instead of single-frequency actuation.

Another relatively simple and straightforward method for measuring acoustic energy density is particle tracking. This method is based on either manual or automated tracking of the position of individual particles over time. Thus, the method requires well-resolved particles and moderate particle concentrations (i.e., no particle-particle overlaps in the recorded images). The tracking data from a time sequence following a particle from its initial position into the pressure node can then be translated into a radiation force based on balancing Equation (1) with the viscous drag [17]. This method has been used for, e.g., measuring the quality factor ($Q$-value) of an acoustophoretic resonance in a microdevice by measuring the energy density as a function of the actuation frequency [33]. For the multi-well microplate discussed in this review, particle tracking was performed for estimating the forces acting on 10 μm polystyrene particles in the wells. The particle tracks in one of the hundred wells are shown in Figure 7 (six repetitions of the same experiment). This data containing tracks of 30 particles resulted in an acoustic energy density between 1 and 4 J m$^{-3}$, which corresponds to acoustic pressure amplitudes of 0.3–0.7 MPa, and acoustic radiation forces from 10 to 50 pN. These values are within the range of biocompatible ultrasonic manipulation of cells [34].

The last method, particle image velocimetry (PIV) [35], analyzes groups of particles from recorded image sequences, rather than individual particles (as for the particle tracking method). When applied to a microsystem using a microscope, the method is often called micro-PIV. The group of particles to be analyzed is defined by a certain interrogation window in the recorded image. Two such corresponding interrogation windows from two image frames separated in time are then inserted into a cross-correlation algorithm that compares light intensities for generating a velocity vector. The full velocity vector field can be used in the same way as for the particle tracking method for calculating the acoustic radiation forces. A strength of PIV is that it allows automated analysis of complex velocity fields. However, it is a time-consuming procedure to acquire reliable PIV data [36].

**Figure 6.** Measurement of the spatial distribution of the acoustic energy density along a micro-channel (*x*-axis), when actuating the chip with (**a**) Single-frequency (SF) actuation; and (**b**) Frequency-modulation (FM) actuation. The light-intensity method was applied to eight 150 μm wide subsections of the recorded images. The averaged energy density for the whole channel, $E_{ac,avg}$, is marked with a dotted black line, and the corresponding $1\sigma$ standard deviation is marked with a grey band. The red error bars are the standard deviations from the four repetitions of each experiment. The figure is reproduced from Ref. [28] by permission from IOP Publishing.

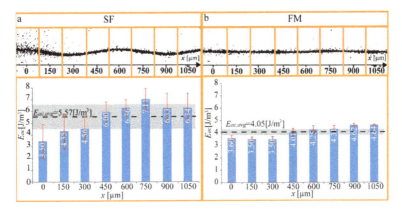

It is also possible to use PIV for measuring acoustic streaming in a microfluidic device. This has been performed in the multi-well microplate together with the particle tracking method described above. Thus, acoustic radiation forces and acoustic streaming velocities can be measured simultaneously when the two methods are combined. This is shown in Figure 7, where the background velocity field is measured by micro-PIV using 1 μm polystyrene beads [17]. The reason that the two methods can be combined is that the 10 μm particles are less influenced by acoustic streaming, and 1 μm particles are less influenced by the acoustic radiation force at the utilized frequency range (2–3 MHz) [37].

It is interesting to compare the three methods (light intensity, particle tracking and PIV). Light intensity has the advantage that it can be used with high particle concentrations and limited optical performance of the microscope. It does not require any advanced equipment or skillful operator, and can therefore easily be implemented in any lab. However, an optically transparent chip is needed [28,32]. The next method, particle tracking, is also easy to implement and it is the most suitable method for measuring the local pressure amplitude without any possible disturbance from particle-particle interactions. (Note that all three methods utilize the Gor'kov equation (Equation (1)) which assumes single particles.) However, particle tracking is time-consuming and provides low spatial resolution of the measured energy density. Finally, PIV is the most sophisticated method and can, if performed properly, provide very accurate and reliable data [36]. However, PIV requires

124

careful tuning of the particle concentration and image properties of the microscope, relative the input parameters in the PIV algorithms (primarily the size of the interrogation window defining the spatial resolution of the measure field). Therefore, a PIV-trained operator is needed.

**Figure 7.** Particle tracking for estimation of acoustic radiation forces acting on 10 μm polystyrene particles, and particle image velocimetry (PIV) diagrams showing the background velocity field from acoustic streaming. The diagrams show the particle motion in the same well for six repetitions of the experiment after re-seeding the well with new particles. The tracks of 10 μm particles are indicated by circles (one color per individual particle), and the acoustic streaming is measured by with 1 μm particles used as flow trackers. The diagrams are based on a figure in Ref. [17].

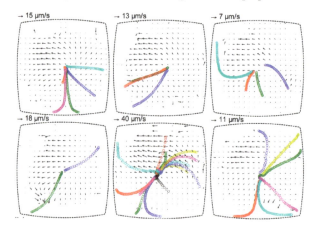

## 3. Biocompatibility

### 3.1. Effect of Ultrasound on Cell Viability and Function

The multi-well microplate is designed to be used for dynamic cell-cell interaction studies by combining ultrasonic trapping and live-cell fluorescence microscopy. This means that the cell-cell interactions are monitored in real-time over time periods lasting from minutes to several days. For this reason, it is of outmost importance that the ultrasound is not causing any harm or interferes with the studied biological process of interest. A more detailed review about biocompatibility of acoustofluidic microdevices is found in Ref. [7]. In brief, the bioeffects of ultrasound techniques for different medical or biomedical applications can differ a lot. For example, diagnostic ultrasound imaging, that uses similar frequencies and energies as in ultrasonic cell manipulation, is today considered as one of the safest imaging methods, and is widely used in clinics around the world. On the other hand, ultrasound can also be used for the purpose of specific destruction of biological material. Examples include shock-wave lithotripsy and high-intensity focused ultrasound (HIFU), where ultrasound is used for, e.g., destroying kidney stones and gall stones.

When using ultrasound for cell manipulation in a microdevice, the two most important parameters to control in terms of biocompatibility are the temperature and the pressure amplitude [7]. The ultrasound may cause heating of the cell sample, and high pressure amplitudes may lead to cavitation. Concerning temperature, the most common sources of heating in an acoustically driven micro-device are losses in the piezoceramic plate, and absorption in lossy supporting structures such as glue layers and polymer-based layers. It is an advantage to minimize the size and amount of such layers. The other parameter of importance for the biocompatibility is the pressure amplitude, which has relevance for the risk of having cavitation in the fluid. Generally, cavitation can be defined as the formation and/or activity of gas/vapor filled cavities, i.e., bubbles, in a fluid medium. Here, ultrasound is one out of many means to initiate and drive cavitation [7]. This stimulated bubble activity leads to local fluid jets causing shear stresses on cells and high local pressures and temperatures that can lead to direct cell death. Although cavitation is primarily associated with low-frequency ultrasound (e.g., "sonication" at 20–50 kHz), it can still be initiated even at MHz-frequencies typically employed for ultrasonic manipulation of cells. The threshold for initiating cavitation is dependent on frequency, pressure amplitude, but also on the size of potential pre-existing bubbles in the fluid. The latter is of high importance, and care should be taken to degas the fluid medium properly before injecting it to the chip. The acoustic pressure amplitudes used in the multi-well microplate (up to 0.7 MPa at 2.5 MHz actuation) are safe given that the fluid does not contain any gas bubbles with sizes of the order of 1 μm. If such bubbles should exist, the cavitation threshold could in theory be as low as 0.4 MPa at 2.5 MHz actuation [38].

In order to optimize biocompatibility of the multi-well microplate, we place the device in an environmental chamber matching the microscope stage where temperature and $CO_2$-level are controlled around 37 °C and 5%, respectively [16,18]. These values are the same as in a standard cell culture incubator. Furthermore, we use temperature probes (thermocouples) positioned as close to the fluid chamber as possible, in order to confirm that the ultrasound is not causing any temperature elevation above 37 °C. If so, the set-point temperature of the environmental chamber needs to be lowered with the same amount as the ultrasound-induced temperature increase. For estimating the risk of having cavitation, the pressure amplitude in the wells can be calibrated by the use of the particle tracking method described in Section 2.3. In a recent paper by Ohlin *et al.* [17], the highest measured pressure amplitude in the ring-transducer microplate was 0.7 MPa. This was measured for an actuation voltage approx. one order of magnitude higher than used during normal operation of the device with cells [16,18]. This means that cavitation is in practice impossible during normal operation of our device.

## 3.2. Measuring Cell Viability and Function with Optical Microscopy

Although we can control heating and avoid cavitation, it is still important to measure the cell viability and cell functions when the cells are exposed to ultrasound for prolonged times. Our first study was performed by Hultström *et al.* [34], who measured the viability and proliferation rate of adherent monkey kidney cells (COS-7) at different ultrasound exposure times. Here, the viability was monitored during the ultrasound exposure by the viability probe calcein-AM, and the proliferation rate was quantified by measuring the cell doubling time after ultrasound exposure. We concluded that exposure times up to 75 min at 0.85 MPa pressure amplitude and 3 MHz frequency did not alter viability or change the expected cell doubling time (24–48 h). Instead, the control cells not exposed to ultrasound showed lower doubling times, potentially because they were not first aggregated as for the ultrasound-exposed cells. Thus, it is reasonable to believe that the cell-cell contact induced by the ultrasound could be beneficial for cell proliferation of adherent cells. In a follow-up study, Vanherberghen et al. [16] used the multi-well microplate for studying the viability and proliferation of immune cells (a calcein-AM-labeled B cell line). Here, we concluded that the ultrasound (similar amplitudes and frequencies as in the previous study) did not cause any noticeable effect on B cells exposed to ultrasound continuously for up to three days (see Figure 8).

**Figure 8.** B cells growing in the multi-well microplate driven with the wedge transducer continuously at 10 $V_{pp}$, 2.5 MHz (frequency modulation) for 60 h. The figure is based on results presented in Ref. [16].

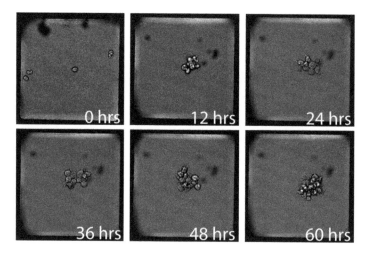

Besides viability and proliferation, it is important that the cell functions are intact when the cells are exposed to ultrasound. Several studies have been performed where different cell types and cell functions have been investigated after short-term ultrasound (seconds to minutes). For example, Augustsson et al. [39] and Burguillos et al. [40] used the XTT assay for measuring the mitochondrial dehydrogenase activity present in cells from prostate cancer cells and BV2 microglial cells, respectively. In another study, Bazou et al. [41] performed different biochemical assays on HEP-G2 liver cell aggregates (e.g., detection of hypoxia, cytokeratin-18, glucose and lactate). In the following section (Section 4), we investigate the functions of natural killer (NK) cells interacting with different target cells during long-term ultrasound exposure. Besides viability and proliferation, we have studied the ability to form immune synapses and the ability of NK cells to selectively kill different target cells.

## 4. Natural Killer (NK) Cell—Cancer Cell Interaction Studies

NK cells are lymphocytes of the immune system and they serve the role of cytotoxic effector cells against virus-infected or cancerous cells as well as cytokine producers for triggering other immune responses. NK cells are characterized by the capability of direct killing of aberrant cells through release of cytotoxic granular content (e.g., perforin and granzymes) at the tight intercellular contact (called "immune synapse" or sometimes "immunological synapse") formed between the NK cell and target cell [42]. The immune synapse was initially described as the junction between T helper lymphocytes and antigen presenting cells (APC) where T cell receptors (TCRs) are interacting with major histocompatibility complex (MHC) molecules on APC carrying foreign or malignant peptides [43,44]. Some viruses have developed mechanisms to suppress the expression of MHC proteins at the cell surface, effectively hiding any virus-associated antigenic peptides and therefore avoiding recognition by T cells. However, NK cells express a range of activating and inhibitory cell-surface receptors that are used to probe the "health" status of potential target cells. Reduced levels of MHC in combination with activating signals can trigger delivery of granules to the immune synapse followed by granule content release that will initiate a signaling cascade inside the target cells, which eventually leads to apoptosis. In an immune synapse dominated by inhibitory signals NK cells will eventually detach leaving the target cell unharmed [45]. The outcome of the immune synapse depends on a balance between activating and inhibitory signals mediated by receptor-ligand interactions at the NK-target interface. The two different outcomes described here, inhibition and activation, are schematically illustrated in Figure 9a,b, respectively.

**Figure 9.** Schematic illustration of an inhibitory (**a**) and an activating (**b**) interaction between a natural killer (NK) cell and a target cell. The three different steps (marked with arrows) are (I): Initiation of cell-cell contact, (II): Development of an inhibitory (green) or activating (red) immune synapse, and (III): Detachment (**a**) or killing (**b**) of the target cell. The ultrasound is used for synchronizing step I in all wells simultaneously (*i.e.,* synchronizing $t_{contact}$) and for retaining the cell-cell interaction from step I to step III.

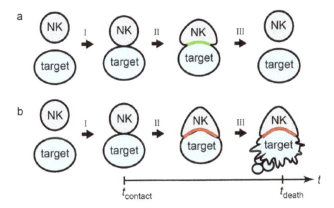

Conventional methods of investigating NK cell properties and functions (such as 51Cr release cytotoxicity assay) are based on bulk averages that hide information related to characteristics of individual NK cells. High NK heterogeneity has been shown by experiments performed on human [46,47] and mouse [48] NK cells indicating the need of more efficient, high throughput and well controlled techniques for single cell analysis. With the multi-well microplate device presented in the previous sections, we can induce synchronized NK-target cell interactions in parallel. Our method allows imaging of isolated events within the individual wells. Thus, we are able to observe and record up to one hundred individual interactions between NK cells and target cells and the resulting NK responses within a specific time frame depending on the experiment [18]. Furthermore, current high-resolution imaging techniques are limited by the tendency of cells to migrate or drift away from the imaging area (field of view). We have shown that besides inducing cell-cell contact and thus initiation of the interaction, we can also maintain the cell conjugates within a well-controlled area in each well allowing high resolution confocal imaging [18].

As mentioned in Section 3, we are able to maintain appropriate cell environmental conditions during the entire experiments performed in the microplate-microscope setup. In addition, we have quantified the trapping performance of the device for two cell types with different adherent properties. The human embryonic kidney cell line 293T with adherent properties were poorly trapped compared to the suspension B cell line 721.221. This strongly indicates that acoustic forces applied on the cells are balanced to natural biological forces such as cell adherence to a glass substrate.

## 4.1. High-Resolution Imaging of the Inhibitory Immune Synapse

In our recent study [18] a human NK cell line (YTS) transfected to express the inhibitory NK cell receptor KIR2DL was imaged while interacting with a human B cell line 721.221, deficient in endogenous surface expression of MHC class I proteins and transfected to express MHC/HLA-Cw6 (cognate ligand to KIR2DL1) coupled to green fluorescent protein (GFP). Accumulation of GFP (green color) in the immune synapses indicates the interaction between MHC proteins on the target cells with KIR2DL1 receptors on the NK cell. Figure 10 (unpublished data) presents a time-lapse interaction between a single YTS-KIR2DL1 cell (unlabeled) with five target cells (721.221/Cw6-GFP) forming four to five synapses. The upper panel (Figure 10a) indicates the morphology of the cells (bright field images) during the NK-target cell interaction (white arrows point out target cells). Figure 10b presents the accumulation of MHC/HLACw6-GFP proteins in the immune synapses at different time points (white arrows). Interestingly, we observed separation of the GFP protein accumulations on the immune synapses of two target cells, caused by the NK cell division into two daughter cells. The divided immune synapses where shown to be preserved between the two target cells and each NK daughter cell (Figure 10, $t = 100$ min, black arrows). The lower panel (Figure 10c) shows in false-color coding the green fluorescence from MHC/HLACw6-GFP clustering at the immune synapse. The divided synapses at $t = 100$ min are again highlighted with black arrows. Enhanced fluorescence is observed in other target cell sites besides the immune synapse. This can be explained by the heterogeneous GFP expression on target cells as well as by the different focal positions of target cells during imaging. The results in Figure 10 show that normal cellular functions such as immune synapse formation and mitosis are retained during the ultrasound exposure. These findings are in agreement with the conclusions drawn in Ref. [18].

**Figure 10.** Time-lapse recordings of the inhibitory interaction between a single NK cell (YTS KIR2DL cell line) and five target cells (721.221/Cw6-GFP). (**a**) Bright field image of the interaction indicating the morphology of the cells. White arrows point out the target cells. At $t$ = 100 min the NK cell has divided into two NK cells; (**b**) Merged images of bright field and green channel indicating the accumulation of GFP protein (white arrows) in the interface between each target cell and the NK cell (the immune synapse). At $t$ = 100 min, two of the synapses (of two target cells) are shown to have divided (black arrows) at the site of the NK cell division (GFP gap); (**c**) False-color coding of the green fluorescence clustering at the immune synapse. Again the divided synapses are highlighted with black arrows.

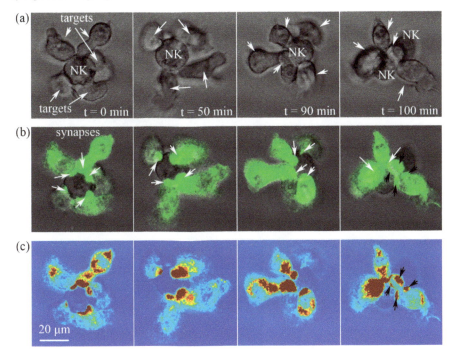

## 4.2. Studying the Killing Dynamics of Individual Natural Killer (NK) Cells

In the study by Christakou *et al.* [18], we characterized NK cells as cytotoxic effector cells by quantifying cytotoxic behaviors of individual NK cells against target cells. We performed several experiments in the multi-well microdevice using IL-2 activated polyclonal primary human NK cells isolated from lymphocyte enriched buffy coat residues derived from healthy donors. As target cells we used the 721.221 B cell line. We observed a significant heterogeneity in the natural killer cell population in their ability to induce cytotoxicity within a four hour assay of continuous contact with at least one target cell [18]. Analysis of four experiments (from two different donors) revealed that 64% of the NK cell population was able to kill at least one target cell, where the rest 36% remained non-cytotoxic during the entire experiment although in continues contact with one or more target

130

cells. Interestingly, a small fraction of the NK cells showed a high killing performance eliminating all their surrounding target cells during the assay.

**Figure 11.** Time-lapse recordings of three parallel events among the 100 wells of the ultrasonic microplate in a 5 h cytotoxic assay. NK cells are shown in orange (orange calcein-AM), living target cells are shown in green (green calcein-AM) and dead target cells in red (far-red DDAO-SE). (**a**) Continuous interaction of a non-active NK cell (non-killer) with four to five targets (target cell division at $t = 132$ min) during the entire assay does not result to any NK cell mediated death; (**b**) Normal killer induces killing at $t = 19$ and 57 min, but remains inactive (although in contact with living target) for the remaining experiment; (**c**) Serial killer eliminating all four target cells within 75 min.

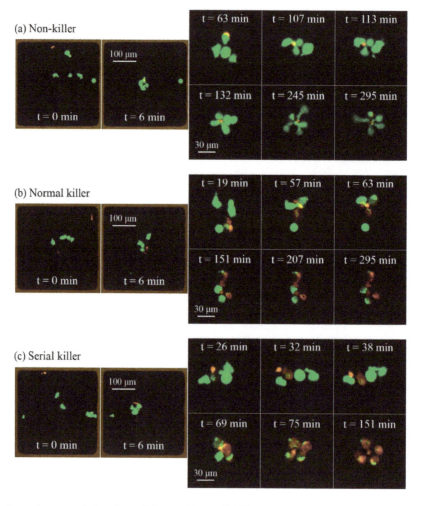

Time-lapse images of the three different NK cell killer types characterized by their cytotoxic abilities in a 5-h killing assay are exemplified in Figure 11. This is an equivalent experiment as reported in Ref. [18], but with one extra hour assay time. Here, NK cells were stained with orange calcein-AM while target cells were stained in a solution of green calcein-AM and Far red DDAO-SE. The property of calcein-AM to rapidly leak out when the cell membrane is raptured combined with increased DDAO intensity allows identification of cell death [7]. At $t = 0$ min, ultrasound was turned off and cells (NKs and targets) are distributed in different positions in the wells. At $t = 6$ min ultrasound was turned on inducing NK-target cell contact. An inactive NK cell is presented in Figure 11a. Although it is in contact with several targets, it remained unable to induce death during the entire assay (at $t = 295$ min, green calcein-AM is still present in all target cells). A normal killer is presented in Figure 11b. The NK cell showed increased activity during the first hour ($t = 57$ min) of the assay killing two out of four target cells, but stayed inactive for the remaining 4 h (expected bleaching of the calcein-AM after long assays should not be confused with cell death). A serial killer, presented in Figure 11, eliminates all surrounding targets within only 75 min.

The property of some NK cells to rapidly kill targets cells is presented more detailed in Figure 12, where wells with individual NK cells and three or more target cells where analyzed and killing events, as well as the times of the killing events ($t_{death} - t_{contact}$, see Figure 9) where scored. Different colors indicate the number of kills induced by NK cells. Results indicate that NK cells, killing up to three target cells, show slower cytotoxic capability, killing every one to three hours, where some particular cells kill every 30 to 60 min eliminating most or all of their surrounding targets.

Figure 12. Timing of the killing events where the bars represent time from cluster formation until target cell death (mean and standard deviation for 1–3 kills). The different colors of the bars represent the order of the NK mediated target cell death within a cluster with red representing the first kills, blue the second, green the third, magenta the fourth, cyan the fifth, and yellow the sixth, respectively. The figure is reproduced from Ref. [18] with permission from RSC.

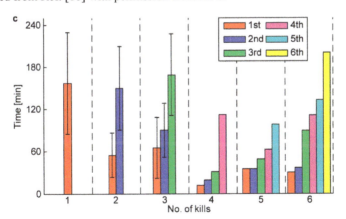

## 5. Conclusions

In this review, we have shown that ultrasound is a powerful and gentle tool for individual cell handling in a multi-well microplate. The described platform has been specifically designed for controlling cell-cell interactions, which are studied by high-resolution confocal and/or fluorescence microscopy. By distributing a few (typically 1–10) cells per well in a 100-well microplate, individual interactions can be monitored in real time and in parallel over time periods lasting for up to several days. The simple seeding method based on gravitational settlement allows for studying different constellations of interactions. For example, individual natural killer (NK) cells have been studied when interacting simultaneously with different numbers of target cells. This made it possible to study the heterogeneity in cytotoxicity of NK cells, but also their ability to form one or several immune synapses simultaneously. Another strength of the platform is that ultrasound can be used not only for retaining an interaction and accurate positioning of the cell aggregate, but also for synchronizing the starting time of the cell–cell contacts in all 100 wells simultaneously. This made it possible to measure the time from the start of interaction to target cell death in a systematic and controlled way.

Of high importance is to evaluate any possible impact of the ultrasound exposure on the cell viability, proliferation rate and function. We have performed extensive measurements of these parameters over the last seven years. We have used different cell types, including animal cells and human cells, adherent cells and non-adherent cells, different cell lines and primary cells. The general conclusion made so far is that if ultrasound is driven in a controlled and well-calibrated manner (which primarily includes controlling the temperature and pressure amplitude at the employed actuation voltage and frequency), cells of various kinds can be continuously exposed to ultrasound for hours and even days without any noticeable effect on the studied parameters. Thus, we believe that our described platform may be of wide and general interest for any type of dynamic cell or cell–cell interaction study where a large number of cells need to be investigated in parallel and at the individual-cell level over extended periods in time.

## Acknowledgments

We thank the Swedish Foundation for Strategic Research, the EU FP-7 RAPP-ID project, the Swedish Research Council, the Göran Gustafsson Foundation, the Jeansson Foundation, the Clas Groschinsky Foundation and the Åke Wiberg Foundation for financial support.

## Conflicts of Interest

The authors declare no conflict of interest.

## References

1.  Single-Cell Analysis, Methods and Protocols. In *Methods in Molecular Biology*; Lindström, S., Andersson-Svahn, H., Eds.; Humana Press Inc.: New York, NY, USA, 2012.
2.  Berridge, M.J.; Bootman, M.D.; Lipp, P. Calcium—A life and death signal. *Nature* **1998**, *395*, 645–648.
3.  Pardee, A.B. G1 events and regulation of cell proliferation. *Science* **1989**, *246*, 603–608.
4.  Ronowicz, E.; Coutinho, A. Functional analysis of B cell heterogeneity. *Immunol. Rev.* **1975**, *24*, 3–40.

5. Davey, H.M.; Kell, D.B. Flow cytometry and cell sorting of heterogeneous microbial populations: The importance of single-cell analyses. *Microbiol. Mol. Biol. Rev.* **1996**, *60*, 641–696.

6. Wiklund, M.; Brismar, H.; Önfelt, B. Acoustofluidics 18: Microscopy for acoustofluidic micro-devices. *Lab Chip* **2012**, *12*, 3221–3234.

7. Wiklund, M. Acoustofluidics 12: Biocompatibility and cell viability in microfluidic acoustic resonators. *Lab Chip* **2012**, *12*, 2018–2028.

8. Crowther, J.R. The ELISA Guidebook. In *Methods in Molecular Biology*; Humana Press Inc.: Totowa, NJ, USA, 2001.

9. Forslund, E.; Guldevall, K.; Olofsson, P.E.; Frisk, T.; Christakou, A.E.; Wiklund M.; Önfelt, B. Novel microchip-based tools facilitating live cell imaging and assessment of functional heterogeneity within NK cell populations. *Front. Immunol.* **2012**, *3*, 300; doi:10.3389/fimmu.2012.00300.

10. Lindström, S.; Larsson, R.; Andersson Svahn, H. Towards high-throughput single cell/clone cultivation and analysis. *Electrophoresis* **2008**, *29*, 1219–1227.

11. Guldevall, K.; Vanherberghen, B.; Frisk, T.; Hurtig, J.; Christakou, A.; Manneberg, O. Lindström, S.; Andersson-Svahn, H.; Wiklund, M.; Önfelt, B. Imaging immune surveillance of individual natural killer cells confined in microwell arrays. *PLoS One* **2010**, *5*, e15453; doi:10.1371/journal.pone.0015453.

12. Frisk, T.; Khorshidi, M.A.; Guldevall, K.; Vanherberghen, B.; Önfelt, B. A silicon-glass microwell platform for high-resolution imaging and high-content screening with single cell resolution. *Biomed. Microdevices* **2011**, *13*, 683–693.

13. Vanherberghen, B.; Olofsson, P.E.; Forslund, E.; Sternberg-Simon, M.; Khorshidi, M.A.; Pacouret, S.; Guldevall, K.; Enqvist, M.; Malmberg, K.-J.; Mehr, R.; *et al.* Classification of human natural killer cells based on migration behavior and cytotoxic response. *Blood* **2013**, *121*, 1326–1334.

14. Yamanaka, Y.J.; Berger, C.T.; Sips, M.; Cheney, P.C.; Alter, G.; Love, J.C. Single-cell analysis of the dynamics and functional outcomes of interactions between human natural killer cells and target cells. *Integr. Biol.* **2012**, *4*, 1175–1184.

15. Khorshidi, M.A.; Vanherberghen, B.; Kowalewski, J.M.; Garrod, K.R.; Lindström, S.; Andersson-Svahn, H.; Brismar, H.; Cahalan, M.D.; Önfelt, M. Analysis of transient migration behavior of natural killer cells imaged *in situ* and *in vitro*. *Integr. Biol.* **2011**, *3*, 770–778.

16. Vanherberghen, B.; Manneberg, O.; Christakou, A.; Frisk, T.; Ohlin, M.; Hertz, H.M.; Önfelt, B.; Wiklund, M. Ultrasound-controlled cell aggregation in a multi-well chip. *Lab Chip* **2010**, *10*, 2727–2732.

17. Ohlin, M.; Christakou, A.E.; Frisk, T.; Önfelt, B.; Wiklund, M. Influence of acoustic streaming on ultrasonic particle manipulation in a 100-well ring-transducer microplate. *J. Micromech. Microeng.* **2013**, *23*, 035008; doi:10.1088/0960-1317/23/3/035008.

18. Christakou, A.E.; Ohlin, M.; Vanherberghen, B.; Khorshidi, M.A.; Kadri, N.; Frisk, T.; Wiklund, M.; Önfelt, B. Live cell imaging in a micro-array of acoustic traps facilitates quantification of natural killer cell heterogeneity. *Integr. Biol.* **2013**, *5*, 712–719.

19. Lord Rayleigh. On the momentum and pressure of gaseous vibrations, and on the connexion with virial theorem. *Philos. Mag.* **1905**, *10*, 364–374.

20. Beyer, R.T. Radiation pressure—The history of a mislabeled tensor. *J. Acoust. Soc. Am.* **1978**, *63*, 1025–1030.

21. Gor'kov, L.P. On the forces acting on a small particle in an acoustical field in an ideal fluid. *Sov. Phys. Dokl.* **1962**, *6*, 773–775.

22. Manneberg, O.; Svennebring, J.; Hertz, H.M.; Wiklund, M. Wedge transducer design for two-dimensional ultrasonic manipulation in a microfluidic chip. *J. Micromech. Microeng.* **2008**, *18*, 095025; doi:10.1088/0960-1317/18/9/095025.

23. Nyborg, W.L. Theoretical criterion for acoustic aggregation. *Ultrasound Med. Biol.* **1989**, *15*, 93–99.

24. Manneberg, O.; Vanherberghen, B.; Svennebring, J.; Hertz, H.M.; Önfelt, B.; Wiklund, M. A three-dimensional ultrasonic cage for characterization of individual cells. *Appl. Phys. Lett.* **2008**, *93*, 063901; doi:10.1063/1.2971030.

25. Barnkob, R.; Augustsson, P.; Magnusson, C.; Lilja, H.; Laurell, T.; Bruus, H. Measuring Density and Compressibility of White Blood Cells and Prostate Cancer Cells by Microchannel Acoustophoresis. In Proceedings of the 15th MicroTAS, Seattle, WA, USA, 2–6 October 2011.

26. Hartono, D.; Liu, Y.; Tan, P.L.; Then, X.Y.S.; Yung, L.Y.L.; Lim, K.M. On-chip measurements of cell compressibility via acoustic radiation. *Lab Chip* **2011**, *11*, 4072–4080.

27. Mishra, P.; Glynne-Jones, P.; Boltryk, R.J.; Hill, M. Efficient finite element modeling of acoustic radiation forces on inhomogeneous elastic particles. *AIP Conf. Proc.* **2012**, *1433*, 753–756.

28. Iranmanesh, I.; Barnkob, R.; Bruus, H.; Wiklund, M. Tunable-angle wedge transducer for improved acoustophoretic control in a microfluidic chip. *J. Micromech. Microeng.* **2013**, *23*, 105002; doi:10.1088/0960-1317/23/10/105002.

29. Bruus, H. Acoustofluidics 2: Perturbation theory and ultrasound resonance modes. *Lab Chip* **2012**, *12*, 20–28.

30. Wiklund, M.; Green, R.; Ohlin, M. Acoustofluidics 14: Applications of acoustic streaming in microfluidic devices. *Lab Chip* **2012**, *12*, 2438–2451.

31. Ohlin, M.; Christakou, A.E.; Frisk, T.; Önfelt, B.; Wiklund, M. Controlling Acoustic Streaming in a Multi-well Microplate for Improving Live Cell Assays. In Proceedings of the 15th International Conference on Miniaturized Systems for Chemistry and Life, Sciences (MicroTAS 2011), Seattle, WA, USA, 2–6 October 2011.

32. Barnkob, R.; Iranmanesh, I.; Wiklund, M.; Bruus, H. Measuring acoustic energy density in microchannel acoustophoresis using a simple and rapid light-intensity method. *Lab Chip* **2012**, *12*, 2337–2344.

33. Barnkob, R.; Augustsson, P.; Laurell, T.; Bruus, H. Measuring the local pressure amplitude in microchannel acoustophoresis. *Lab Chip* **2010**, *10*, 563–570.

34. Hultström, J.; Manneberg, O.; Dopf, K.; Hertz, H.M.; Brismar, H.; Wiklund, M. Proliferation and viability of adherent cells manipulated by standing-wave ultrasound in a microfluidic chip. *Ultrasound Med. Biol.* **2007**, *33*, 145–151.

35. Raffel, M.; Willert, C.E.; Wereley, S.T.; Kompenhans, J. *Particle Image Velocimetry*; Springer: Berlin, Germany, 2007.

36. Augustsson, P.; Barnkob, R.; Wereley, S.T.; Bruus, H.; Laurell, T. Automated and temperature-controlled micro-PIV measurements enabling long-term-stable microchannel acoustophoresis characterization. *Lab Chip* **2011**, *11*, 4152–4164.

37. Barnkob, R.; Augustsson, P.; Laurell, T.; Bruus, H. Acoustic radiation- and streaming-induced microparticle velocities determined by microparticle image velocimetry in an ultrasound symmetry plane. *Phys. Rev. E* **2012**, *86*, 056307; doi:10.1103/PhysRevE.86.056307.

38. Apfel, R.E.; Holland, C.K. Gauging the likelihood of cavitation from short-pulse, low-duty cycle diagnostic ultrasound. *Ultrasound Med. Biol.* **1991**, *17*, 179–185.

39. Augustsson, P.; Magnusson, C.; Nordin, M.; Lilja, H.; Laurell, T. Microfluidic, label-free enrichment of prostate cancer cells in blood based on acoustophoresis. *Anal. Chem.* **2012**, *84*, 7954–7962.

40. Burguillos, M.A.; Magnusson, C.; Nordin, M.; Lenshof, A.; Augustsson, P.; Hansson, M.J.; Elmér, E.; Lilja, H.; Brundin, P.; Laurell T.; Deierborg, T. Microchannel acoustophoresis does not impact survival or function of microglia, leukocytes or tumor cells. *PLoS One* **2013**, *8*, e64233; doi:10.1371/journal.pone.0064233.

41. Bazou, D. Biochemical properties of encapsulated high-density 3-D HepG2 aggregates formed in an ultrasound trap for application in hepatotoxicity studies. *Cell Biol. Toxicol.* **2010**, *26*, 127–141.

42. Orange, J. Formation and function of the lytic NK-cell immunological synapse. *Nat. Rev. Immunol.* **2008**, *8*, 713–725.

43. Monks, C.R.; Freiberg, B.A.; Kupfer, H.; Sciaky, N.; Kupfer, A. Three-dimensional segregation of supramolecular activation clusters in T cells. *Nature* **1998**, *395*, 82–86.

44. Grakoui, A.; Bromley, S.K.; Sumen, C.; Davis, M.M.; Shaw, A.S.; Allen, P.M.; Dustin, M.L. The immunological synapse: A molecular machine controlling T cell activation. *Science* **1999**, *285*, 221–227.

45. Ljunggren, H.-G.; Kärre, K. In search of the "missing self": MHC molecules and NK cell recognition. *Immunol. Today* **1990**, *11*, 237–244.

46. Bhat, R.; Watzl, C. Serial killing of tumor cells by human natural killer cells—Enhancement by therapeutic antibodies. *PLoS One* **2007**, *2*, e326; doi:10.1371/journal.pone.0000326.

47. Yawata, M.; Yawata, N.; Draghi, M.; Partheniou, F.; Little, A.-M.; Parham, P. MHC class I-specific inhibitory receptors and their ligands structure diverse human NK-cell repertoires toward a balance of missing self-response. *Blood* **2008**, *112*, 2369–2380.

48. Brodin, P.; Lakshmikanth, T.; Johansson, S.; Kärre, K.; Höglund, P. The strength of inhibitory input during education quantitatively tunes the functional responsiveness of individual natural killer cells. *Blood* **2009**, *113*, 2434–2441.

# A Single-Cell Study of a Highly Effective Hog1 Inhibitor for *in Situ* Yeast Cell Manipulation

**Charlotte Hamngren Blomqvist, Peter Dinér, Morten Grøtli, Mattias Goksör and Caroline B. Adiels**

**Abstract:** We present a single cell study of a highly effective Hog1 inhibitor. For this application, we used sequential treatment of a *Saccharomyces cerevisiae* cell array, with the Hog1 inhibitor and osmotic stress. For this purpose, a four-inlet microfluidic chamber with controlled introduction of two different cell strains within the same experimental setting and a subsequent rapid switching between treatments was designed. Multiple cell strains within the same experiment is a unique feature which is necessary for determining the expected absent cellular response. The nuclear translocation of the cytosolic MAPK, Hog1, was monitored by fluorescence imaging of Hog1-GFP on a single-cell level. An optical tweezers setup was used for controlled cell capture and array formation. Nuclear Hog1-GFP localization was impaired for treated cells, providing evidence of a congenial microfluidic setup, where the control cells within the experiments validated its appropriateness. The chamber enables multiple treatments with incubation times .in the order of seconds and the possibility to remove either of the treatments during measurement. This flexibility and the possibility to use internal control cells ensures it a valuable scientific tool for unraveling the HOG pathway, similar signal transduction pathways and other biological mechanisms where temporal resolution and real time imaging is a prerequisite.

Reprinted from *Micromachines.* Cite as: Blomqvist, C.H.; Dinér, P.; Grøtli, M.; Goksör, M.; Adiels, C.B. A Single-Cell Study of a Highly Effective Hog1 Inhibitor for *in Situ* Yeast Cell Manipulation. *Micromachines* **2014**, *5*, 81-96.

## 1. Introduction

The emerging interest for single-cell analytical data calls for novel data acquiring methods. Microfluidics can effectively be used in studies of signal transduction pathways by the fast and reproducible introduction of different perturbations on the studied system. Single-cell analysis of yeast was first reported in the early 50's [1], and includes several different single-cell assays [2]. The spatial and temporal resolutions of such analyses are widely exceeding that of traditional cell culture methodologies [3]. In addition, single-cell analysis provides information on cell-to-cell variability that will be obscured in averaged results from population analyses [4]. This heterogeneity in cell response can be attributed to intrinsic and extrinsic noise [5], e.g., in which phase the individual cells are in their cell cycle. Single-cell analyses have been improved further by the use of microfluidics. The microfluidic chambers are cheap to produce, customizable and compatible with different spectrometric methods and, in addition, they also enable the possibility of accomplishing fast and accurate concentration changes of, e.g., nutrients and different substances that affect the biological event studied. In order to control not only the microenvironment around the cells in the microfluidic chamber, but also the cell positions, optical tweezers (OT) are used [6]. This enables selective cell manipulation in a non-intrusive way [7].

The study of biological signaling pathways is complicated, and *Saccharomyces cerevisiae* (*S. cerevisiae*), also known as budding yeast due to its reproduction mechanism, is a frequently used eukaryote model organism [8–10] for studying biological mechanisms that could have future impact on human disease prevention [11]. The High Osmolarity Glycerol (HOG) Mitogen Activated Protein Kinase (MAPK) pathway of *S. cerevisiae*, a functional homolog of the stress activated MAPK signaling pathway Jun *N*-terminal kinase (JNK) and the MAPK p38 pathways of mammals [12], is involved in the cellular adaptation to hyperosmotic stress. Because of the high degree of conservation of the MAPK kinase cascades, the yeast HOG pathway is a good model for studying osmotic adaptation processes. The HOG pathway responds to changes in external osmolarity by activating the MAPK Hog1, triggering the cellular response that includes both transcriptional upregulation of approximately six hundred osmoresponsive genes [13–15], and events extending beyond gene transcription. The closure of the glycerol export channels in the plasma membrane [16] and rerouting of the metabolite utilization in glycolysis [17] will contribute to an increased cellular glycerol content and cell adaptation to the new environment. Three transmembrane proteins, Sln1, Msb2 and Hkr1 sense the increased external osmolarity [18,19]. The activation signal is transduced via two branches (the Sln1 and Sho1 branch respectively) that merge by the phosphorylation of the MAPK kinase (MAPKK) Pbs2. Pbs2 subsequently phosphorylates and activates the MAPK Hog1, which rapidly translocates from the cytoplasm into the nucleus [20] via the nuclear envelope transport protein, Nmd5p [21]. A simplified schematic of the HOG signaling pathway can be seen in Figure 1. The phosphorylation of Hog1 is required for its nuclear envelope translocation [21]. The influence of the used Hog1 inhibitor on the translocation of Hog1 has been described by Dinér *et al.* [22]. Migration studies upon Hog1 pathway activation, where the intensity ratio of nucleic to cytosolic Hog1-GFP is plotted, would reveal if the effects of Hog1 inhibition (*i.e.*, a prolonged phosphorylation and hence nuclear localization of Hog1) were mirrored in the protein's location.

In this article, we report on a single-cell evaluation of the highly effective Hog1 inhibitor 4-(1-benzyl-4-phenyl-1H-1,2,3-triazol-5-yl)-*N*-isopropylpyridin-2-amine [22] for the HOG pathway. A four-inlet microfluidic chamber, enabling rapid switching between different treatments, was utilized for analyzing the stress-induced translocation process of Hog1 as a function of time. Cell responses due to osmotic stress after and during exposure with a Hog1-specific inhibitor was studied using two distinguishable cell strains within the same chamber. Sequential Hog1 inhibitor and osmotic stress treatment of an *S. cerevisiae* cell array were performed, with temporal resolution and an experimental precision down to a few seconds. This temporal precision was essential in order to determine the most efficient incubation time for Hog1 inhibition and to have comparable measurements with a minimized temporal variation of incubation times between the different single-cell experiments.

**Figure 1.** A simplified scheme of the HOG signaling pathway. The HOG pathway responds to changes in external osmolarity. The activation signal is transduced via the Sln1 and Sho1 branch respectively, that merge by the phosphorylation of the MAPKK Pbs2. Pbs2 subsequently phosphorylates and activates the MAPK Hog1, which rapidly translocates from the cytoplasm into the nucleus. The inhibitor acts on Hog1 and will inhibit its downstream kinase activity.

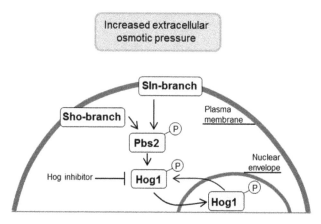

Our setup enables actively choosing single cells from two different cell strains and following the responses of individual cells over time. This possibility makes the setup advantageous for unraveling the mechanisms of the HOG and similar dynamic signal transduction pathways. Any heterogeneous response of the single cells is revealed by using the intensity ratio of fluorescently tagged proteins within the cell as a tool for tracing protein movement. For the possible event of complete inhibition, a method to ensure that cells were responding to the inflowing chemical as intended had to be established. The solution was to introduce a second cell strain using the additional inlet of the four-inlet chamber. These control cells were imaged alongside the cells of interest when the Hog1 inhibitor was used. This increase in versatility and the use of *in situ* control cells ensures our chamber a valuable tool for providing insight into biological problems, e.g., the complexity of the signaling pathways of *S. cerevisiae*.

A key improvement over our previously described three-inlet chamber [7], is that the four-inlet microfluidic chamber allows for rapid switching between two treatments, which leads to a great gain in temporal resolution.

## 2. Experimental Section

The cells were captured and positioned using OT (400 mW Ytterbium fibre laser LP, 1070 nm, IPG Laser) and were sequentially treated with a selective Hog1 kinase inhibitor [22] and sorbitol. These single-cell experiments are the first using this particular Hog1 inhibitor. Responses were monitored on a single-cell level by time-lapse fluorescence microscopy, monitoring the nuclear migration of the reporter protein Hog1-GFP, initiated by osmotic stress. The flow of Hog1 inhibitor was introduced to the cells via one of the four inlets. Two other inlets carried the two cell strains respectively, and the final one introduced the flow of sorbitol (for increased osmotic pressure upon the cells). The microscope was a Leica DMI6000B with control box CTR 6500 (Leica Microsystems, Wetzlar, Germany). The GFP filter cube was a 472/30 nm exciter, 520/35 nm emitter and 495LP dichroic mirror (Semrock IDEX Corporation, Rochester, NY, USA). The mCherry filter cube was a 560/40 nm exciter, 630/75 nm emitter and 585LP dichroic mirror (Chroma, Bellows Falls, VT, USA). A 100× HCX plan fluotar oil immersion objective (Leica Microsystems, Wetzlar, Germany) with a numerical aperture of 1.30 was used.

## 2.1. Strains and Cell Culture

Two different yeast strains in BY4741 background were used; the HOG1-GFP-HIS3 NRD1-mCherry-hphNT1 strain, for monitoring Hog1 migration, and the MSN2-GFP-HIS3 NRD1-mCherry-hphNT1 strain as control cells. Both strains were grown in Yeast Nitrogen Base (YNB, 6.7 g/L) with Complete Supplement Mixture (CSM, 1.54 g/L) and 2% Glucose (pH = 6), at 30 °C on a shaker (220 rpm). The two cell strains were collected at $OD_{600}$ = 0.5–1.0. The Hog1-GFP cells were then concentrated to twice the initial concentration by centrifugation at a relative centrifugal force of 2400× g for 30 s, followed by removal of the supernatant and addition of fresh growth medium. The cell density of the Hog1-GFP cells were 3 to 4 times the cell density of the Msn2-GFP cells.

## 2.2. Inhibitor

The selective Hog1 inhibitor 4-(1-benzyl-4-phenyl-1H-1,2,3-triazol-5-yl)-N-isopropylpyridin-2-amine [22] (M = 478.67 g/mol) (see Figure S1 for chemical structure) was dissolved in dimethyl sulfoxide (DMSO) to a suitable stock solution. Final concentrations range between 10 nM and 25 μM and control experiments contained the corresponding maximum volume of DMSO. The approximated diffusion coefficient was determined to 260 $\mu m^2/s$ (measured at 22 °C).

## 2.3. Microfluidic Fabrication and Setup

The manufacturing protocol for the microfluidic chamber and the experimental procedure has previously been reported [7,23,24]. The disposable microfluidic chambers were made from polydimethylsiloxane (PDMS) using soft lithography and sealed off with a cover glass. A reusable master relief pattern of 27 μm height was formed on a silicon wafer and PDMS was poured onto it using a formwork holding pins to form the four inlet holes and the outlet of the microfluidic chamber. After polymerization, the PDMS structure and a glass slide were treated with air plasma and thereafter immediately placed in physical contact with each other, spontaneously forming a strong irreversible seal [25]. Figure 2 shows a schematic image of the four-inlet microfluidic chamber and workflow setup, and a colored overlay where both the cells of interest and the control cells are shown.

**Figure 2.** Schematic image of the setup in relation to the workflow. (**A**) The syringes filled with cells and substances are placed in a syringe pump. Cells are trapped by OT and positioned in an array within the microfluidic chamber. The cells and their reporter proteins are imaged in transmission light and fluorescent light while the pump flow rates are automatically controlled and altered; (**B**) a colored overlay of the bright field, GFP and mCherry images. Cells were actively placed in an array using the OT. In the four first columns, cells are expressing Hog1-GFP and in the rightmost column, control cells are instead expressing Msn2-GFP. The two cell types are visually distinguishable by the different GFP expression. Both cell types express the nucleic protein Nrd1-mCherry. The scale bar is 10 μm.

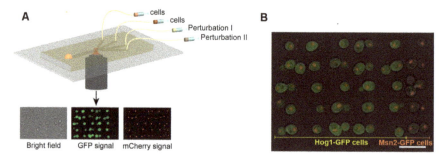

The inner lining of the chamber was initially saturated with the lectin concanavalin A, which promotes cell adhesion between the cell wall sugar residues and the surfaces [26]. Then, four 250 μL Hamilton glass syringes (Hamilton Company, Reno, NV, USA) containing the specific cells and different media respectively, were attached to the microfluidic chamber via polytetrafluoroethylene tubing [24].

*2.4. Forming a Two-Type Cell Array Using Optical Tweezers*

Using the 1070 nm OT (infrared light), single cells were individually chosen; captured and automatically moved from the inlet flow to the cell array site, see Figure 3. Cells are trapped in the focus of the optical trap, 6 μm from the bottom surface. The microscope stage is then automatically elevated 13 μm in order for the bottom surface of the chamber to come in close contact with the cell surface. This assures both small and large yeast cells adhering to the concanavalin A treated glass surface. If the cell is large, the cell is slightly moved out from the focus of the OT even more than a smaller cell, but the forces acting upon it by the microscope stage is neither more or less for differently sized cells. By automating this action for repetition, an array of cells was formed on the chamber floor. The trapping laser exposes each cell to the infrared light only for a few seconds. Experiments confirming that yeast cell viability stays unaffected by this short exposure to the 1070 nm OT have been performed for short time exposure ($t \leq 10$ s) [7].

**Figure 3.** Shows the channel junction and the cell array site. The inlets are for a: Cells of interest (Hog1-GFP cells), b: Control cells (Msn2-GFP cells), c: Chemical agent one (Hog1-inhibitor), d: Chemical agent one and agent two (sorbitol). The coordinate system (x, y, z) of the microfluidic chamber has its origin at the junction between the two middle inlet channels (marked with +). The array is placed with the upper most left cell at (150, −14, 0). Cells are not drawn to scale.

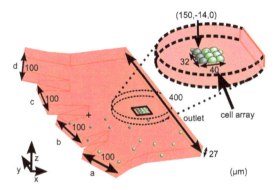

The cell array consisted of a 5-by-5 matrix for the Hog1-GFP single or budding cells and an extra column for the Msn2-GFP control cells, see Figure 2B. Depending on the number of currently budding cells, the cell count in each experiment differs. First, approximately five Msn2-GFP cells were captured in the control cell channel (b) in Figure 3, and positioned in the cell array using the OT. Finally, approximately 25 Hog1-GFP cells were positioned in the same array. Figure 2B shows the cell array after 20 min of inhibitor treatment but just before sorbitol treatment ($t = -30$ s). The cells in the rightmost column are the Msn2-GFP control cells. During imaging, most cells move slightly (hence, the need for a cell tracing software) and occasionally, some cells might even be lost depending on differences in adhesion strength due to presence and/or size of any buds.

## 2.5. The Use of Control Cells within the Cell Array

An issue that had to be resolved when investigating inhibitory events was the fact that a complete inhibition followed by stress treatment will cause the exact same response as a situation where the cells are not exposed to any stress. In order to identify that the array is indeed treated with sorbitol, a column of control cells expressing Msn2-GFP can in our setup be added to the cell array when a complete Hog1 nuclear localization is anticipated. Msn2 is a transcription factor that regulates the yeast general stress responses and is regulated by several pathways [27–29]. Msn2 activation is thus induced by several different stresses of which one is high osmolarity. Msn2 translocates from the cytosol to the nucleus upon activation, just like Hog1, where it together with its related transcription factor, Msn4, regulates the expression of ~200 genes [27,30]. Hence, if Hog1 in inhibitor treated cells do not migrate following stress treatment; an Msn2 migration in the control cells ensures that the cells are de facto exposed to the stress agent. Hence, the usage of control cells for signal detection is a unique and useful approach. In this set of experiments their response is only analyzed qualitatively, due to the high complexity of the Msn2 signaling pathway [31].

## 2.6. Flow Simulations, Flow Setup and Array Location

Changing the flow velocities in the inlet channels creates the change in the media flow around the immobilized cells, which is necessary to trigger intracellular protein migration. In this way, the microenvironment could rapidly be changed from neutral media to a media containing Hog1 inhibitor (for inhibition of Hog1), or sorbitol (for inducing osmotic stress) or a mixture thereof. A sorbitol concentration of 500 mM was used for exposing the cells to osmotic shock. This, quite low, sorbitol concentration was chosen since a higher sorbitol concentration could complicate image analysis due to large changes in cell volume. The automation software OpenLab (PerkinElmer, Waltham, MA, USA) enabled a completely automated setup and maximized the control of the experimental process. OpenLab was used for controlling the mechanical syringe pumps (CMA Microdialysis, Kista, Sweden), the microscope and the EM-CCD camera (C9100-12, Hamamatsu Photonics, Shizuoka, Japan).

The position of the cell array was chosen after performing flow simulations using COMSOL Multiphysics; Chemical Engineering module with application modes "Incompressible Navier-Stokes" and "Convection-Diffusion". The simulations were also used for determining the concentration distributions of the sorbitol and the inhibitor respectively, as well as the velocity field within the device. Computer simulations of the flow profiles and concentration gradients were essential for deciding the location of the cell array. The concentration gradients depend on the flow rates as well as on the diffusion coefficients of sorbitol and the inhibitor respectively. The main advantages with using sorbitol over the commonly used stress agent NaCl (mean diffusion coefficient 1600 $\mu m^2/s$ [32]) is that sorbitol will provide narrower concentration gradients due to the lower diffusion coefficient and hence lower flow speeds can be used. This is beneficial, since higher flow speeds are more likely to flush the adhered cells away. Another advantage with using sorbitol over NaCl is that it is not taken up by the cells [33], and does therefore not contribute to the quenching of the GFP signal.

The cell array was positioned to be exposed to a specific concentration from only one inlet channel at a time (e.g., culture medium, inhibitor solution or the sorbitol-inhibitor mixture). Simulations of three different flow configurations of sorbitol and Hog1 inhibitor were performed for the four-inlet microfluidic chamber, respectively (Figure 4):

I.   The configuration used when trapping cells with the OT and placing them in an array required flow rates of 80 nL/min in the inlet channels containing cells and control cells respectively, and 40 nL/min in the inlet channels containing inhibitor and stress.

II.  The configuration for inhibitor incubation required flow rates of 40 nL/min in the cell, control cell and stress channel respectively and 400 nL/min in the inhibitor channel.

III. The configuration for stress treatment required flow rates of 40 nL/min in all inlet channels except the stress channel, which required 800 nL/min.

In order to have strictly laminar and stable flows at all time points, the flow in any inlet channel was kept to a minimum of 40 nL/min. According to simulations, the flow velocities at the site of the cell array (5 µm above the adhesion surface) are approximately 0.8 mm/s during inhibitor treatment and 1 mm/s during stress treatment. Gustavsson *et al.* [34] confirmed that sustained glycolytic oscillations in yeast cells stayed unaffected by this 0.2 mm/s increase in flow velocity at the cell site. Our measurements confirm that neither the Hog1 response is affected, see Figure 5. A complete detachment of the cell array will occur if increasing the flow rate ten times (8000 nL/min in the stress channel).

**Figure 4.** Simulation data on concentrations and flow velocities in the microfluidic chamber are shown. The arrow lengths are proportional to the flow velocities given at half of the channel height (a distance of 13.5 µm from the bottom surface). The concentration distribution is given at a distance of 0.1 µm from the bottom surface. The green area represents the position of the yeast cells and the pump rates are shown in nL/min for each inlet channel. The coloring represents the sorbitol flow from 0 to 500 mM (**upper row**) and the Hog1 inhibitor flow from 0 to 10 µM (**lower row**) respectively. The first configuration (**column I**) is used for positioning the cell array using OT, the second configuration (**column II**) is used for inhibitor incubation and the third configuration (**column III**) is used for sorbitol treatment and imaging.

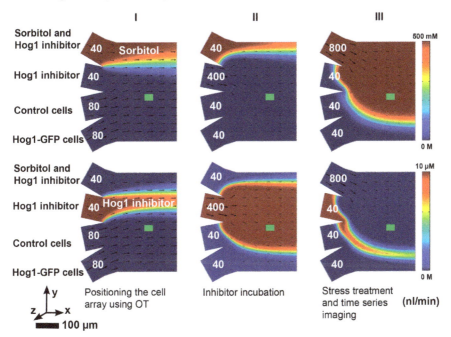

**Figure 5.** Single-cell response curves for dose-response and inhibition time dependence, respectively. Data were acquired from $t = -30$ s to $t = 2700$ s and the sorbitol-inhibitor mixture (500 mM sorbitol) was introduced into the microfluidic chamber at $t = 0$ s. (**Upper row**) Dose-response comparison between (from the left): sorbitol stress only, two different inhibitor concentrations, and the inhibitor only, respectively. The presented data clearly show inhibitor uptake by the cells during 20 min flow inhibitor exposure. For the experiment with only inhibitor (no sorbitol), the concentration was set to 25 µM. The figure shows that even a treatment with as low as 5 µM Hog1 inhibitor solution induces a partial inhibitory response in the cells. The number of cells in the each plot was from left to right: 86, 52, 51 and 96. (**Lower row**) Time response comparison of Hog1-GFP nuclear localization due to increased Hog1 inhibitor incubation times from 0 to 20 min. Immediately adding the sorbitol-inhibitor mixture (500 mM sorbitol) without prior inhibitor incubation, did barely affect the Hog1-GFP nuclear localization, but already after 5 min of inhibitor treatment, a slight decrease of the Hog1-GFP nuclear localization can be seen. The most dramatic decrease in Hog1-GFP nuclear localization could be seen after 10 min of inhibitor treatment compared to the sorbitol only treated cells and the results from the 20 min incubation time experiments. The number of cells differs depending on the number of budding cells in each experiment, the number of repetitions of the measurements, and was from left to right: 86, 30, 36, 43, 51 and 96.

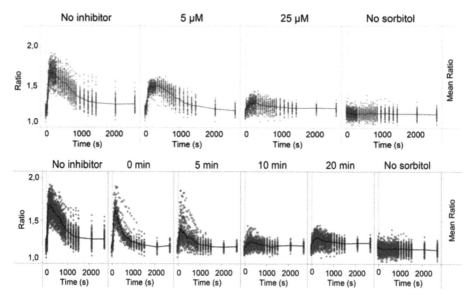

One of the main advantages with the setup is that this single-cell analysis method has a temporal resolution superior to traditional techniques. Additional fluorescein measurements revealed that within only four seconds after pump speed change, the whole cell array is covered with the new intended microenvironment. These measurements also showed that there is no gradient present in the near proximity of the site of the cell array before or after the microenvironment change, confirming the selection of the experimental area as adequate.

## 2.7. Hog1 Inhibitor Incubation

The Hog1 inhibitor incubation times were varied between 0 and 20 min. The time-lapse imaging started after the inhibitor incubation, at $t = -30$ s and a sorbitol-inhibitor mixture was introduced at $t = 0$ s. Using a sorbitol-inhibitor mixture instead of pure sorbitol induces osmotic pressure without removing the inhibitory signal. The inhibitor incubation time could be controlled down to a few seconds, as opposed to the previously developed three-inlet microfluidic chamber [7], where the cells had to be pre-treated with the Hog1 inhibitor prior to being introduced to the microfluidic chamber. The temporal control of the inhibitor pre-treatment in this previous chamber was very poor and the mean pre-incubation time was $29 \pm 13$ min (see Supplementary Information, Section S2, Figures S2–S4). In this approach, incubations times ranging from 0 to 20 min were investigated.

## 2.8. Imaging and Analysis

Exposures were taken every 30 s for 5 min; every minute for 10 min, every other minute for yet another 10 min and every tenth minute for 20 min. In order to capture the Hog1 dynamics while minimizing the bleaching of the fluorophores, the exposures were less frequent as the measurement progressed. The acquiring of the images was performed using the highest level of the attenuator of the EL6000 mercury metal halide bulb, in order for the fluorescent intensity results to be comparable with earlier published single-cell measurements [7]. In order to reduce the photo-bleaching rate, the intensity of the excitation light was kept to a minimum throughout the time-lapse imaging. However, when Hog1-GFP is concentrated to the nucleus, the total bleaching is likely to be faster than when the reporter protein is distributed in the cytosol [35]. The control cells are clearly distinguishable from the Hog1-GFP cells during analysis, by their location and GFP intensity.

For each time point during the time-lapse imaging, an axial stack of seven optical sections with an internal distance of 0.8 μm was acquired for bright field, GFP and mCherry respectively [24]. Every image sequence contained 21 photos ($3 \times 7$ photos) per time point, and the maximum imaging frequency was two image sequences per minute. In total, 609 images were analyzed for each experiment. The fluorescence images show the Hog1-GFP/Msn2-GFP and Nrd1-mCherry (a fluorescently marked protein restricted to the nucleus) intensities in every time point. In order to interpret the migration of Hog1-GFP, the exact locations of the cell wall and the nuclear membrane had to be known. This information was retrieved from the outline of the cell contours from a bright field image and the contours of the Nrd1-mCherry intensity, respectively.

The GFP fluorescence intensity was used as a measure of the number of Hog1 proteins in a subcellular location. The images were analyzed using CellStress, an open source image-analysis software for single-cell analysis developed by Smedh et al. [36], and Cellstat. The software automatically identifies optical section where the nucleus is in focus (focal plane), for each individual cell. The mean GFP fluorescence intensity of the cytosol for this particular section is automatically calculated. CellStress uses both the GFP fluorescence images and the bright field images for calculating the ratio ($R$) between the intensity of the cytosol of the cell focal plane and the nuclear subsection of the cocal plane. The fraction R is therefore used as an indicator of protein migration.

$$R = \frac{\text{Mean intensity in the nuclear area}}{\text{Mean intensity in the cytosol area}} \propto \frac{[\text{Hog1 in cuclear area}]}{[\text{Hog1 in cytosol area}]} \tag{1}$$

## 3. Results and Discussion

Yeast cells were captured using OT and were sequentially treated with a selective Hog1 kinase inhibitor and sorbitol. As a result, Hog1-GFP nuclear migration upon sorbitol treatment was impaired post inhibitor exposure. Cellular responses were monitored on a single-cell level by fluorescence microscopy. The results were supported by the use of control cells providing evidence of a congenial setup. A video of the fluorescent response can be found as part of the Supplementary Information (Section S3, Figure S5).

The problem of pre-treatment outside of the microfluidic chamber is now eliminated as a consequence of the introduction of the fourth inlet. The second inlet is still kept neutral, but is now also used for the introduction of the control cells.

### 3.1. Constant Flow Situation: Hog1 Inhibitor Treatment of the Adhered Yeast Cell Array

It was earlier shown that the Hog1 inhibitor could be taken up from a constant flow [24]. However, those measurements were performed without the presence of any control cells. Our following measurements, with control cells, confirm the conclusion that the inhibitor can be taken up from a constant flow. The inhibitor can also be taken up from a stationary environment, where a concentration of 25 µM seemed to be the optimal concentration, and the highest concentration where precipitation did not occur (see Supplementary Information, Section S2, Figures S3–S4). Our measurements conclude that an incubation time of ten minutes is the most efficient for maximizing the Hog1 inhibition.

#### 3.1.1. Dose Response

Single-cell experiments of an adhered cell array were performed as explained in Section 2. The single-cell data in Figure 5 clearly illustrates the dose dependency of the inhibitory response of the cells. The figure also shows that even a treatment with as low as 5 µM Hog1 inhibitor solution induces a partial inhibitory response in the cells.

Altogether, the nuclear migration of Hog1 is dramatically decreased and inhibited by approximately 75% (from the mean ratio values at $t = 150$ s) by a 25 µM concentrate of the Hog1 inhibitor 4-(1-benzyl-4-phenyl-1H-1,2,3-triazol-5-yl)-$N$-isopropylpyridin-2-amine, when administrated in a flow in the four-inlet microfluidic chamber. This is in agreement with previous results obtained with the Hog1 inhibitor, from experiments performed on in vitro kinase assays and a yeast cell biofilm [22]. In the aforementioned study, the $IC_{50}$-value was established to $7.4 \pm 0.41$ nM. Using whole cells in the microfluidic chamber, our determined $IC_{50}$-value was 180 nM.

Experiments performed using a three-channel system with inhibitor pre-incubation of the cells outside of the system are shown in Supplementary Information, Section S2. A few differences between the cell responses can be seen. Plausible explanations to the differences in inhibition/cellular uptake and initial stress level are the very poor time resolution for the pre-incubation step needed in the three-channel microfluidic chamber, or the difference in flow rates when administering the stress. The difference in cellular uptake of the inhibitor could also be caused by one of, or a combination of two things: The flow with which the inhibitor is administrated to the cells in the microfluidic chamber (400 nL/min), or the fact that not all of the cell surface is exposed to the inhibitor due to the cells being adhered to the bottom surface. However, it is possible to partly counteract this effect by increasing the inhibitor concentration within the range of solubility of the inhibitor.

### 3.1.2. Time Response

To investigate if the Hog1-GFP nuclear localization response would decrease even further as a function of a shorter inhibitor incubation time, experiments were performed where the inhibitor (25 μM) was administrated to the cells 0, 5, 10 and 20 min respectively, before the sorbitol-inhibitor mixture was introduced (Figure 5): Immediately adding the sorbitol-inhibitor mixture without prior inhibitor incubation, did barely affect the amplitude of the mean intensity ratio curve of Hog1-GFP nuclear localization, but a slightly heterogeneous response can be seen here and for 5 min incubation. Already after 5 min of inhibitor treatment, a slight decrease of the Hog1-GFP nuclear localization could be seen. However, the most dramatic decrease in Hog1-GFP nuclear localization (86% inhibition) could be seen after 10 min of inhibitor treatment compared to the sorbitol only treated cells. A plausible explanation to this might be that inhibitor molecules taken up by the cell could for instance be rapidly exported by the members of the ABC transporter superfamily [37,38]. The Hog1 inhibitor treatment could in future studies be accompanied with ABC transporter inhibitor treatment (or use mutant yeast cells deficient in export protein/proteins [22]) to facilitate the intracellular residence time of the kinase inhibitor. No correlation between the location of the individual cells in the array and the cell response has been detected.

### 4. Conclusions

In this article, a single-cell study of a selective Hog1 kinase inhibitor [22] was presented using a four-channel microfluidic system, enabling multiple signal inputs (*i.e.*, the Hog1 kinase inhibitor and sorbitol) to a yeast signal transduction pathway and for studying the subsequent dynamic single-cell responses during time-lapse imaging. The presence or absence of a cellular response—activation of the HOG signaling pathway—was monitored by imaging the nuclear translocation of the cytosolic MAPK, Hog1 (fluorescently tagged with GFP) on a single-cell level. This single-cell setup enables cells to be individually traced during the full time period of the experiment. The fourth channel does not only enable controlled, multiple sequential treatments of the cells, it also facilitates a controlled introduction of two different cell strains (e.g., control cells, a mutant or cells treated differently), side by side within the same cell array. Multiple cell strains within the same experiment is a unique feature which is a necessity for, as in this case, determining an expected absent cellular response. The control cells within each experiment had their reporter proteins localized to the nuclei after the equivalent treatment, since the signaling pathway of that reporter protein is not affected by the inhibitor. Hence, the inclusion of these cells further validated the appropriateness of the setup. The data obtained in four-inlet microfluidic chambers are also validated by comparison to results reported in the literature. Hence, the experimental setup of a four-inlet microfluidic chamber, which allows switching between two treatments, greatly improves the temporal resolution compared to a system where switching between different perturbation agents is not possible [7].

The main biological conclusions are that a Hog1 inhibitor concentration of 25 μM impaired the nuclear Hog1-GFP localization for treated cells with a maximum effect after ten minutes of treatment (86% inhibition). We have shown that our achieved temporal resolution in the order of seconds was essential in order to determine the most efficient incubation time for Hog1 inhibition. The $IC_{50}$-value was established to 180 nM, in comparison to the earlier *in vitro* determined value of $7.4 \pm 0.41$ nM [22]. In this case, due to single-cell measurements, we can conclude that the Hog1 response is mostly homogenous. In addition, kinase inhibition using our approach is a viable alternative to genetic mutation methods when analyzing cellular pathways, circumventing compensatory mechanisms.

Our setup enables a temporal resolution controlled on the level of seconds, with a microscopy resolution on a sub cellular basis. A temporal resolution in this range proved extremely useful for determining the optimal inhibitor treatment time (of a fixed concentration) to be decided. The automatic setup enables very low inter-experimental variation and the custom made automations will provide the opportunities to elaborate with a removal of either perturbation during measurement. This would be extremely hard—not to say impossible—to accomplish using traditional biological methods.

## Acknowledgments

We would like to thank Fraunhofer Chalmers Research Centre Industrial Mathematics (Gothenburg, Sweden) for providing the Cellstat software, and Stefan Hohmann and Peter Dahl at the department of Cell and Molecular Biology (Gothenburg, Sweden) for developing and providing the yeast strains. We would also like to thank the Swedish NMR center (Gothenburg, Sweden) for the diffusion coefficient measurements and Martin Adiels for Tableau support.

This work was supported by the Swedish Research Council (VR), Carl Trygger Foundation for Scientific Research and the European Commission programs AMPKIN and UNICELLSYS. The microfluidic devices were developed at the research facility Centre for Biophysical Imaging, sponsored by the University of Gothenburg.

## Conflicts of Interest

The authors declare no conflict of interest.

# References

1. Ephrussi, B.; Hottinguer, H. Direct demonstration of the mutagenic action of euflavine on baker's yeast. *Nature* **1950**, *166*, 956–956.

2. Lindstrom, S.; Andersson-Svahn, H. Overview of single-cell analyses: Microdevices and applications. *Lab Chip* **2010**, *10*, 3363–3372.

3. Svahn, H.A.; van den Berg, A. Single cells or large populations? *Lab Chip* **2007**, *7*, 544–546.

4. Di Carlo, D.; Lee, L.P. Dynamic single-cell analysis for quantitative biology. *Anal. Chem.* **2006**, *78*, 7918–7925.

5. Raser, J.M.; O'Shea, E.K. Control of stochasticity in eukaryotic gene expression. *Science* **2004**, *304*, 1811–1814.

6. Ashkin, A.; Dziedzic, J.M.; Yamane, T. Optical trapping and manipulation of single cells using infrared-laser beams. *Nature* **1987**, *330*, 769–771.

7. Eriksson, E.; Sott, K.; Lundqvist, F.; Sveningsson, M.; Scrimgeour, J.; Hanstorp, D.; Goksor, M.; Graneli, A. A microfluidic device for reversible environmental changes around single cells using optical tweezers for cell selection and positioning. *Lab Chip* **2010**, *10*, 617–625.

8. Mell, J.C.; Burgess, S.M. Yeast as a Model Genetic Organism. In *eLS*; John Wiley & Sons, Ltd.: Hoboken, NJ, USA, 2001.

9. Botstein, D.; Chervitz, S.A.; Cherry, J.M. Genetics—Yeast as a model organism. *Science* **1997**, *277*, 1259–1260.

10. Mager, W.H.; Winderickx, J. Yeast as a model for medical and medicinal research. *Trends Pharmacol. Sci.* **2005**, *26*, 265–273.

11. Hartwell, L.H. Yeast and cancer. *Biosci. Rep.* **2004**, *24*, 523–544.

12. De Nadal, E.; Real, F.X.; Posas, F. Mucins, osmosensors in eukaryotic cells? *Trends Cell Biol.* **2007**, *17*, 571–574.

13. Westfall, P.J.; Ballon, D.R.; Thorner, J. When the stress of your environment makes you go HOG wild. *Science* **2004**, *306*, 1511–1512.

14. Rep, M.; Krantz, M.; Thevelein, J.M.; Hohmann, S. The transcriptional response of Saccharomyces cerevisiae to osmotic shock—Hot1p and Msn2p/Msn4p are required for the induction of subsets of high osmolarity glycerol pathway-dependent genes. *J. Biol. Chem.* **2000**, *275*, 8290–8300.

15. Rep, M.; Reiser, V.; Gartner, U.; Thevelein, J.M.; Hohmann, S.; Ammerer, G.; Ruis, H. Osmotic stress-induced gene expression in *Saccharomyces cerevisiae* requires Msn1p and the novel nuclear factor Hot1p. *Mol. Cell. Biol.* **1999**, *19*, 5474–5485.

16. Thorsen, M.; Di, Y.; Tangemo, C.; Morillas, M.; Ahmadpour, D.; van der Does, C.; Wagner, A.; Johansson, E.; Boman, J.; Posas, F.; *et al.* The MAPK Hog1p modulates Fps1p-dependent arsenite uptake and tolerance in yeast. *Mol. Biol. Cell* **2006**, *17*, 4400–4410.

17. Dihazi, H.; Kessler, R.; Eschrich, K. High osmolarity glycerol (HOG) pathway-induced phosphorylation and activation of 6-phosphofructo-2-kinase are essential for glycerol accumulation and yeast cell proliferation under hyperosmotic stress. *J. Biol. Chem.* **2004**, *279*, 23961–23968.

18. Posas, F.; WurglerMurphy, S.M.; Maeda, T.; Witten, E.A.; Thai, T.C.; Saito, H. Yeast HOG1 MAP kinase cascade is regulated by a multistep phosphorelay mechanism in the SLN1-YPD1-SSK1 "two-component" osmosensor. *Cell* **1996**, *86*, 865–875.
19. Tatebayashi, K.; Tanaka, K.; Yang, H.-Y.; Yamamoto, K.; Matsushita, Y.; Tomida, T.; Imai, M.; Saito, H. Transmembrane mucins Hkr1 and Msb2 are putative osmosensors in the SHO1 branch of yeast HOG pathway. *EMBO J.* **2007**, *26*, 3521–3533.
20. Klipp, E.; Nordlander, B.; Kruger, R.; Gennemark, P.; Hohmann, S. Integrative model of the response of yeast to osmotic shock. *Nat. Biotechnol.* **2005**, *23*, 975–982.
21. Ferrigno, P.; Posas, F.; Koepp, D.; Saito, H.; Silver, P.A. Regulated nucleo/cytoplasmic exchange of HOG1 MAPK requires the importin beta homologs NMD5 and XPO1. *EMBO J.* **1998**, *17*, 5606–5614.
22. Dinér, P.; Veide Vilg, J.; Kjellén, J.; Migdal, I.; Andersson, T.; Gebbia, M.; Giaever, G.; Nislow, C.; Hohmann, S.; Wysocki, R.; *et al.* Design, synthesis, and characterization of a highly effective Hog1 inhibitor: A powerful tool for analyzing MAP kinase signaling in yeast. *PLoS One* **2011**, *6*, e20012; doi:10.1371/journal.pone.0020012.
23. Sott, K.; Eriksson, E.; Goksör, M. Biomolecular Separation and Analysis. In *Lab-on-a-Chip Technology*; Herold, K., Rasooly, A., Eds.; Caister Academic Press: Norwich, UK, 2009.
24. Hamngren, C.; Diner, P.; Grotli, M.; Goksor, M.; Adiels, C.B. Design and Evaluation of a Microfluidic System for Inhibition Studies of Yeast Cell Signaling. In Proceedings of Optical Trapping and Optical Micromanipulation IX, San Diego, CA, USA, 12 August 2012; Dholakia, K., Spalding, G.C., Eds.; SPIE: San Diego, CA, USA, 2012; Volume 8458.
25. Duffy, D.C.; McDonald, J.C.; Schueller, O.J.A.; Whitesides, G.M. Rapid prototyping of microfluidic systems in poly(dimethylsiloxane). *Anal. Chem.* **1998**, *70*, 4974–4984.
26. Mislovicova, D.; Masarova, J.; Svitel, J.; Gemeiner, P. Influence of mannan epitopes in glycoproteins—Concanavalin A interaction. Comparison of natural and synthetic glycosylated proteins. *Int. J. Biol. Macromol.* **2002**, *30*, 251–258.
27. Gorner, W.; Durchschlag, E.; Martinez-Pastor, M.T.; Estruch, F.; Ammerer, G.; Hamilton, B.; Ruis, H.; Schuller, C. Nuclear localization of the C2H2 zinc finger protein Msn2p is regulated by stress and protein kinase A activity. *Gene Dev.* **1998**, *12*, 586–597.
28. Gorner, W.; Durchschlag, E.; Wolf, J.; Brown, E.L.; Ammerer, G.; Ruis, H.; Schuller, C. Acute glucose starvation activates the nuclear localization signal of a stress-specific yeast transcription factor. *EMBO J.* **2002**, *21*, 135–144.
29. Hirata, Y.; Andoh, T.; Asahara, T.; Kikuchi, A. Yeast glycogen synthase kinase-3 activates Msn2p-dependent transcription of stress responsive genes. *Mol. Biol. Cell* **2003**, *14*, 302–312.
30. MartinezPastor, M.T.; Marchler, G.; Schuller, C.; MarchlerBauer, A.; Ruis, H.; Estruch, F. The *Saccharomyces cerevisiae* zinc finger proteins Msn2p and Msn4p are required for transcriptional induction through the stress-response element (STRE). *EMBO J.* **1996**, *15*, 2227–2235.
31. Petrenko, N.; Chereji, R.V.; McClean, M.N.; Morozov, A.V.; Broach, J.R. Noise and interlocking signaling pathways promote distinct transcription factor dynamics in response to different stresses. *Mol. Biol. Cell* **2013**, *24*, 2045–2057.

32. Vanýsek, P. *CRC Handbook of Chemistry and Physics*; Lide, D.R., Ed.; CRC Press: Boca Raton, FL, USA, 2005.

33. Karlgren, S.; Pettersson, N.; Nordlander, B.; Mathai, J.C.; Brodsky, J.L.; Zeidel, M.L.; Bill, R.M.; Hohmann, S. Conditional osmotic stress in yeast—A system to study transport through aquaglyceroporins and osmostress signaling. *J. Biol. Chem.* **2005**, *280*, 7186–7193.

34. Gustavsson, A.-K.; Adiels, C.B.; Goksor, M. Induction of Sustained Glycolytic Oscillations in Single Yeast Cells Using Microfluidics and Optical Tweezers. In Proceedings of Optical Trapping and Optical Micromanipulation IX, San Diego, CA, USA, 12 August 2012; Dholakia, K., Spalding, G.C., Eds.; SPIE: San Diego, CA, USA, 2012; Volume 8458.

35. Frey, S.; Sott, K.; Smedh, M.; Millat, T.; Dahl, P.; Wolkenhauer, O.; Goksor, M. A mathematical analysis of nuclear intensity dynamics for Mig1-GFP under consideration of bleaching effects and background noise in Saccharomyces cerevisiae. *Mol. Biosyst.* **2011**, *7*, 215–223.

36. Smedh, M.; Beck, C.; Sott, K.; Goksör, M. CellStress—Open Source Image Analysis Program for Single-Cell Analysis. In Proceedings of Optical Trapping and Optical Micromanipulation VII, San Diego, CA, USA, 1 August 2010; Dholakia, K., Spalding, G.C., Eds.; SPIE: San Diego, CA, USA, 2010; Volume 7762.

37. Decottignies, A.; Goffeau, A. Complete inventory of the yeast ABC proteins. *Nat. Genet.* **1997**, *15*, 137–145.

38. Nelissen, B.; DeWachter, R.; Goffeau, A. Classification of all putative permeases and other membrane plurispanners of the major facilitator superfamily encoded by the complete genome of Saccharomyces cerevisiae. *FEMS Microbiol. Rev.* **1997**, *21*, 113–134.

MDPI AG
Klybeckstrasse 64
4057 Basel, Switzerland
Tel. +41 61 683 77 34
Fax +41 61 302 89 18
http://www.mdpi.com/

*Micromachines* Editorial Office
E-mail: micromachines@mdpi.com
http://www.mdpi.com/journal/micromachines

www.ingramcontent.com/pod-product-compliance
Lightning Source LLC
LaVergne TN
LVHW061658070326
832904LV00035B/303